Climate-Based Judicial Review and Liberal Democracy

# International Environmental Law

*Series Editor*

Makane Moïse Mbengue

VOLUME 23

The titles published in this series are listed at *brill.com/iel*

# Climate-Based Judicial Review and Liberal Democracy

*By*

Patrick Lentz

BRILL | NIJHOFF

ISSN 1873-6599
ISBN 978-90-04-76532-0
ISBN 978-90-04-77171-0 (PDF)
DOI https://doi.org/10.1163/9789004771710

Library of Congress Control Number: 2026948199



Brill Nijhoff and Koninklijke Brill BV are part of De Gruyter Brill.
www.degruyterbrill.com

Questions about General Product Safety Regulation: productsafety@degruyterbrill.com

*For our young and future generations*

*Your courage and heartfelt dedication to safeguarding a healthy climate,*
*not just for yourselves but for all of us, including our future generations*
*deserves our sincere respect and gratitude*

# Contents

# Abstract

Climate protection lawsuits are being brought before courts worldwide. In particular, young people demand that the judiciary grant declaratory and injunctive relief in complex climate-focused judicial review petitions, thus placing courts in a difficult position. Climate protection involves a fundamental restructuring of socioeconomic life and the balancing of interests, which is not for courts to decide. The judiciary, as the third branch of government, has no authority over the purse or the sword of the state. What should courts do?

On the one hand, courts should avoid making counter-majoritarian decisions, respecting the separation of powers and the principle of self-governance through the laws of the people. On the other hand, they should hold political representatives accountable because the competing ideal of government bound by law limits political discretion and imposes duties on courts. When courts take the lead in climate protection, this, of course, raises counter-majoritarian challenges. Every court decision that results in stricter climate measures carries budgetary implications, and public resources might need to be reallocated. When courts, however, decline to intervene and dismiss those cases on standing grounds, this may likewise undermine democracy, as courts have a duty to uphold our rights and liberties, not only against one another but also against the state itself.

This monograph, drawing on the work of John Rawls, Frank Michelman, and Mark Tushnet, aims to develop a climate-based framework for judicial review that considers both democratic ideals and mitigates counter-majoritarian threats. It should promote the respectworthiness of the democratic project and foster cooperation among the branches of government.

# Foreword

This monograph is based on research for my PhD thesis on democracy and climate litigation, titled "*Climate-Based Judicial Review and Liberal Democracy: Towards a New Understanding of the Separation of Powers?*"

This book originated in my mind as part of a broader concern about anthropocentrism and the environmental challenges it creates. My research explores two significant topics that clash in the context of climate change: liberal democracy and climate protection. It highlights the significant role courts can and sometimes must play in addressing human-caused climate change. They exert pressure on the political branches of government, thus raising countermajoritarian issues. I aim to reconcile climate protection with liberal democracy by proposing a benchmark for climate-based judicial review that aligns with the core principles of liberal democracy. We will outline climate-related risks to liberal democracy. Inadequate climate action by the political branches could lead to societal disagreements, including civil disobedience. When courts sidestep climate-related judicial review, this might undermine participatory rights that are crucial democratic rights. If courts, however, grant access to the court and then intervene by adopting an unreasonable stance, this might also affect their legitimacy and their respectworthiness.

The research is important for anyone interested in climate change, climate litigation, and sound democratic processes. Those topics concern us all, both the present and future generations. The court rulings we will discuss are based on both cutting-edge scientific knowledge and the latest applicable international law. Therefore, the book can serve as a valuable resource and reference for environmental lawyers, judges, policymakers, and climate litigators. It also documents a significant part of the history of climate-related judicial review, legal requirements, and scientific knowledge. It furthermore examines the impact of climate change on our typical understanding of liberal democratic law. Of particular concern is the influence of climate activist judicial decisions on the separation of powers.

# Abbreviations

| | |
|---|---|
| APA | Administrative Procedure Act (U.S.) |
| CALCDA | Climate Action and Low Carbon Development Act (Ireland) |
| CAA | Clean Air Act (U.S.) |
| CCC | Climate Change Commission (Pakistan) |
| CFREU | Charter of Fundamental Rights of the European Union |
| CJEU | Court of Justice of the European Union |
| COP | Conferences of the Parties |
| CPP | Clean Power Plan (U.S.) |
| DEA | Department of Environmental Affairs (South Africa) |
| DOJ | Department of Justice (U.S.) |
| EA | Environmental Authorisation |
| ECHR | European Convention on Human Rights |
| ECtHR | European Court of Human Rights |
| EIA | Environmental Impact Assessment |
| ELAW | Environmental Law Association Worldwide |
| EMA | Emission Allowance |
| EO | Executive Order (U.S.) |
| EPA | Environmental Protection Agency (U.S.) |
| ETS | Emissions Trading System |
| EU | European Union |
| FAO | Food and Agriculture Organization |
| FIE | Friends of the Irish Environment |
| GFCC | German Federal Constitutional Court |
| GHG | greenhouse gases |
| HAP | hazardous air pollutants (U.S.) |
| ICAO | International Civil Aviation Organization |
| ICC | International Criminal Court |
| ICCPR | International Covenant on Civil and Political Rights (UN) |
| ICJ | International Court of Justice (UN) |
| IPCC | Intergovernmental Panel on Climate Change (UN) |
| IUCN | International Union for Conservation of Nature |
| KSG | Klimaschutzgesetz (Federal Republic of Germany) |
| MEPA | Montana Environmental Policy Act |
| NAAQS | National Ambient Air Quality Standards (U.S.) |
| NDC | Nationally Determined Contributions |
| NEMA | National Environmental Management Act (South Africa) |
| NGO | non-governmental organisation |

| | |
|---|---|
| NMP | National Mitigation Plan (Ireland) |
| NTO | National Transition Objective (Ireland) |
| PUC | Public Utilities Commission (State of Hawai'i) |
| SCCC | Standing Committee on Climate Change (Pakistan) |
| TEU | Treaty of the European Union |
| TFEU | Treaty on the Functioning of the European Union |
| TLA | Timber License Agreement (the Philippines) |
| UN | United Nations |
| UNCRC | UN Committee on the Rights of the Child |
| UNEP | United Nations Environment Programme |
| UNFCCC | UN Framework Convention on Climate Change |
| UNICEF | United Nations International Children's Emergency Fund |
| Urgenda | Urgenda Foundation |
| U.S. | United States of America |
| WHO | World Health Organization |

# General Introduction

Why are people resorting to courts to challenge their government's stance on climate change? Governmental inertia or weak climate protection efforts fuel disapproval among parts of the population and increase demand for effective, prompt climate action. Concerning competing interests (i.e., economic priorities), political decision-makers may hesitate to implement strong, immediate greenhouse gas (GHG) emission reductions, thereby delaying more substantial cuts for the future. To avoid imposing drastic reductions that could harm their economies, some governments argue that ambitious GHG cuts will not effectively protect the climate, especially if GHG emissions are rising elsewhere, such as in India or China.

## 1 A Three-Step Democratisation Process

People expressing discontent with the current government's approach to climate protection might show disapproval through a three-step democratisation process. We will identify the three steps, then focus on the second: climate-based judicial review.

### 1.1 First Step

In the first step, people might raise their concerns directly with the political branches of government. Beyond voting at the polls, they can submit rulemaking petitions directly to governmental authorities or organise protests in the streets, as they did in large numbers on the first Earth Day (April 22, 1970). This event mobilised millions of people to call for better protection of the planet. People marched in the streets en masse to demand environmental protection measures. These protests led to significant change. In the United States, for example, Congress passed 28 important federal environmental protection laws over a 10-year period. During this time, Republicans and Democrats worked together on environmental issues.[1]

These laws remain in place, but according to Professor Mary Christina Wood, they ultimately failed to achieve their aim. The environmental protec-

1 Kennedy Jr. Robert; *Crimes against Nature: How George W. Bush and His Corporate Pals Are Plundering the Country and Hijacking Our Democracy;* New title Edition (New York, Harper, 2004); page 22.

 | HTTPS://DOI.ORG/10.1163/9789004771710-002

tion system exposed the government and its agencies to pressure from powerful corporations and lobbyists. Instead of safeguarding the environment, this led to its further exploitation. Influence from the private sector hindered environmental protection agencies' ability to regulate carbon dioxide emissions. Consequently, environmental laws did not effectively safeguard the climate. The delegation of discretion to executive agencies, rather than to courts (common law protection), led to the misappropriation of environmental law, as agencies could permit harmful activities and thereby legalise ecological destruction.[2]

Be that as it may, environmental protection events and protest movements have increased significantly over the past decade.[3] Generally, youth organisations organise these events to call for governmental climate action.[4] This is understandable, as scientific experts have demonstrated that children are at greater risk from climate change. Global warming impacts children's health, potentially leading to lifelong consequences. Expert witnesses provided detailed testimonies regarding the adverse effects on children in climate cases.[5] The underaged do not have an equal political voice and cannot yet participate in political elections.

Nevertheless, they aim to express their opinions and use these movements to urge political leaders to address the concerns of young people and future generations. Consider the "*Fridays for Future*" or "*Youth for Climate*" movements, which organise street protests in many countries. Participants in these movements even miss school to demand climate protection measures to defend their interests. Children have become a "*powerful force in the fight against climate change*."[6]

Concerned citizens have also advised government authorities to implement climate protection measures. A notable example was the rulemaking petition submitted to the U.S. Environmental Protection Agency (*EPA*), calling

---

2 See, for instance, Wood, Mary Christina; *Nature's Trust: Environmental Law For A New Ecological Age* (New York, Cambridge University Press, 2013); page i.

3 See, for instance, Rochfeld Judith; *Justice pour le climat: Les nouvelles formes de mobilisation citoyenne;* (Paris, Jacob, 2019); pages 7–9.

4 See, for instance, Greta Thunberg and *Fridays for Future* or *Youth for Climate.*

5 See, for instance, *Rikki Held, et al. v. State of Montana, et al.*, CDV-2020-307; Montana 1st Judicial District Court, Lewis & Clark County, 14.08.2023; ["*Held v. State of Montana* (2023)"]; pages 26–46 & Rikki Held, et al. v. State of Montana, et al., DA 23-0575; Supreme Court of the State of Montana, 18.12.2024; ["*Held v. State of Montana* (2024-2)"]; pages 37 &38.

6 Smith Don; *Held v Montana: the beginning of a climate change lawsuit trend in US state level courts or a one-shot wonder?;* Journal of Energy & Natural Resources Law, 41:4, (2023); 369–378; page 373.

for the regulation of GHG emissions from new vehicles. When this initial step failed, petitioners turned to the courts, the second stage in the democratic process. EPA's rejection of the rulemaking petition ultimately led to the Supreme Court's decision in *Massachusetts v. EPA*.[7] Part 1 offers a more detailed analysis of this case.

### 1.2 Second Step

The second step involves challenging governmental climate protection decisions through judicial review. Climate protection lawsuits target the lack, or inadequacy, of climate recovery plans, insufficient GHG reduction targets, failures to meet intermediate goals, delays in implementing immediate GHG reductions, and flaws in transparency and planning security. Petitioners emphasise potential breaches of constitutional rights and international obligations, to ensure a sustainable climate for present and future generations (public trust). Even if the judicial review outcome is unfavourable to the petitioners, it still impacts society. The increase in public awareness may be enough to encourage change through normal democratic channels. In the U.S., governments have repeatedly filed motions to dismiss climate protection cases at the preliminary stage, preventing them from reaching trial.[8] Nonetheless, those cases attracted public attention; some members of the U.S. House of Representatives and senators supported the petitions and encouraged then-President Biden to take action. The literature describes this type of case as public interest litigation. Dr Hussain Faquir, for instance, defines public interest litigation in a broad sense as "*litigation in the interest of the public*," where "[*t*]*he word 'public' means public at large, including all classes and sections of society without any distinction of gender, social status, economic background, ethnic origin, religious credence or cultural orientation*."[9]

### 1.3 Third Step

Failed litigation can lead to civil disobedience, with citizens willing to break the law to raise awareness of climate issues. Consider the "*Extinction Rebel-*

7 *Massachusetts v. EPA*, 49 U.S. 497; United States Supreme Court; 02.04.2007; ["Massachusetts v EPA (2007)"].

8 See, notably, the proceedings in *Juliana v. United States*, which we will discuss in more detail in Section 2 of Chapter 1.

9 Hussain, Faquir, *Public Interest Litigation in Pakistan, Sustainable Development Policy Institute*, Work Paper Series, 5, (1993).

*lion*" movement, or instances in Germany where people glued themselves to the streets or vandalised artworks in museums.

These three steps generate political pressure and raise public awareness. When people turn to the courts or engage in civil disobedience, they move beyond the ordinary political debate. The difference between steps two and three is that in the former, people exercise their participatory rights and seek to enforce their legal rights through a proper judicial process, believing the law is on their side. In the third step, they express their discontent with the law by breaking it.[10]

We focus on the second stage: when people turn to courts. How do and should courts handle the complex climate protection lawsuits submitted to their scrutiny, and how is this sustainable in a (liberal) democracy? Can the proper dose of judicial activism help keep diverse societies together and prevent the intensification of civil disobedience, or will it accomplish little beyond violating the separation of powers principle and harming the integrity of the legislative and executive branches of government?

We will argue that the second step could enhance climate protection and political discourse by fostering a new understanding of the separation of powers that also emphasises their cooperation, thereby empowering all branches of government to address climate change more effectively.

## 2 Climate-Based Judicial Review

We shall see that in recent climate protection lawsuits, parties have largely agreed on the nature and severity of the climate threats and acknowledged the need to limit and reduce atmospheric GHG concentrations. They disagreed, however, about the speed, percentage, and trajectory of those GHG reductions. In some cases, claimants challenged specific instances of positive state action, such as state concessions and authorisations leading to increased GHG emissions, carbon sink destruction, or implementation deficits. In other cases, they challenged state inaction (sometimes considered an implicit refusal to act).

In response to these claims, state authorities and officials consistently petitioned the courts not to involve themselves in climate protection. They questioned the legitimacy of courts interfering with policy choices or providing the redress sought by petitioners. They also expressed doubts about the justicia-

10 Burgers Laura; *Should Judges Make Climate Change Law?;* Transnational Environmental Law 9, No. 1 (March 2020); 55–75, pages 66–69.

bility of climate protection issues, arguing that such questions would force the court into a polycentric decision-making process that it is not suited for. This would require balancing interests, adopting and implementing multisectoral policy plans, and offering long-term planning security. It is not the court's role to prescribe legislative and policy reforms to the government. Judicial remedies could unduly influence political discretion and the separation of powers. They also questioned whether any national climate measures ordered by courts could effectively halt or curb global warming.

Judicial review of climate protection cases could indeed lead to countermajoritarian difficulties. The separation of powers, a critical principle in liberal democracy, is a significant concern as it affects the role of courts, the scope of judicial decisions and the extent of political discretion. If courts repeatedly find that the government's policies fall short of adequate climate protection measures, that its actions are wrongful, or even violate human rights, this could impact the legitimacy of all three branches of government, as we shall show.

The classical notion of the separation of powers and respect for the discretion granted to the political branches suggests that court intervention in the political arena should remain rare and strictly confined to cases of clear abuse of discretion or obvious errors. However, climate change and its consequences could become so severe that we need to reconsider our traditional understanding of the separation of powers and the judicial branch's role.

To what extent can the judiciary intervene to encourage or even compel government authorities to adopt science-based climate protection measures without undermining the legitimacy of the three branches of government? Do activist judicial review decisions inevitably weaken democracy, or could we perhaps envisage a legitimate format for activist climate-focused judicial review?

As we will show later, it is essential to distinguish between procedural due process and substantive judicial review. The former concerns whether political actors complied with the Constitution's procedural requirements when adopting a normative act. The latter concerns whether the political action or inaction complies with substantive constitutional essentials. According to Frank Michelman, constitutional essentials include "*equal rights and liberties of citizenship*" that "*all people may reasonably be expected to endorse.*"[11] Substantive judicial review is controversial because it gives rise to irresolvable debates over what constitutes a constitutional essential and what its defin-

11 Michelman Frank; *Constitutional Essentials: On the Constitutional Theory of Political Liberalism*; (New York, Oxford University Press, 2022); page 3.

ition, nature, and scope are. It implies more leeway for judicial interpretation and less discretion for political decision-makers.

We will argue that judicial review might be less problematic if courts promote participatory rights, such as the right to information and political participation. We will also assert that access to court is an important participatory right. Examining whether the political branches followed proper procedures when authorising environmentally sensitive activities is less contentious than making decisions on the substance of government policies. Citizens should be informed about the state's plans to tackle global warming over time. The state ought to provide specific details on the projected climate adaptation and protection measures. Courts could evaluate whether the state's climate plan is detailed enough for interested citizens to gather the necessary information and anticipate the impacts of the proposed measures.[12] Participatory rights support effective climate protection policies and help defend individual rights. Decision-makers should evaluate the climate impacts of activities before approving those with high GHG emissions.

However, limited procedural judicial review may be insufficient, as climate change threatens the rights and liberties enshrined in the Constitution's substantive part. Lawsuits concerning climate-related rights, public trust duties, and the implementation or sufficiency of climate recovery plans are more controversial than procedural due-process cases and could pose counter-majoritarian challenges.

## 3 Definitions

For this book, we will define the key concepts of liberal democracy, judicial activism, judicial restraint, state sovereignty, and the separation of powers.

### 3.1 Liberal Democracy

A liberal democratic state is a complex society of *"just and equal citizens, profoundly divided by reasonable though incompatible religious, philosophical,*

12 See, for example, the *"Friends of the Irish Environment"* case (*Friends of the Irish Environment CLG v. the Government of Ireland, Ireland and the attorney general*; [Appeal No: 205/19]; Supreme Court; 31.07.2020); and the *"Neubauer"* case (*Neubauer, et al. v. Germany,* ECLI:DE:BVerfG:2021:rs20210324. 1bvr265618; Bundesverfassungsgericht; 24.03.2021).

*and moral doctrines.*"[13] Liberal democracy rests on the belief that citizens should govern themselves in a society of equals. They have the right to participate in political discourse that shapes political will, with due regard for diverse political opinions. Political representatives must consider and weigh all relevant factors and interests in political debate to justify their majoritarian decisions. According to Frank Michelman, "[*d*]*emocracy, it is said, attempts to reconcile individual autonomy with collective self-determination by subordinating governmental decision making to communicative processes sufficient to instil in citizens a sense of participation, legitimacy, and identification.*"[14]

The state's policies are, at best, a momentary compromise in the life of divided societies. Through civilised political discourse, a political majority makes a decision that prevails over the dissenting minorities. Although minorities may dissent from majoritarian decisions, they generally accept and submit to majoritarian decisions that are rightfully adopted, reasonable, and worthy of respect. The democratic system can only function if most people respect the democratically adopted norms and submit to them over time, because, as John Rawls might put it, they are *at least reasonable*.

In (liberal) democracies, the ideals of self-government by laws of the people and of government bound by law are two sides of the same coin. The former typically requires courts to exercise judicial self-restraint and to remain strictly faithful to the Constitution's text. Conversely, the latter opens the door to judicial activism and moral readings of the Constitution. For a liberal democratic society to stay coherent, this dichotomy clearly calls for an ethics of collaboration and a sensible division of labour. In other words, any theoretical concern with the threat or challenge that climate change presents to liberal democracy must articulate a framework of governmental and judicial compromise that respects the democratic core of liberal democracy, especially the democratic dialogue between political majorities and minorities and the responsibility of the people's representatives to decide political questions.

Constitutional theorists distinguish between the procedural and substantive aspects of the Constitution. Those who favour the procedural approach prioritise the ideal of self-government by the laws of the people. At the same time, those who emphasise the significance of substantive constitutional essentials promote the ideal of a government bound by law.

---

13 Michelman Frank; *Legitimacy, The Social Turn and Constitutional Review: What Political Liberalism Suggests;* Kritische Vierteljahresschrift für Gesetzgebung und Rechtswissenschaft 98, No. 3 (2015); 183–205; page 192.

14 Michelman Frank; *Dilemmas of Belonging: Moral Truth, Human Rights, and Why We Might Not Want a Representative Judiciary; UCLA Law Review* 47, no. 5; page 1238.

Frank Michelman argues that basing democracy merely on a constitutional procedure of popular decision-making might be insufficient. There is a need for constitutional morality in the form of a bill of rights that guarantees essential constitutional values and rights. The principle of equality, for instance, is a prerequisite to democracy.[15] Constitutional rights frame governmental action and reduce the number of possible political choices: "[*t*]*he category 'human rights' takes in those norms that might sometimes require states to deviate from otherwise permissible and even commendable choices of laws, policies, and practices, in deference to certain specially favoured interests, needs, or claims attributed to persons just as such.*"[16] Hence, for political decisions to be reasonable and worthy of respect, majoritarian decisions must, on the one hand, comply with proper deliberative procedures and, on the other, respect substantive constitutional essentials.

We will constantly keep this concept of liberal democracy in mind. However, we will also discuss judicial decisions issued by states that do not fit the bill for this concept of liberal democracy.

## 3.2 Judicial Activism versus Judicial Restraint

> The distinction between judicial activism and judicial restraint is a classic one. The latter is a court posture to avoid interfering with the political branches and to promote legitimate judicial decision-making. In the past, courts sometimes departed from their tolerant posture and decided to intervene despite the political colourations of the case.[17]

Frank Michelman distinguishes between the activist and the quiescent judicial posture. On the one hand, activism might relate to the judiciary's conception of standing and justiciability because courts broaden the standards to address the case. On the other hand, it would concern an expansion of the substantive constitutional essentials.

---

15 Michelman Frank; *Dilemmas of Belonging: Moral Truth, Human Rights, and Why We Might Not Want a Representative Judiciary;* pages 1238 & 1239.

16 Michelman Frank, *Human Rights and Constitutional Rights: A Proceduralizing Function for Substantive Constitutional Law?; Human Rights, Democracy, and Legitimacy in a World of Disorder;* Gerald L. Neuman und Silja Voeneky; 73–96. (Cambridge; Cambridge University Press; 2018); page 75.

17 Fuller Lon and Winston Kenneth; *The Forms and Limits of Adjudication*; Harvard Law Review, Dec. 1978, Vol. 92, No. 2 (Dec. 1978); pp. 353–409; page 367.

Keenan D. Kmiec argues that the meaning of judicial activism is unclear. He identified the following five core meanings of court activism: "(1) *invalidation of the arguably constitutional actions of other branches,* (2) *failure to adhere to precedent,* (3) *judicial 'legislation,'* (4) *departures from accepted interpretive methodology, and* (5) *result-oriented judging* [...]. *In the context of public interest litigation, judicial activism can be broadly characterised as judges pushing the boundaries of existing law for political purposes.*"[18]

In this book, we consider court decisions that deviate from settled precedent, loosen standing criteria, or expand the interpretation of rights and principles as judicial activism. We shall argue that differentiating solely between judicial activism and self-restraint is too simplistic and that the form of judicial review is a crucial consideration. We will, therefore, distinguish between strong and weak court stances, as well as different forms of judicial decision-making. Weak-form court decisions, i.e., those that declare the law or outline constitutional and human rights risks, promote political debate and cause less concern about the separation of powers. The political arms of government remain in charge of policy balancing and political decision-making. Strong-form court decisions, on the other hand, close the debate because the court issues a decision that political decision-makers should endorse in spirit and letter. This type of decision binds the political branches of government over time, thereby raising additional counter-majoritarian concerns.

### 3.3 State Sovereignty

State sovereignty, the underlying principle of political discretion, might hamper climate protection for obvious reasons. If the sovereign prefers, he may well prioritise economic concerns over environmental considerations.

The concept of sovereignty has two key dimensions in climate-related judicial review.

According to the internal aspect of state sovereignty, political representatives have considerable (though not absolute) discretion to define state policies and norms within the constitutional framework. The political branches are entitled to exploit their territorial natural resources, and elected representatives may permit further oil drilling operations[19] or grant timber-logging

18 Kmiec Keenan; *The Origin and Current Meanings of Judicial Activism*; California Law Review 92, No. 5 (2004); 1441–1477; page 1444.

19 See, for instance, *Greenpeace Nordic Ass'n and Natur og Ungdom v. Ministry of Petroleum and Energy*, 20-051052SIV-HRET; Supreme Court; 22.12.2020 (*People v. Arctic Oil*). Despite the threats of climate change, the Norwegian government awarded new petroleum production licences on the continental shelf in the Barents Sea. Economic concerns

licences[20] despite recognising the reality of climate change. Those political decisions can again give rise to dissent. Authors such as Mary Christina Wood and Gustave Speth are highly critical of this type of administrative discretion, calling for a shift from unconstrained legislative and administrative freedom to a public trust framework protected by judicial review.

Public trust obligations and the principle of self-determination potentially limit the sovereign's unconstrained freedom to address domestic concerns in any manner he chooses. In other words, they might constrain the sovereign's discretion. We shall see that in Germany, some courts have even granted standing to foreigners to challenge the constitutionality of the German sovereign's domestic discretion. In the *Neubauer*[21] case, the Constitutional Court allowed foreigners to challenge the constitutionality of the German Climate Protection Act (Klimaschutzgesetz). In *Luciano Lliuya v. RWE*,[22] the Oberlandesgericht Hamm likewise allowed a foreign national to seek damages from RWE, a German electricity company.

The external aspect of state sovereignty protects national policies, including internal discretion, from interference by other states. This international law setting, along with the constitutional principle of the separation of powers, undoubtedly supports political discretion in the elected branches of government when defining state environmental policy. However, if a state commits itself through a treaty, it must respect its engagements. The UN Framework Convention on Climate Change (*UNFCCC*), the Kyoto Protocol, the Paris Agreement, and their most recent updates constitute relevant law. The international climate treaties leave some discretion to their parties. For instance, the Paris Agreement states that it does not impose disproportionate burdens on its state parties. It still binds the parties and imposes burdens on them.[23]

---

were prioritised over ecological ones. The court granted the government broad discretion to shape energy policies.

20 See, for instance, *Minors Oposa v. Factoran, G.R. No. 101083, 33 I.L.M. 173;* the Philippines, Supreme Court; 30.07.1993.

21 *Neubauer, et al. v. Germany,* ECLI:DE:BVerfG:2021:rs20210324. 1bvr265618; Bundesverfassungsgericht; 24.03.2021 ("*Neubauer*"). We will expound on this case in Section 2 of Chapter 2.

22 *Luciano Lliuya v. RWE,* No. 2 O 285/15; Oberlandesgericht Hamm (D); 25.05.2025; ("*Huaraz* case"). We will describe the case in more detail in Chapter 3.

23 See, for instance, article 13 of the Paris Agreement about the establishment of a transparency framework to promote effective implementation: "*The transparency framework shall build on and enhance the transparency arrangements under the Convention, recognizing the special circumstances of the least developed countries and small island developing States, and be implemented in a facilitative, non-intrusive, non-punitive manner, respectful of national sovereignty, and avoid placing undue burden on Parties.*"

Hence, some states claim that the Paris Agreement amounts to law. We shall, for instance, study the *Urgenda* case, in which the Dutch Supreme Court applied international treaty obligations to order a reduction in the State's GHG emissions at a level higher than political decision-makers intended.[24] We shall also see that regional courts, such as the European Court of Human Rights (*ECtHR*) in *KlimaSeniorinnen*[25] and the International Court of Justice (*ICJ*) in its advisory opinion, highlighted states' obligations in the context of climate change, drawing on the above-mentioned international conventions. Both rulings affect states' discretion in climate matters.

We will see that the states' domestic discretion and their international obligations clash in climate-related litigation.

### 3.4 The Separation of Powers

How we handle the doctrine of the separation of powers is central to my work, as court intervention in climate matters pivots around counter-majoritarian concerns. Courts are often reluctant to admit climate cases to trial because they raise underlying political questions.

The separation of powers is a fundamental and multilayered principle of democracy. It aims to prevent the concentration of power and introduces checks and balances through separate branches of government to avoid arbitrariness and abuse of power. State powers are constituted, not constituent. Constituted authorities must respect the constitutional framework and the rule of law. These arguments support the ideal of government bound by law and advocate for court intervention.

We shall see that many sub-concepts connect to the idea of the *trias politica,* such as justiciability or standing. Justiciability relates to the type of question that is admissible to the court's scrutiny. Legal questions are distinguished from political ones. Courts are indisputably competent in the former, but their competence to review the latter is a matter of controversy. We will address political discretion as another connector of the separation of powers.

I argue that we might need to depart from rigid conceptions of the *trias politica* towards a more flexible "*cooperation of powers*" approach. My research

24 *The State of the Netherlands v. the Urgenda Foundation*, 19/00135, ECLI:NL:HR:2019:2007; Supreme Court (Hoge Raad); 13.01.2020; ("*Urgenda 2020*").

25 *Verein KlimaSeniorinnen Schweiz and Others v. Switzerland*, application no. 53600/20; *ECtHR*; 09.04.2024 ("*KlimaSeniorinnen*").

does not stand alone with this claim. Since the early 20th century, theorists have argued that Montesquieu's conception of the "*separation of powers*" is no longer adequate.[26]

## 4 Statement of Aims

Acknowledging that climate change is an environmental concern linked to environmental destruction and loss of biodiversity, and understanding that it is one of several significant threats the world faces, I will nonetheless focus specifically on the threats posed by unchecked global warming. Global warming poses an existential threat to the rights and liberties of current and future generations, the liberal democratic project, and global peace: An increase in average global temperature disrupts the water cycle, which is vital to life on Earth. More water evaporates, leading to severe weather distortions and droughts. If the polar ice caps melt, sea levels rise. Coastal habitats are at risk, which in turn poses a threat to world peace and challenges human solidarity. People may have to settle in unsafe locations. The risk and potentiality of displaced persons and climate refugees are increasing.[27]

My research neither assesses whether review powers should be entrusted to courts or other institutions nor whether courts should have the authority to invalidate or replace majority decisions. Instead, it investigates whether transitioning from a separation of powers to a collaboration of powers framework, based on seemingly weak forms of judicial review, could offer sufficient relief in climate cases without triggering the counter-majoritarian problem. Suffice it for now to say that I consider a weak form of judicial review to be a court decision that does not terminate the political debate but instead promotes the discursive process. Political actors remain in charge and accountable. A weak-form court decision could offer guidance and set limits, but it does not impose a mandatory solution that binds the state in the long run. It is open to political change.

I do not provide a micro-legal analysis of different systems, but rather conceptualise how courts, within a (liberal) democratic system based on the separation of powers, address climate-related lawsuits and the inherent political questions that arise in these cases. In this regard, my research develops a glo-

26 See, for instance, Ackerman Bruce; *Goodbye, Montesquieu;* Rose-Ackerman Susan and Lindseth Peter; *Comparative Administrative Law;* Research Handbooks in Comparative Law series (Edward Elgar Publishing, 25.08.2017).

27 See, for instance, Valéry Laramée de Tannenberg: *Le changement climatique: menace pour la démocratie?*, Collection Dans le vif (Paris: Buchet-Chastel, 2017), pages 11 & 103.

bal framework. I believe this is necessary and doable because global warming is a global problem. The scientific facts about global warming are, after all, the same for each state. The *UNFCCC* and later texts added a significant international dimension to domestic climate action. Although the different state concepts are not identical, I believe it is possible to extract solutions from their domestic climate litigation cases that could contribute to efficient climate protection litigation without disproportionately impairing democratic systems.

Aware that distinguishing between developed and developing states might appear out-of-date, even problematic, this distinction might nevertheless be necessary in climate matters. Building on the international climate protection framework, which holds that every state should preserve a viable climate for current and future generations, the argument will be that there are differentiated climate responsibilities. Industrialised states can and should shoulder higher burdens than developing states. Significant climate treaties, such as the 1992 UN Framework Convention on Climate Change, the 1997 Kyoto Protocol, and the 2015 Paris Agreement, set different obligations for developed and developing states. By (historically) emitting a significantly higher proportion of GHGs, and even more so when calculated per capita, the industrialised states contributed disproportionately to atmospheric pollution. They are allegedly responsible for around 70% of atmospheric GHG concentrations, thereby owing an ecological debt to developing countries. Moreover, their wealth would enable developed states to implement more costly climate protection measures. Hence, the relevant climate treaties specify greater climate responsibilities, i.e., GHG-emission reduction targets for developed states.

Developing countries are unequally affected by the adverse climatic effects and must take more urgent climate adaptation measures. Developed states should support developing states and vulnerable populations.[28] Nonetheless, developing states, such as Pakistan, acknowledged their duty to protect the climate.[29] Even if the latter states cannot always be qualified as liberal democ-

28 See, for instance, *Greenpeace Netherlands and eight citizens of Bonaire v. State of the Netherlands;* C/09/659832 / HA ZA 24-53 (ENG); the Hague District Court (Rechtbank Den Haag); 28.01.2026.

29 See, for instance, Pakistan, Lahore High Court, *Ashgar Leghari v Federation of Pakistan*, W.P. No. 25/01/2018; page 7: "*Notwithstanding the fact that Pakistan's contribution to global greenhouse gas emissions is very small, its role as a responsible member of the global community in combating climate change has been highlighted by giving due importance to mitigation efforts in sectors such as energy, forestry, transport, industries, urban planning, agriculture and livestock.*"

racies, I believe we can still draw essential insights from these rulings and from how those courts addressed the doctrine of the separation of powers.

We will explore methods to address concerns about the separation of powers in climate change cases without compromising the need for urgent action. This controversy about the proper role of courts and judicial review is not new, but the climate crisis has amplified the debate. Separation of powers concerns are inherent to climate-based judicial review because petitioners ask courts to act as quasi-political actors on issues typically entrusted to the executive and legislative branches of government. Courts would intervene in the political sphere by ordering a decrease in GHG emissions, thereby limiting political discretion.

We will primarily refer to John Rawls's theory of political liberalism and the subsequent contributions of Frank Michelman to legal theory, particularly in the context of liberal democracy. In addition to Rawls' and Michelman's writings, Mark Tushnet's series on weak forms of judicial review also contributed significantly to the understanding of climate-based judicial review developed in this book. I do not assume that these thinkers would endorse my readings of their work; the same counts for all the other authors to whom I refer. Nevertheless, despite these words of caution, I trust that my research can help us establish a sound framework for climate-based judicial review.

The debate surrounding judicial review and socioeconomic rights is important for understanding the developments I propose in the context of climate-based judicial review, because the concerns raised in the socioeconomic rights debate mirror those found in climate protection and climate rights. Both pertain to polycentric cases that demand profound social restructuring and considerable costs. According to one school of thought, courts would be ill-suited to address socioeconomic rights because they would lack the necessary capacity and legitimacy to do so.[30] Another line of argument defends judicial review in these matters, and the authors attempt to develop a framework to mitigate counter-majoritarian concerns by distinguishing between weak, strong, and experimentalist (or dynamic) forms of judicial review. The works of Frank Michelman (on the experimental mode of judicial review) and of

30 See, for instance, Bickel Alexander; *The Least Dangerous Branch: The Supreme Court at the Bar of Politics;* 2nd Edition (New Haven, Yale Univ. Press, 1986); Waldron Jeremy; *The Core of the Case against Judicial Review;* The Yale Law Journal 115, No. 6 (2006); 1346–1406; https://doi.org/10.2307/20455656; Friedman Barry; *The History of the Counter-majoritarian Difficulty, Part One; The Road to Judicial Supremacy; NYU Law Review* 73, Number 2 (May 1998); 333–433 & Whittington Keith; *Repugnant Laws: Judicial Review of Acts of Congress from the Founding to the Present*; Illustrated Edition. (Kansas, Univ. Press of Kansas, 2019).

Mark Tushnet (on the weak forms of judicial review) in the context of socio-economic rights will be crucial to our proposal of a legitimate format for climate-related judicial review. We will expound on this later.

Considering the political nature of climate protection, courts must decide whether to exercise self-restraint or to intervene. If the court decides to refrain from assessing its merits and dismisses the case, this could affect its credibility and respectworthiness in the eyes of the public. Addressing the climate crisis in the present and over time could, as I will argue, require cooperation among the three powers through *prima facie* weak-form judicial review. Each power could, according to its competencies, strive for climate protection. The court could declare what the law is and what the rule of law requires, and then leave follow-up decisions to the deliberative process of the state's political representatives, thereby promoting political accountability, legitimacy, and respect for the state branches and their respective decisions.

This *modus operandi* might transform the separation of powers into a concept of cooperation of powers, as weak forms of review could lead to an ongoing discourse among state powers. This could aid the democratic process and avoid a "*juristocracy.*" It could enable the state to maintain the functioning of a liberal democratic system while addressing complex, polycentric questions related to climate change.

There is a vast body of literature on climate change and a wide variety of types of climate-relevant litigation, and this book cannot cover it all. We will focus primarily on climate protection, judicial review, and the doctrine of separation of powers. We will mainly discuss climate-related court decisions that impact our understanding of the separation of powers. However, this does not mean the following developments ignore cases we will not explicitly refer to. In the framework of this research, I have coded different kinds of environmental cases in a spreadsheet before making a selection based on the following criteria: The recentness of the case, the pivotal effect within the state or the international sphere (for instance, the references to the decision), and the court level of the decision (is it a final decision of a High Court or a Constitutional Court?).

I trust my case selection covers the most essential climate change rulings issued to date, including significant follow-up decisions. Throughout this book, I have occasionally included longer quotations from judicial decisions. I have deliberately done so to guide you to key sections of often lengthy and complex judgments. My research, beyond offering a respectworthy framework for climate-related judicial review, also aims to shed light on the emerging area of climate protection litigation. It documents how courts have dealt with such cases to date.

## 5 Book Structure

Given the increasing number of climate-related judicial review petitions entering court dockets worldwide, **Part 1** analyses a selection of pivotal decisions to grasp the stakes, arguments, court postures, and effects of those decisions. It furthermore explores the grounds that entitle courts to review the actions or inactions of elected political representatives and the factors that prompt them to intervene or exercise self-restraint. This analysis remains the backbone of my research from start to finish. On the one hand, it records the strengths and successes of climate litigation, while on the other, it highlights the limitations of judicial proceedings in these cases. It informs our development of a format for climate-based judicial review that aligns with the fundamental principles of democracy.

In climate protection cases, the primary objective is not to allocate damages but to prevent future harms that are uncertain in terms of occurrence, timing, location, and causality. Traditional judicial mechanisms are ill-suited for these cases, as the potential injuries are generalised, and causation is diffuse. Moreover, many enterprises responsible for GHG emissions in the past may no longer exist and therefore cannot be held accountable. Moreover, even if they were, why should only they be held accountable? The atmosphere does not belong to anyone, and it is not self-evident who carries responsibility for it.[31]

The uncertain damages resulting from a deregulated climate extend beyond time and space, raising accountability issues linked to the principle of sovereignty. We will see that the list of potential claimants is "*wide and varied,*"[32] ranging from very young to very old people, from individuals to states, and from current to future generations. Allocating damages for fault, injury, causation, and redress is complex and challenging. Fulfilling the classic tort law conditions ("*responsabilité civile,*" "*responsabilité publique*") is difficult.[33] Who is a victim of climate change, who deserves standing and who should bear the costs of generalised climate injuries? These are some of the questions courts have to address. Consequently, courts may need to re-evaluate classic tests and requirements in light of changing realities, which implies an inevitable elem-

31 Rochfeld Judith; *Justice pour le climat: Les nouvelles formes de mobilisation citoyenne;* page 40.

32 Castagno Davide; *Challenging Legal Standing in Climate Change Litigation: A Comparative Approach to the Italian Case 'Giudizio Universale*; International Journal of Procedural Law 14, No 1 (5 September 2024); 47–72; page 47.

33 Rochfeld Judith; *Justice pour le climat: Les nouvelles formes de mobilisation citoyenne*; pages 81, 103, 109.

ent of judicial activism. For instance, the *ECtHR* held in *KlimaSeniorinnen* that the key characteristics and circumstances of climate cases differ significantly from those of other cases, particularly in terms of the sources of harm and temporal or spatial predictability. It developed a test to determine *"victim status."* Furthermore, it emphasised the importance of collective bodies, such as non-governmental organisations. It strengthened their standing by developing a three-step test, thereby allowing associations to take greater recourse to legal action in climate change matters.[34]

It should also be noted that GHG-intensive activities are not illegal; many remain necessary to satisfy basic societal needs, such as agriculture and livestock farming.[35] Those activities result from how states define their carbon budgets, which the judiciary should not interfere with. Suing companies that emit large quantities of GHGs appears unmanageable, particularly when those companies comply with the rules. So, people would need to turn against the state to challenge those rules, which, of course, carries counter-majoritarian risks.

Courts have not shied away from these challenges. They have shown themselves willing to engage with them in innovative ways that are indeed not politically neutral. Hence, the number of pivotal judicial decisions is increasing.

The most significant court rulings on climate protection related to GHG reductions stem from courts in developed countries, primarily those in the EU and the U.S. The most significant climate protection developments regarding carbon sink protection are related to court decisions in developing states.

Although there are many types of climate-relevant cases with different aims, my research primarily concerns three types of climate protection cases. First and foremost are cases involving adequate climate protection efforts, including the adoption of consistent climate recovery plans that specify significant GHG reduction targets. The second type concerns petitions to protect and expand carbon sinks. The third type concerns lawsuits related to individual state decisions that authorise harmful, carbon-intensive activities. The political authorisations expose the conflict between decarbonisation and the state's economic and energy interests.

I focus essentially on the first type. We primarily, but not exclusively, deal with cases from the U.S. and the EU because these are the regions where

34 *Verein KlimaSeniorinnen Schweiz and Others v. Switzerland*, application no. 53600/20, 09.04.2024; ECtHR; (*"KlimaSeniorinnen"*).

35 See, for instance, *Greenpeace Netherlands and eight citizens of Bonaire v.State of the Netherlands;* C/09/659832 / HA ZA 24-53 (ENG); the Hague District Court (Rechtbank Den Haag); 28.01.2026; point 10.8.4.

significant court developments have occurred, and because they involve developed states and liberal democracies based on the separation of powers, among which one branch includes a court system with judicial review powers.

Since the cases in the second and third categories present similar challenges, we will address them only briefly. The second category mainly concerns developing states.[36] They have contributed to the development of international environmental law provisions aiming at preserving and expanding carbon sinks. These cases relate to deforestation, forestation, and even international criminal law. According to the fourth *IPCC* report on climate change, deforestation is the second-largest source of anthropogenic carbon emissions after fossil fuel emissions. Rainforest destruction accounts for about a quarter of greenhouse gas emissions, and deforestation is occurring at a rapid rate. Climate protection, therefore, goes hand in hand with protecting and expanding carbon sinks. Destroying carbon sinks releases stored GHGs into the atmosphere. Hence, protecting carbon sinks, such as forests, is vital in two ways. Firstly, carbon sinks naturally capture and store carbon. Secondly, they prevent those GHGs from concentrating in the atmosphere. If we destroy them, the stored carbon is released. The oil and coal deposits we extract from the ground originated from plant life, which captured high concentrations of carbon dioxide in our planet's atmosphere. Plants stored it in the ground as coal and oil.

Despite poverty and security challenges, courts in developing countries have taken an activist stance in environmental lawsuits, prioritising the protection of carbon sinks, ecosystems, and biodiversity. They have supported the development of international environmental law by concretising ecological principles, such as intergenerational justice and the right to a balanced and healthy environment. For a long time, developed states have dominated international law; however, developing states have taken the lead in international environmental law.

The third category involves lawsuits related to government authorisations for GHG-intensive activities, such as fossil fuel extraction and the construction of carbon-fuelled power plants. These cases focus less on profound societal restructuring and more on individual administrative decisions driven by economic concerns. The cases in this third category concern specific policy decisions linked to harmful, GHG-intensive activities permitted or carried out by the state and involve political discretion, climate impact assessments, and the proper balancing of interests. Environmental interests, including climate

36 Their carbon emissions *per capita* are lower than those of developed countries.

change considerations, compete with other core interests of sovereign states, such as economic and energy concerns, as well as the marketing of national fossil-based resources. Interest balancing is a function of the political branches of government. Courts tend to exercise judicial self-restraint and conclude that the elected branches, notably the executive branch, are entitled to considerable discretion in determining the best policy for the state. Court review is essentially procedural; courts assess whether the government based its political decisions on a thorough assessment of environmental impacts and whether there is a less harmful alternative to the projected activity.

**Part 2** discusses climate-based judicial review and its possible risks to (liberal) democracy. State sovereignty and political discretion set the outer bounds to climate-based judicial review. In a democratic country, the political branches of government are responsible for defining, enacting, and implementing the laws and policies. If other states cannot intervene, who can? Who can people turn to if their political institutions fail to protect the climate, uphold climate-related human rights, or fulfil natural trust obligations? What recourse is available if their state fails to preserve the environment at the expense of future generations?

There is a tension between climate protection, political discretion, and judicial review. Can courts promote climate protection without jeopardising the essence of liberal democracy? We will examine the risks associated with climate-based judicial review. Identifying caveats to judicial review in climate protection matters is crucial for developing a climate litigation and judicial framework that promotes, rather than undermines, democracy. We will, therefore, elaborate with reference to Frank Michelman, a conceptual framework that does three things: (1) recognises the normative demands of a liberal democratic system; (2) recognises the need for reasonable and respectworthy decisions by all three branches of government, and (3) harmonises the competing democratic ideals of self-government by laws of the people and government bound by law. On the one hand, self-government by laws of the people would require the judicial branch to exercise self-restraint, taking into account the political nature of climate protection cases. On the other hand, the ideal of a government bound by law would require the court to take a more activist approach to upholding the rule of law and distinguishing it from the rule of persons.

Frank Michelman's thoughts on the court enforcement of socioeconomic rights and the discussions about an "*experimentalist*" model of judicial review will serve as a basis for our subsequent discussions on climate protection and climate rights.

**Part 3** takes the task of articulating a workable standard for climate-related judicial review one step further by exploring the potential of a judicial stance that steers clear of both the extremes of judicial activism and judicial restraint. Taken on its own, neither judicial activism nor judicial restraint can adequately address the needs of liberal democracy in the face of climate change.

We will argue that even if a court adopts an activist stance, it can still issue reasonable and respectable decisions because the court's posture matters. The court must consider whether to grant declaratory or injunctive relief, a question of ripeness. We will also move beyond the dichotomy of strong and weak forms of judicial review. Drawing on Frank Michelman and Mark Tushnet, we will revisit the concept of *experimentalist* or dynamic forms of judicial review in the context of socioeconomic rights and apply it to the context of climate change and the right to a healthy and stable environment. The aim is, on the one hand, to stimulate the progressive realisation of climate protection and climate-related rights, and, on the other hand, to promote the respectworthiness of the democratic system through a cooperative approach among powers.

Shifting court postures might alleviate tensions associated with the counter-majoritarian nature of judicial review. However, choosing a proper court posture does not exempt the court from its duty to answer legal questions based on legal arguments, which can be distinguished from political questions and decisions.

# PART 1

# Study of Pivotal Court Decisions

"Exercising my "reasoned judgment," [...] I have no doubt that the right to a climate system capable of sustaining human life is fundamental to a free and ordered society. Just as marriage is the "foundation of the family," a stable climate system is quite literally the foundation "of society, without which there would be neither civilisation nor progress."[1]

"The majority portrays any relief we can offer as just a drop in the bucket. [...] In a previous generation, perhaps that characterisation would carry the day and we would hold ourselves impotent to address plaintiffs' injuries. But we are perilously close to an overflowing bucket. These final drops matter a lot. Properly framed, a court order – even one that merely postpones the day when remedial measures become insufficiently effective – would likely have a real impact on preventing the impending cataclysm. Accordingly, I conclude that the court could do something to help the plaintiffs before us."[2]

"But the public are entitled to know what current thinking is and, indeed, form a judgment both on whether the Plan is realistic and whether the types of technology considered in the Plan are appropriate and likely to be effective. In my view, a reasonable and interested observer would not really have a sufficient view of just how it is currently hoped that such measures might contribute towards achieving the NTO [National Transition Objective] to form a considered judgment."[3]

1 United States District Judge Ann Aiken in *Kelsey Cascadia Rose Juliana, et al. v. United States et al.*, Case 6:15-cv-01517-TC; District Court of Oregon; 10.11.2016; page 32.

2 Dissenting opinion of Judge Josephine Staton in *Kelsey Cascadia Rose Juliana, et al. v. United States et al.*, Case: 18-36082, D.C. No. 6:15-cv-01517-AA; United States Court of Appeals for the Ninth Circuit; 17.01.2020; pages 45–46.

3 *Friends of the Irish Environment CLG v. the Government of Ireland, Ireland and the Attorney General*, Appeal No: 205/19; Supreme Court; 31.07.2020; point 6.47.

 | HTTPS://DOI.ORG/10.1163/9789004771710-003

# Introduction

In climate litigation, particularly in climate protection cases involving climate recovery plans, the parties and courts invariably debate the scope of the separation of powers. Governmental parties argue that courts should dismiss those cases because they involve non-justiciable political questions and that courts lack the authority to balance competing interests. They argue that claimants lack standing and that courts are ill-suited to provide the remedies the petitioners demand. Petitioners claim that abuse of political discretion affects the rule of law, that the state violates constitutional rights, and that it disrespects its public trust obligations. They insist that the judicial branch should intervene and promote climate protection by providing injunctive and declaratory relief.

We shall see that the courts have carefully discussed whether they can, should, or must intervene in climate matters. Aware of their role and limits, the judicial approach was prudent. Courts tended to be especially careful in designing judicial remedies. They grounded their intervention in well-explained considerations and cited external sources, especially scientific literature.

Based on a selection of pivotal decisions, this part examines how courts have addressed the new wave of climate-based judicial review petitions. The approach we take is holistic. We will discuss the issues, claims, arguments, judicial outcomes, follow-up decisions, and the effects of the court rulings. The aim is to assess whether a trend exists among courts adjudicating these cases and how they have explained their activist or conservative approach. In other words, what factors led courts to take an activist stance or exercise self-restraint? What encouraged them to adopt new interpretations or change the traditional judicial approach? Was the new approach accepted, or did other courts roll back?

This part unfolds in three chapters.

Chapter 1 studies lawsuits related to the regulation or non-regulation of GHG emissions. This category primarily concerns claims urging the government to adopt specific climate protection measures or to adopt a climate recovery plan. These lawsuits are of significant concern in the U.S. because it has yet to adopt a federal climate protection plan.

Chapter 2 discusses lawsuits about the consistency of the GHG recovery plan and its implementation. Petitioners challenged the GHG reduction targets, the speed and immediacy of the GHG reductions, and the compliance

 | HTTPS://DOI.ORG/10.1163/9789004771710-004

with national and international commitments. Those lawsuits arose in EU member states after the adoption of climate recovery plans.

Chapter 3 provides an overall analysis of the critical elements we identified in our study. We will also include elements of court decisions that we did not discuss. The analysis will focus on the typical difficulties the courts have encountered in climate-protection litigation. We will also draw preliminary conclusions. These findings provide background information for the second and third parts.

CHAPTER 1

# Regulating or Not Regulating GHG Emissions

## Introduction

This chapter addresses lawsuits and court decisions regarding the reduction of GHG emissions through regulation and climate remedial plans. Climate protection plans are complex aggregates of short-, medium-, and long-term measures across various political fields and economic sectors, including agriculture, transportation, industry, construction, and energy production.

In the U.S., before petitioners demanded the adoption of a multi-sector climate protection plan, there was a dispute over whether the Environmental Protection Agency (EPA) had the authority to regulate GHG emissions. This was the essential question to which discussed in Section 1 below responded.

Section 1 discusses the first U.S. Supreme Court climate case, *Massachusetts v. EPA,* which concerns the EPA's denial of a rulemaking petition to regulate GHG emissions from new vehicles. In that case, the Supreme Court pointed to the EPA's regulatory responsibilities under the Clean Air Act (*CAA*). It brought climate protection back on track after the U.S. denounced the Kyoto Protocol, and the political branches barred the EPA from implementing the protocol through the back door by regulating carbon emissions.

Section 2 addresses the new wave of youth cases, which demand the adoption of a consistent climate protection plan. In the U.S., the movement began with the *Juliana* case at the federal level. The specificity of these cases lies in the fact that courts should recognise specific climate rights and extend the state's public trust obligations to the atmosphere.

 | HTTPS://DOI.ORG/10.1163/9789004771710-005

## Section 1: Regulating Specific GHG Emissions

### *Massachusetts v. EPA*[1]

### 1 Introduction

The Supreme Court opinion in *Massachusetts v. EPA* is one of the most significant U.S. climate decisions. For the first time, the U.S. Supreme Court has accepted a case related to global warming. According to Richard J. Lazarus, the Supreme Court chooses only 1% of the cases. In four decades, the Supreme Court has never taken up requests from environmentalists who lost their cases against the EPA. It was the second time in the Supreme Court's history that it granted review to an environmentalist petition (and the first case about global warming).[2]

It is a case about the agency's refusal to regulate GHG emissions from new cars; in other words, it is a case about the EPA's discretion in deciding whether to regulate those carbon emissions. Agencies derive their powers from acts of legislation. In the case at bar, the *CAA* empowered the EPA to issue endangerment findings regarding air pollutants and to determine their regulation.

Beyond the importance of the Supreme Court's opinion, the case highlights the challenges liberal democracy faces in the context of climate change. Both the Court of Appeals for the District of Columbia Circuit's judgment and the Supreme Court's opinion reveal disagreements among the federal judges at that time. Despite these disagreements, both courts issued majority decisions. This case shows that dissenting opinions can help shift perspectives and prompt climate protection measures. We will examine each decision separately to show the crucial influence of dissenting judges. These disagreements occurred even though the issue was relatively straightforward compared to later, more complex, climate-related lawsuits: It involved the interpretation of the *CAA*, a single act, rather than an aggregate of the executive branch's actions and inactions.

Before discussing the judicial decisions, it is worth providing background information on the U.S. federal state's climate position during the proceedings.

1 *Massachusetts v. EPA*, 49 U.S. 497; Supreme Court; 02.04.2007; ["*Massachusetts v EPA* (2007)"]; *Commonwealth of Massachusetts, et al. v. EPA and alliance of automobile manufacturers et al.*, 415 F.3d 50 (2005) & Court of Appeals for the District of Columbia circuit; 15.07.2005; ["*Massachusetts v EPA* (2005)"].

2 Lazarus Richard; *The Rule of Five: Making Climate History at the Supreme Court*; (Cambridge, Massachusetts, Belknap Press, 2020); page 111.

Despite being a major GHG emitter, the U.S. has been hesitant to adopt bold climate protection measures, such as GHG reduction policies or a climate recovery plan.[3] In 1969, when the study of climate change was in its early stages, Congress enacted the Clean Air Act. In 1990, under the administration of President George H. W. Bush, Congress amended the *CAA "to curb four major threats to the environment and to the health of millions of Americans: acid rain, urban air pollution, toxic air emissions, and stratospheric ozone depletion."*[4] Congress authorised further climate-relevant investigations but refrained from adopting binding GHG limitations.

One of the key questions in the case was whether the EPA had the authority to regulate GHGs. In 1998, then-EPA Administrator Carol Browner stated that the Clean Air Act authorised the EPA to regulate GHGs as air pollutants. Likewise, in 1999, EPA General Counsel Jonathan Z. Cannon issued a memorandum asserting that carbon dioxide meets the definition of an air pollutant and, therefore, the EPA would be competent to regulate it. The following EPA General Counsel, Gary Guzy, endorsed this memorandum.[5]

Congress, however, prevented the EPA from regulating GHG emissions.[6] Without the Kyoto Protocol's approval and ratification, the Executive should refrain from implementing it in secret.[7]

## 2 The Rulemaking Petition

On October 20, 1999, nineteen private organisations submitted a rulemaking petition to the EPA requesting that it limit GHG emissions from new motor vehicles.[8]

---

3 Lazarus Richard; *The Rule of Five: Making Climate History at the Supreme Court;* pages 1–2.

4 Environmental Protection Agency; *The Clean Air Act – Highlights of the 1990 Amendments*; o. J.; https://www.epa.gov.

5 Smith Joel; *Massachusetts v. EPA: A Change of Climate at EPA Clouds the D.C. Circuit's Review of Risk-Based Policy Decisions*; Ecology Law Quarterly 33, no. 3 (2006); 653–674, page 660.

6 Lazarus Richard; *The Rule of Five: Making Climate History at the Supreme Court*, pages 13–15.

7 Ibid., page 34: *"President Bush indicated in a letter to Republican Senators that the EPA had no authority to regulate greenhouse gas emissions because greenhouse gases are not pollutants. As the highest authority of the executive branch of government, the President bound the EPA to its authoritative interpretation."*

See also Smith Joel; *Massachusetts v. the EPA:* The Clinton administration did not make a decision and wanted to leave the matter to the Bush administration.

8 Rulemaking petition to the EPA, https://www.ciel.org/Publications/greenhouse_petition_EPA.pdf, 20.10.1999.

Although the EPA had already affirmed its competence to regulate GHGs, it denied the rulemaking petition on two grounds. First, the EPA argued that it had retracted its earlier statement claiming authority under the *CAA* to regulate GHGs.[9] It further reasoned that even if it had had that authority, it would not have regulated at that time. Second, solely focusing on the GHG emissions of new motor vehicles would *"result in an 'inefficient piecemeal approach'* to climate change.[10]

This denial of the rulemaking petition led to an appeal to the United States Court of Appeals for the District of Columbia Circuit by twelve states, three cities, an American territory, and numerous environmental organisations. Ten states and several trade associations intervened on the respondent's side. Eventually, the Supreme Court issued a decision as a last resort.

## 3 The Court Decisions

The United States Court of Appeals for the District of Columbia Circuit[11] ruled in favour of the respondent's argumentation (Section 3.1). The Supreme Court[12] eventually ruled in favour of the claimants (Section 3.2).

### 3.1 *Massachusetts v. EPA* (2005)

The United States Court of Appeals for the District of Columbia Circuit upheld the EPA's denial to regulate GHG in a split decision.

Standing was a significant issue. Access to *Article III* judicial review by a U.S. federal court requires that the petition be classified as a case or controversy, and that the plaintiffs meet three standing requirements. The court decision, written by Circuit Judge Randolph, bypassed the standing issue to examine the case's merits directly, as standing and assessments of the merits would overlap in the case at bar. The question of whether petitioners have standing was thus not resolved. On the case's merits, the court acknowledged

---

9 See Smith, *Massachusetts v. EPA*, page 661 and Meltz Robert; *Climate Change Litigation: A Growing Phenomenon*; (Bibliogov, 2013): In August 2003, EPA General Counsel Robert E. Fabricant issued a memorandum stating that he retracted from the "*Cannon memorandum*" by holding that the *EPA* has no authority to regulate GHG emissions.

10 United States, Environmental Protection Agency, Denial Rulemaking Petition, https://www.govinfo.gov/content/pkg/FR-2003-09-08/pdf/03-22764.pdf, 08.09.2003; Federal Register, Vol. 68, No. 173, Monday, September 8, 2003, Notices, Page 52931.

11 *Commonwealth of Massachusetts, et al. v. EPA and alliance of automobile manufacturers et al.*, 415 F.3d 50 (2005); Court of Appeals for the District of Columbia Circuit; 15.07.2005; ["*Massachusetts v EPA* (2005)"].

12 *Massachusetts v. EPA*, 49 U.S. 497; Supreme Court; 02.04.2007; ["*Massachusetts v EPA* (2007)"].

that scientific uncertainties persisted regarding the most effective approach to addressing climate change. It held that the EPA Administrator had presented sufficient and convincing arguments for not regulating GHG emissions from new motor vehicles, thereby correctly exercising his discretion.

In a separate opinion, Justice Sentelle argued that the petitioners did not meet the standing requirements because the issue was a matter of general interest for the political branches of government to address, not for a court. He argued that petitioners would not satisfy the standing requirements because they failed to establish a direct, concrete, and particularised injury from EPA's rulemaking denial. The claimed injury would be common to all members of the public and, therefore, be neither personal nor individual. In other words, according to Circuit Judge Sentelle, global warming does not qualify for Article III standing because it is "*harmful to humanity at large.*"[13] Legislatures and Presidents should address questions of general interest. The public at large must be considered and not solely the interests of the actual petitioners. Circuit Judge Sentelle would thus have dismissed the case on standing grounds, arguing that it was not the court's role to assess the merits. He, therefore, would neither have granted nor denied the petition. He nonetheless decided to concur with Circuit Judge Randolph on the point that the court must uphold EPA's rulemaking denial. Justice Sentelle concurred in part, allowing the court to issue a judicial decision. He thus joined Circuit Judge Randolph's opinion, which was closest to his own.

Circuit Judge Tatel dissented on standing and merits. According to his dissent, at least the State of Massachusetts fulfilled *Article III* standing because Massachusetts faced a loss of coastal land, which individualised it and caused a particularised injury. Global warming would affect other states differently, and reducing GHG from new motor vehicles would help mitigate or delay the effects of climate change. Partial redress would suffice.

Circuit Judge Tatel would also grant the rule-making petition on the merits because EPA's denial was "*arbitrary, capricious, an abuse of discretion or otherwise not in accordance with the law.*" Carbon dioxide and other GHGs would meet the broad definition of an air pollutant, and Congress had explicitly listed them as such. The EPA Administrator's discretion would be limited to determining whether an air pollutant endangers public health or welfare, and policy

13 *Massachusetts v EPA* (2005); Sentelle, Circuit Judge, dissenting in part and concurring in the judgment, page 3.

considerations would not count. The EPA should have made that endangerment finding.[14]

### 3.1.1 Effects of Disagreeing Judges

In the Court of Appeals for the District of Columbia Circuit, there was a clear division among the three judges. However, such disagreements, especially if recurrent, could lead to disenchantment with the judicial branch, indicating that judges have differing perceptions of the law. In the case at bar, all three judges interpreted the facts differently. On the other hand, one could also view it as a feature of democratic decision-making within the judicial branch. There is a clear record of both the majority's and the dissenting minority's opinions. Minorities still have a voice, as they can express their thoughts. Such dissent might become significant in the further development of the law. It may be that the time was not yet ripe for the dissenting opinion to become a precedent, but it might pave the way for a new interpretation of the law.

Even if there was a court judgment, it was relatively weak because the two concurring Circuit Judges could not even agree on the grounds for upholding EPA's decision. The court could only issue a decision because Circuit Judge Sentelle was willing to concur with Circuit Judge Randolph's opinion. Circuit Judge Sentelle nevertheless felt obliged to write a partial dissent.

According to *The Rule of Five* by Richard Lazarus, Judge Tatel wrote his dissent for the Justices of the Supreme Court: "*Tatel also explained that the intended audience of his dissenting opinion extended to the Supreme Court Justices. If the Massachusetts petitioners decided to seek Supreme Court review, "Tatel wanted any Justice on the fence about hearing the case to be persuaded by his dissent that Supreme Court review was appropriate and that Justices should overturn the EPA's denial of* [*the*] *petition.*"[15]

Most Supreme Court Justices have indeed considered and endorsed Judge Tatel's dissent. The court itself explained that it took up the case because of

14 Ibid., Circuit Judge Tatel, dissenting, page 34: "*I have grave difficulty seeing how EPA, while treating the NRC Report as an objective and independent assessment of the relevant science,*[…] *could possibly fail to conclude that global warming may reasonably be anticipated to endanger public health or welfare,*[…] *with effects on welfare including "effects on soil, water, crops, vegetation, manmade materials, animals, wildlife, weather, visibility, and climate, damage to and deterioration of property, and hazards to transportation, as well as effects on economic values and on personal comfort and well-being.*"

15 Lazarus Richard; *The Rule of Five: Making Climate History at the Supreme Court*, pages 102 & 111.

the significance of its subject matter: "The *unusual importance of the underlying issue persuaded us to grant the writ*."[16]

### 3.2 *Massachusetts v. EPA* (2007)

According to the Supreme Court opinion, written by Justice Stevens and supported by Justices Kennedy, Souter, Ginsburg, and Breyer, the petitioners established *Article III* standing. The Supreme Court ruled that the EPA had not sufficiently justified the denial of the rule-making petition. This denial was, therefore, "*arbitrary, capricious, an abuse of discretion, or otherwise not in accordance with the law*."[17] GHGs meet the definition of pollutants under the *CAA*, and therefore, the EPA should have assessed whether GHG emissions from new vehicles endanger public health or welfare. If the finding is affirmative, the EPA must regulate those emissions.

The remaining four Justices (Chief Justice Roberts, Justice Scalia, Justice Thomas, and Justice Alito) wrote two dissents, one by Chief Justice Roberts on standing and one by Justice Scalia on the merits. Each time, the three remaining Justices joined. Through the lens of dissenting opinions, the novelty and pivotal effect of the court's decision become apparent.

In his dissenting opinion, Chief Justice Roberts made clear from the outset that, even if climate change is an important issue, this does not permit turning non-justiciable questions into justiciable ones. Additionally, Scalia emphasised in his dissent that, regardless of the significance of climate change, this would not justify altering the rules of the game.[18]

Before we discuss the outcome of the Supreme Court decision, the case's justiciability regarding both standing (Section 3.2.1) and the merits (Section 3.2.2) warrants our attention.

16 *Massachusetts v. EPA* (2007); page 2.

17 Ballotpedia; *Arbitrary-or-Capricious Test;* https://ballotpedia.org/Arbitrary-or-capricious_test, <29092021>: "*The arbitrary-or-capricious test is a legal standard of review used by judges to assess the actions of administrative agencies. It was originally defined in a provision of the 1946 Administrative Procedure Act (APA), which instructs courts reviewing agency actions to invalidate any that they find to be 'arbitrary, capricious, an abuse of discretion, or otherwise not in accordance with the law.' The test is most frequently employed to assess the factual basis of an agency's rulemaking, especially informal rulemakings.*"

18 *Massachusetts v. EPA* (2005); Justice Scalia's dissenting opinion, page 13: "[*n*]*o matter how important the underlying policy issues at stake, the Court has no business substituting its own desired outcome for the reasoned judgment of the responsible agency.*"

### 3.2.1 Justiciability

The majority and dissenting opinions highlight the same rules but reach different conclusions on justiciability. The majority stated that the question at issue was whether the EPA correctly interpreted the *CAA*. In Chief Justice Roberts' dissent, he argued that this question is not one for the court to address because it is neither a case nor a controversy. Therefore, the court should stick to the traditional conception of the separation of powers. The role of courts is to decide specific cases, not to serve as a forum for policy debates.

Justiciability and standing are interconnected in the U.S. federal court system. The test for standing requires petitioners to demonstrate the minimum *Article III* requirements of *"injury in fact,"* *"causation,"* and *"redressability,"* and courts have developed specific criteria for each of these conditions. The Supreme Court granted *"parens patriae"* standing to the State of Massachusetts.

Building on Judge Tatel's dissent at the appellate court level, the Supreme Court attributed specific standing to states. As a quasi-sovereign, the State of Massachusetts would have an interest independent of its citizens. This may justify granting a unique standing position. *Parens patriae* requires the state to protect its citizens' interests. Due to the threat of land loss linked to rising sea levels, the state has the right, and even the duty, to protect its territory. Since Massachusetts has transferred certain sovereign prerogatives to the federal government, its ability to address the issue and protect its interests is limited. In return, this entitles the state to broader rules on standing.

The dissenters strongly opposed this new development. According to Chief Justice Roberts' dissent, the Supreme Court's standing jurisprudence requires that Congress or the Executive Branch resolve the petition at issue rather than a court. Petitioners do not meet the standing criteria, and the court cannot provide sufficient grounds to change the rules by granting standing to the State of Massachusetts. This judicial extension of federal jurisdiction lacks a foundation in the court's jurisprudence. The case of *Georgia v. Tennessee Copper,*[19] upon which the court relied in its opinion, would not be comparable to the current issue because it did not involve an *Article III* injury.

Moreover, the dissenting judges argued that parens patriae standing should make it more difficult, rather than easier, to establish *standing.* Massachusetts would need to establish its own standing and that of its citizens, similar to an organisation that must prove that at least one of its members meets the fed-

19 *Georgia v. Tennessee Copper Co.*, 206 U.S. 230 (1907); United States Supreme Court; 13.05.1907.

eral court standing requirements. The dissenters saw no reason to adopt a new theory of *Article III* standing; they argued that the majority's reasoning actually proved that the petitioners lacked standing. Therefore, they continued to assess each standing requirement and concluded that the petitioners did not satisfy any of them.

Regarding *injury in fact*, Chief Justice Roberts referred to Circuit Judge Sentelle's partly concurring opinion to argue that global warming is incompatible with the requirement of a particularised injury, as it affects each person indiscriminately. Thus, according to Chief Justice Roberts's dissent, courts cannot address climate change.

Regarding causation, he argued that only a tiny fraction of global GHG emissions is attributable to motor vehicles.[20] Given the complex relationship between worldwide GHG emissions and the fact that these gases remain in the atmosphere for 50 to 200 years, Chief Justice Roberts concluded that petitioners could not establish causation.[21]

He argued that the petitioners also failed to satisfy the redressability requirement. Chief Justice Roberts did not accept that reducing domestic GHG emissions from new vehicles would slow or reduce global warming if other states increased their emissions.

### 3.2.2 The Merits

The merits of the case concern two interrelated questions. First, whether the EPA has the statutory authority to regulate greenhouse gas emissions from new motor vehicles under the *CAA*, and second, whether the EPA's reasons for not regulating are consistent with that statute.

EPA's refusal to regulate is a matter of agency discretion. The Majority distinguished between an agency's decision not to take enforcement action and the denial of a rulemaking petition. The court granted greater discretion to the former than the latter. It submitted the second type of agency decision to

20 *Massachusetts v. EPA* (2007); Chief Justice Roberts' dissenting opinion, point III: "*According to one of the petitioners' declarations, domestic motor vehicles contribute about 6 percent of global carbon dioxide emissions and 4 percent of global greenhouse gas emissions. The amount of global emissions at issue here is smaller still; §202(a)(1) of the Clean Air Act covers only new motor vehicles and new motor vehicle engines, so petitioners' desired emission standards might reduce only a fraction of 4 percent of global emissions.*"

21 Ibid., point III: "*Petitioners are never able to trace their alleged injuries back through this complex web to the fractional amount of global emissions that might have been limited with EPA standards. In light of the bit-part domestic new motor vehicle greenhouse gas emissions have played in what petitioners describe as a 150-year global phenomenon and the myriad additional factors bearing on petitioners' alleged injury – the loss of Massachusetts coastal land – the connection is far too speculative to establish causation.*"

further formalities, notably the need to provide a public explanation. According to the Supreme Court, the EPA must provide a reasoned explanation for denying a rulemaking petition. To do so, the EPA has three options: it can conclude that the pollutant endangers public health or public welfare and then make an endangerment finding, which obliges it to take regulatory action. Alternatively, it can conclude that it does not endanger public health or public welfare; in that case, it must not regulate. Or it can provide sufficient reasons for choosing not to regulate. Justice Scalia said the EPA provided sufficient reasons not to regulate.

The EPA's authority to regulate GHG turned on the question of whether they qualify as pollutants under the *CAA*.[22] Justice Scalia's dissenting opinion answered the question in the negative. GHGs are not pollutants, he argued. Pollutants must disperse into the ambient air, meaning the air near the ground level, not the higher atmosphere. It is the notion that an air pollutant must pollute the air. Justice Scalia argued that even if GHGs are emitted into the ambient air, this does not necessarily mean they must be considered air pollution agents. In other words, even if GHGs meet the second half of the definition, this does not necessarily mean they fit into the definition altogether. Therefore, Justice Scalia concluded that the court wrongfully favoured solely one possible interpretation of the definition.

## 4 Effects of the Supreme Court Opinion

*EPA v. Massachusetts* relaxed the standing requirements for states, limited the Executive's discretion in interpreting the *CAA*, and imposed stricter conditions for denying a rule-making petition.

One could view *EPA v. Massachusetts* as an activist court decision (Section 4.1) that provided the impetus for regulating GHGs, even though the political branches declined to do so. It could be said that the Supreme Court's opinion partly alleviated an unsatisfactory situation: the adoption of the *CAA* effectively ended federal common-law public nuisance claims in U.S. courts. At the same time, the EPA refrained from regulating GHG emissions (Section 4.2). If the Supreme Court spurred the GHG regulation process (Section 4.3). The Supreme Court later barred the *EPA* from implementing an energy shift without express congressional authorisation (Section 4.4).

---

22 Ibid., point I: The term air pollutant is defined by the Act as "*any air pollution agent or combination of such agents, including any physical, chemical, biological, radioactive (including source material, special nuclear material, and byproduct material) substance or matter which is emitted into or otherwise enters the ambient air.*"

### 4.1 An Activist Decision?

Circuit Judge Tatel argued that *EPA v. Massachusetts* falls within the traditional cases brought to federal courts, specifically judicial review of an administrative denial of a rulemaking petition where the EPA had not sufficiently justified its action. Scrutiny of whether the federal agency EPA has complied with the *CAA* does not require extraordinary court intervention.[23] Considering the outcome of the case, I would argue that *Massachusetts v. EPA* already fits into the current worldwide wave of climate protection cases, in which petitioners seek judicial review of broader policy decisions of the executive and legislative branches. These cases extend beyond petitions to review administrative action. Petitioners ask the courts to order the governments to adopt consistent policies and to issue adequate rules through primary or secondary legislation. *Massachusetts v. EPA* was the first U.S. Supreme Court case addressing global warming, garnering immense public attention. The court's opinion is exceptional in many regards.

The extension of *parens patriae* standing might be a significant innovation in this case, as a matter of public interest may now qualify for admission to court. Particular injury to a specific group or individual is no longer considered an absolute requirement. A state can use its general interest and that of its citizens to meet the standing requirements, which matters given global warming's impact on each of us. This extension is particularly essential, especially in a federation like the United States, because individual states lack discretion over the subject matter. During the Bush administration, twelve state attorneys general warned that they would join lawsuits if the federal government did not act.[24] Accepting that an abstract entity, such as a state, can fulfil the standing requirements could significantly promote future climate protection. Loosened notions of standing could thus pave the way for climate-related judicial review, especially in intergenerational cases.

*Parens patriae* standing, as developed by the Supreme Court, has already been applied by federal courts in subsequent climate change lawsuits, such as

---

23 *Massachusetts v. EPA* (2005); Circuit Judge Tatel's dissenting opinion, page 38: "*Although this case comes to us in the context of a highly controversial question – global warming – it actually presents a quite traditional legal issue: has the Environmental Protection Agency complied with the Clean Air Act? For the reasons given above, I believe that EPA has both misinterpreted the scope of its statutory authority and failed to provide a statutorily-based justification for refusing to make an endangerment finding. I would thus grant the petitions for review.*"

24 Smith Joel; *Massachusetts v. EPA;* page 655.

in *Connecticut v. American Electric Power Co.*[25] The Supreme Court's opinion directly affected similar ongoing cases, such as *New York v. EPA,* where the Court of Appeals for the Columbia Circuit ordered that the *"case be remanded to EPA for further proceedings in light of Massachusetts v. EPA."*[26] In the subsequent proceedings, the petitioners and the EPA reached an agreement.

### 4.2 An Expertise-Forcing Ruling

Reference to scientific knowledge played a key role in both the majority and dissenting opinions, but for different purposes. The majority cited science to underscore the need for judicial intervention. The dissenters pointed to scientific uncertainties and called for judicial restraint. Justice Stevens made clear from the beginning of his opinion that science has documented the reality of dangerous climate change.[27] Justice Scalia, however, pointed to scientific uncertainties and urged the court to refrain from interfering with the EPA's decision to deny the rule-making petition, quoting parts of a 2001 report by the National Research Council.[28]

Considering the reproaches that the Bush administration influenced scientific experts and tied their hands by altering their reports, silencing their voices, or suppressing inconvenient evidence, some authors argued that *Massachusetts v. EPA* is part of a series of decisions in which the Supreme Court intervened to stop the politicisation of expertise and that in the case at bar climate science ought to be unconstrained from political guardianship to force scientific expertise.[29]

The Supreme Court's ruling did not interfere with the Legislature but with the highest federal executive authority. It overturned the U.S. President's interpretation of the *CAA*. Consequently, the Supreme Court ultimately limited

---

25 See, for example, *Connecticut v. American Electric Power Co.*, 05-5104-cv, 05-5119-cv; United States Court of Appeals 2nd Circuit; 21.09.2009; page 139: "*The States have parens patriae and Article III standing, in their quasi-sovereign and proprietary capacities respectively.*"

26 *New York v. EPA,* USCA case number 06-1322; United States Court of Appeals for the District of Columbia Circuit; 24.09.2007.

27 *Massachusetts v. EPA* (2007); Introduction: "*A well-documented rise in global temperatures has coincided with a significant increase in the concentration of carbon dioxide in the atmosphere. Respected scientists believe the two trends are related.*"

28 Ibid., Justice Scalia's dissenting opinion, point I B: "*The science of climate change is extraordinarily complex and still evolving. Although there have been substantial advances in climate change science, there continue to be important uncertainties in our understanding of the factors that may affect future climate change and how it should be addressed.*"

29 Freeman Jody and Vermeule Adrian; *Massachusetts v. EPA: From Politics to Expertise*, Supreme Court Review (2007); pages 51–110.

the Executive's discretion by disqualifying its interpretation of the *CAA*'s definition.

The Supreme Court made the U.S. federal agencies' discretionary decision not to regulate judicially reviewable despite the *"nondelegation rulings"* through which the Supreme Court formerly used to force Congress to settle an agency's competencies unequivocally.[30] Here, the court did the opposite. *Massachusetts v.* EPA could therefore be seen as an *"anti-delegation case"* because the court effectively passed the opposite of a nondelegation ruling by holding that the EPA had the authority to regulate GHG emissions, forcing the EPA to decide on the dangerousness of those emissions.

The Supreme Court could perhaps rely on the EPA staff's willingness to regulate GHG once the political block was lifted. There were well-known accusations against the Bush administration for dictating the scientific position on climate change, and the EPA was barred from referring to climate change in official documents.

## 4.3 Judicial Rule-Making Impetus

The governmental situation in the U.S. reflects the typical tensions that often burden liberal democracies. Legislatures and administrative authorities often compete. Climate protection requires consistent decision-making, and the state powers must pull in the same direction to reshape society. Rival interests and rival expressions of legislative and executive intent obstruct this process.[31]

*EPA v. Massachusetts* underlines the obstacles that frustrate initiatives to address global warming. Congress and the government postponed climate protection measures for years, even decades. Although the EPA had already confirmed its power to regulate GHG, its chief executive took the opposite position.[32] However, the Supreme Court's decision in *EPA v. Massachusetts* fundamentally changed the situation.

Even though debated, the executive branch accepted the ruling. The Executive branch, the EPA, and the federal government initiated the necessary steps to endorse it. President Bush promised courageous action, convened the EPA Administrator and the secretaries for Transportation, Energy, and Agriculture to a meeting, and subsequently ordered them to take executive action

---

30 Cornell University's Legal Information Institute (see https://www.law.cornell.edu/wex/nondelegation_doctrine; <06/07/2024>) defines the *Nondelegation Doctrine* as follows: *"The non-delegation doctrine stands for the principle that Congress cannot delegate its legislative powers or lawmaking ability to other entities. This prohibition typically involves Congress delegating its powers to administrative agencies or to private organizations."*

31 Smith Joel; *Massachusetts v. EPA*; page 659.

32 Lazarus Richard; *The Rule of Five: Making Climate History at the Supreme Court;* page 261.

to begin regulating GHGs. Perhaps the Supreme Court issued an activist decision because it could rely on past memoranda that exposed the EPA's willingness to regulate GHG emissions. The EPA's civil servants needed to overcome the highest executive authority's interpretation to begin regulating.

Following the court ruling, the EPA issued an endangerment finding regarding the public health and welfare impacts of carbon dioxide and established limits on new motor vehicles and power plants. The legislature did not counter the court decision by amending the *CAA*; thereby, it also accepted that the EPA has the authority to regulate GHG emissions.

### 4.4 The Extent of EPA's Discretion to Regulate Carbon Dioxide

#### 4.4.1 Before *EPA v. Massachusetts*

Before *EPA v. Massachusetts,* the Supreme Court ruled in *American Electric Power Co. v. Connecticut* that Congress had entrusted the EPA with rulemaking powers by adopting the *CAA*. At the same time, the *CAA* effectively ended common law public nuisance claims against GHG emissions.[33] Federal Courts henceforth systematically dismissed federal public nuisance cases.[34] The EPA, however, could not regulate GHGs, leaving the situation unsatisfactory.

#### 4.4.2 After *EPA v. Massachusetts*

*EPA v. Massachusetts* was a landmark decision because it permitted the EPA to exercise the regulatory powers conferred by the *CAA*. However, in 2022, in *West Virginia v. EPA,*[35] the Supreme Court again limited the EPA's regulatory discretion. It red-carded the power-generation shifting policies laid out in the *EPA*'s Clean Power Plan (*CPP*) and barred the EPA from implementing economically and politically significant GHG regulations.

---

33 *American Electric Power Co. v. Connecticut*; 04 Civ. 5669, 04 Civ. 5670; United States District Court of New York (southern district); 19.09.2005.

34 *Native Village of Kivalina v. ExxonMobil Corporation,* No. 09-17490; United States Court of Appeals for the Ninth Circuit; 21.09.2012; page 11654: *"We need not engage in that complex issue and fact-specific analysis in this case, because we have direct Supreme Court guidance. The Supreme Court has already determined that Congress has directly addressed the issue of domestic greenhouse gas emissions from stationary sources and has therefore displaced federal common law. [...] Our conclusion obviously does not aid Kivalina, which itself is being displaced by the rising sea. But the solution to Kivalina's dire circumstance must rest in the hands of the legislative and executive branches of our government, not the federal common law."*

35 *West Virginia v. EPA*, 597 U.S. (2022); United States Supreme Court; 30.06.2022; ["*West Virginia v. EPA* (2022)"].

Under the Obama administration, the EPA introduced the *CPP* in June 2014 to initiate a sector-wide shift toward cleaner energy sources, transitioning from coal to natural gas and renewable energy, primarily wind and solar power. The EPA aimed to restructure the overall mix of U.S. power generation to reduce coal-fired energy from 38% down to 27% by 2030. The EPA also established standards to improve the efficiency of coal-burning power plants. However, because existing coal-fired power plants already operate at near-optimal efficiency, this would yield only small reductions in GHG emissions.

Since existing power stations could not meet the new targets, the *CPP* required them to reduce their energy output, purchase emission allowances (EMA*s*), build new gas, solar, or wind power stations, or invest in existing sustainable power plants. According to the EPA's calculations, this could lead to the shutdown of dozens of coal-fired power plants and significant job losses across various sectors.

The *CPP* did not enter into force as dozens of parties, including 27 states, requested its repeal through judicial review. The DC Circuit Court declined the application for a stay of implementation,[36] which the Supreme Court later overturned. During the Trump administration, the EPA repealed the *CPP*, arguing that, under the "*major questions doctrine,*" it lacked statutory authority to implement it. According to that doctrine, the agency "*must point to a 'clear congressional authorization' for the authority it claims.*"[37] Implementing the energy transition strategies developed in the *CPP* would exceed the powers delegated to the EPA by Congress.[38]

Twelve states and private parties challenged that repeal. On January 19, 2021, shortly before the transition from the Trump to the Biden administration, the DC Circuit Court[39] held that the proceedings at bar would not qualify as a "*major questions* case." According to the court, a reasonable reading of the *CAA* would empower the EPA to implement an energy system transformation. It vacated the EPA's repeal of the *CPP* and remanded the matter to the agency for further consideration.

---

36 *West Virginia v. EPA*, USCA Case 15-1363; Court of Appeals for the District of Columbia Circuit; 21.01.2016; ["*West Virginia v. EPA (2016)*"].

37 *West Virginia v. EPA (2022);* concurring opinion written by Justice Gorsuch, page 1: "*To resolve today's case, the Court invokes the major questions doctrine. Under that doctrine's terms, administrative agencies must be able to point to "clear congressional authorization" when they claim the power to make decisions of vast "economic and political significance."*

38 Ibid., page 9: "*As the Court aptly summarizes it today, the doctrine addresses a particular and recurring problem: agencies asserting highly consequential power beyond what Congress could reasonably be understood to have granted.*"

39 *West Virginia v. EPA*, USCA Case 15-1363; Court of Appeals for the District of Columbia Circuit; 17.09.2019; ["*West Virginia v. EPA (2019)*"].

The states that demanded the repeal of the *CPP* petitioned the Supreme Court, which accepted a *writ of certiorari*. It held that the *CAA* did not grant the EPA the authority to determine how much energy transition the grid could support or how much energy prices could increase. The EPA would only refer to an ancillary provision of the *CAA*, which would be insufficient for decisions of economic and political significance, and it would need direct congressional empowerment to implement a shift from coal power to gas and renewable energy. Therefore, the Supreme Court barred the EPA from implementing an energy system transformation. The concurring opinion written by Justice Gorsuch, with whom Justice Alito joined, provided further precision to the "*major questions doctrine.*"

Justice Kagan wrote a dissent, joined by Justices Breyer and Sotomayor. The dissenting judges emphasised the urgency of addressing global warming and noted that the energy sector was responsible for a quarter of the United States' GHG emissions. The dissenting Justices regretted that the court took up the case without waiting for the EPA's response to the Circuit Court's decision. They argued that the Clean Air Act would sufficiently empower the EPA as the expert agency. The relevant section of the *CAA* cannot be qualified as a "*statutory backwater.*" Instead, it is a "*backstop*" or "*catch-all provision*" that protects against pollutants not covered by other programmes, such as the National Ambient Air Quality Standards (*NAAQS*) or the Hazardous Air Pollutants (*HAP*).[40]

According to Justice Kagan, the Supreme Court acted in an unprecedented fashion on two counts. It first hindered the implementation of the *CPP* while it was still under review in the DC Circuit.[41] Moreover, it invoked the "*major questions doctrine*" to bar the EPA from deciding and implementing similar energy transition initiatives.[42]

---

40 *West Virginia v. EPA* (2022); dissenting opinion written by Justice Kagan; pages 5 & 6.

41 Ibid., page 3: "*This Court has obstructed EPA's effort from the beginning. Right after the Obama administration issued the Clean Power Plan, the Court stayed its implementation. That action was unprecedented: Never before had the Court stayed a regulation then under review in the lower courts.*"

42 Ibid., page 15: "*The majority claims it is just following precedent, but that is not so. The Court has never even used the term 'major questions doctrine' before. And in the relevant cases, the Court has done statutory construction of a familiar sort. It has looked to the text of a delegation. It has addressed how an agency's view of that text works – or fails to do so – in the context of a broader statutory scheme. And it has asked, in a common-sensical (or call it purposive) vein, about what Congress would have made of the agency's view – otherwise said, whether Congress would naturally have delegated authority over some important question to the agency, given its expertise and experience. In short, in assessing the scope of a delegation, the Court has considered – without multiple steps, triggers, or*

Whereas the Supreme Court strengthened the EPA's competence to regulate GHGs in *EPA v. Massachusetts,* in *West Virginia v. EPA,* it limited that discretion by holding that Congress must expressly delegate the power to implement an energy system transformation.

The controversy about the EPA's GHG regulation powers and efforts persists. On October 12, 2023, fifteen minors from California filed a complaint for declaratory relief in the United States District Court for the Central District of California, alleging that the EPA had violated their constitutional rights by permitting harmful levels of *GHG* emissions. The case was dismissed on standing.[43]

On February 12, 2026, during the Trump administration, the EPA revoked the endangerment finding for carbon dioxide under the Clean Air Act. This development will likely give rise to new judicial proceedings. The Massachusetts Attorney General announced that she will request judicial review.[44] On February 18, 2026, 18 young people filed the lawsuit *Venner v. EPA*, asking to invalidate the above-mentioned EPA decision.[45]

The result of *Massachusetts v. EPA* sparked a series of U.S. youth-led climate cases, beginning with *Juliana v. United States.*

---

*special presumptions – the fit between the power claimed, the agency claiming it, and the broader statutory design."*

43 *G. B., et al. v. United States Environmental Protection Agency, et al.,* Case No. CV 23-10345-MWF (AGRx); District Court of the Central District of California; 08.05.2024 & *G. B., et al. v. United States Environmental Protection Agency, et al.,* Case No. CV 23-10345-MWF (AGRx); U.S. District Court of the Central District of California; 11.02.2025.

44 Le Moult Craig; "*Mass. Officials, Environmentalists Criticise EPA's Revocation of Scientific Finding*"; GBH News; 12.02.2026; https://www.wgbh.org/news/local/2026-02-12/mass-officials-environmentalists-criticize-epas-revocation-of-scientific-finding; <16.02.2026>.

45 Our children's Trust; *Venner v. EPA*; https://www.ourchildrenstrust.org/venner-v-epa <26.02.2026>.

## Section 2: Adopting a Climate Protection Plan

### *Juliana v. United States*[46]

### 1 Introduction

*Juliana* is the leading U.S. federal case concerning future generations, climate rights, and public trust obligations. Current environmental policies and decisions predominantly favour the interests, rights, and freedoms of the current electorate[47] which may therefore disproportionately burden future generations who do not yet have a voice. This argument has come to a head in *Juliana*. The case exemplifies worldwide petitions predominantly led by or on behalf of young people protesting inadequate legislative efforts, government action, or inaction. The petitioners seek to raise public awareness, put pressure on the branches of government, overcome policy blocks, and initiate change. So far, the typical responses of affected governments have been to raise separation of powers objections and argue that their national emissions are insignificant relative to global levels.

In the *Juliana* proceedings, plaintiffs relied on scientific evidence to assert that climate change is a fact and that it is caused and accelerated by atmospheric GHG concentrations resulting from the combustion of fossil fuels. They also claimed that the government has known about global warming and its risks for a long time. Still, instead of acting to curb GHG emissions, the political decision-makers have exacerbated the situation by their ongoing promotion of fossil fuels. All these facts were unchallenged by the defendants.[48] Although urgently advised by scientific expertise, the state postponed sharp reductions to the future.

This kind of lawsuit was novel because claimants did not challenge a single decision but rather a broad aggregate of the Executive's actions and inactions. These actions include promoting fossil fuels, leasing public lands for oil, gas,

46 *Kelsey Cascadia Rose Juliana, et al. v. United States et al.*, Case 6:15-cv-01517-TC; District Court of Oregon; 10.11.2016; ["*Juliana* (*2016*)"]; *Kelsey Cascadia Rose Juliana, et al. v. United States et al.*, Case 6:15-cv-01517-AA; District Court of Oregon; 15.10.2018; ["*Juliana* (*2018*)"]; *Kelsey Cascadia Rose Juliana, et al. v. United States et al.*, Case: 18-36082, D.C. No. 6:15-cv -01517-AA; United States Court of Appeals for the Ninth Circuit; 17.01.2020; ["*Juliana* (2020)"] & *Kelsey Cascadia Rose Juliana et al. v. United States et al.*; docket 24-645; order list 604 U.S.; United States Supreme Court; 24.03.2025; ["*Juliana* (2025)"].

47 See, for instance, Gore Albert; *Earth in the Balance: Forging a New Common Purpose;* (London, Earthscan, 2008); pages 2, 3 & 191.

48 *Juliana* (2020); pages 14–16.

and coal production, importing and exporting fossil fuels, and authorising GHG-intensive activities.[49]

On August 12, 2015, the petitioners filed the lawsuit in the United States District Court for the District of Oregon. Proceedings in the case began under the Obama administration, continued through the Trump and Biden administrations, and carried into the second Trump administration. This research examines the lawsuit for three primary reasons. Firstly, the novelty of this type of youth case involves essential separation of powers considerations, questions about intergenerational justice, and public trust obligations. Secondly, it is important in light of the unprecedented opinion issued by District Judge Ann Aiken in the Oregon District Court on November 10, 2016, concerning the declaration of the *right to a climate system capable of sustaining human life*. Thirdly, it considers the dissent about *Article III* standing and the need for court intervention issued by District Judge Josephine Staton, sitting on the Bench of the Court of Appeals for the Ninth Circuit.

We will not address all arguments and decisions, but will focus on the core of the *Juliana* proceedings. The most significant arguments supporting my scholarly work relate to the separation of powers, standing, court intervention, and judicial self-restraint. Two decisions of the Oregon District Court, dated November 10, 2016, and July 20, 2018, are essential. On appeal, the

---

49 *Juliana* (2016); page 3: "*This is no ordinary lawsuit. Plaintiffs challenge the policies, acts, and omissions of the President of the United States, the Council on Environmental Quality, the Office of Management and Budget, the Office of Science and Technology Policy, the Department of Energy, the Department of the Interior, the Department of Transportation ("DOT"), the Department of Agriculture, the Department of Commerce, the Department of Defense, the Department of State, and the Environmental Protection Agency("EPA"). This lawsuit challenges decisions defendants have made across a vast set of topics – decisions like whether and to what extent to regulate* $Co_2$ *emissions from power plants and vehicles, whether to permit fossil fuel extraction and development to take place on federal lands, how much to charge for use of those lands, whether to give tax breaks to the fossil fuel industry, whether to subsidize or directly fund that industry, whether to fund the construction of fossil fuel infrastructure such as natural gas pipelines at home and abroad, whether to permit the export and import of fossil fuels from and to the United States, and whether to authorize new marine coal terminal projects. Plaintiffs assert defendants' decisions on these topics have substantially caused the planet to warm and the oceans to rise. They draw a direct causal link between defendants' policy choices and floods, food shortages, destruction of property, species extinction, and a host of other harms. This lawsuit is not about proving that climate change is happening or that human activity is driving it. For the purposes of this motion, those facts are undisputed. The questions before the Court are whether defendants are responsible for some of the harm caused by climate change, whether plaintiffs may challenge defendants' climate change policy in court, and whether this Court can direct defendants to change their policy without running afoul of the separation of powers doctrine.*"

Court of Appeals for the Ninth Circuit's opinion, dated January 17, 2020, provides further insight.

## 2 The Petition

Twenty-one youth claimants, supported by the non-profit organisation *Our Children's Trust,* challenged the actions and inactions of the President of the United States and several federal departments and agencies. Despite having long-standing knowledge (over 50 years) of climate hazards, the defendants allegedly continued contributing to global warming.[50]

According to the claimants, the political climate stance allegedly violated their substantive rights, specifically their rights to life, liberty, and property, by directly contributing to the dangers of climate change. The court should declare that the state violated the claimants' constitutional rights (declaratory relief). Moreover, the court should order the state to prepare and implement a federal mitigation plan, including a consistent short-term strategy with straight GHG emissions reductions (injunctive relief). The federal government should not further delay the phase-out of fossil fuels.

The claimants further argued that, under the public trust doctrine and the common law doctrine of sovereignty, the federal state, as trustee, must safeguard federal natural resources for future generations and political decision-makers. Such resources, i.e., public property, are vital to citizens' well-being and fundamental rights, such as life and liberty. Petitioners claimed that the federal government breached its public trust obligations by failing to implement effective climate protection policies (actions and inactions).

## 3 Defendants' Separation of Powers Arguments

The separation of powers principle is central to the *Juliana* proceedings. The defendants did not want the case admitted to the trial stage and persistently filed motions to dismiss, for a stay, for summary judgment, and for judgment on the pleadings. The defendants requested dismissal of the case, advancing three separation of powers arguments: first, the case involves a non-justiciable political question. Second, the acting President is not a proper defendant in

50 Ibid., page 2: "*By their exercise of sovereign authority over our county's atmosphere and fossil fuel resources, … permitted, encouraged, and otherwise enabled continued exploitation, production, and combustion of fossil fuels, … deliberately allow*[*ing*] *atmospheric* $Co_2$ *concentrations to escalate to levels unprecedented in human history.*"

the lawsuit. Third, plaintiffs would not meet the *Article III* requirements for standing.

The Oregon District Court acknowledged twice that it must respect the boundaries among the branches of government, especially regarding remedies. Additionally, the Oregon District Court dismissed the acting President, Donald Trump, as a defendant from the lawsuit on *trias politica* grounds.

According to *Our Children's Trust*, the government's efforts to prevent the case from reaching the trial stage were remarkable.[51] Eventually, the government prevented the case from progressing to trial. We will focus on justiciability (Section 3.1) and *Article III* standing (Section 3.2).

### 3.1 Justiciability of the Juliana Claim

The defendants argued that the case was not justiciable because the plaintiffs did not challenge a specific cause of action under the Administrative Procedure Act (*APA*), but rather a broad range of decisions across multiple areas. These decisions concerned actions and inactions – regulating GHG emissions, granting extraction permits, subsidising, and promoting the fossil fuel industry. They argued that the case at bar presented a political question and that the court should dismiss. The Supreme Court established six criteria in its *Baker* decision, indicating that the case at bar could involve a political question. If any of the *Baker* factors are present, the court should exercise judicial self-restraint and dismiss the case before trial.[52]

The Oregon District Court nevertheless decided not to dismiss the case, stating that both review under the *APA* and under constitutional law were possible. After a thorough assessment, the court concluded that the case before it does not pose a nonjusticiable political question. The court emphasised that the judicial branch has a role in evaluating the claimants' allegations. It must determine whether constitutional rights are at stake, a legal question that falls within its domain.[53] District Judge Ann Aiken acknowledged that the court should exercise care when designing a remedy if the plaintiffs prevail on the merits.

---

51 Our Children's Trust; *ACTION ALERT: SAVE America's Climate Case!*; 27.02.2024: "*Today, the U.S. Department of Justice (DOJ) is doing everything in [its] power to silence these youth and shut down their case. They've made 22 extraordinary attempts to get it thrown out – that's more government persecution than* any other case *has faced in U.S. history.*"

52 *Baker v. Carr.*, 369 U.S. 186 (1962); Supreme Court; 26.03.1962; ("*Baker*").

53 *Juliana (2016)*; pages 18–28.

### 3.2 *Article III* Standing

Like in *Massachusetts v. EPA*, standing became a pivotal issue in *Juliana*. The Oregon District Court twice found (in 2016 and 2018) that plaintiffs satisfied all three *Article III* standing requirements: "*injury in fact,*" "*causation,*" and "*redressability.*"

The defendants appealed the finding, and in 2020, the Court of Appeals for the Ninth Circuit reversed it. In a split decision, it held that the petitioners did not, and could not, satisfy the redressability prong because ordering such redress would exceed the competence of an *Article III* court.[54] It would require far-reaching policy decisions to redress the plaintiffs' injuries. The legislative and executive branches must adopt a remedial plan and, among other things, reform the U.S. energy system. After that, the court would need to determine whether the plan effectively addresses the constitutional rights violation. Therefore, the Court of Appeals for the Ninth Circuit refrained from intervening and concluded that the petitioners should address the democratic branches or the electorate directly. Consequently, the court reversed the Oregon District Court's order and remanded the case to that court with instructions to dismiss it for lack of *Article III* standing.

District Judge Josephine Staton wrote a dissent in which she explained that she would grant *Article III* standing because partial redress would suffice to meet the redressability prong. Even if the court cannot halt climate change, Judge Staton emphasised that even partial relief matters. She pointed to the Supreme Court's ruling in *Massachusetts v. EPA*, in which the only relief was the regulation of GHG emissions from new vehicles.[55] She concluded that this was sufficient to allow the case to proceed to trial. The constitutional principle of perpetuity would oblige the government to preserve the Nation. Even though people could express themselves through the ballot box, this

---

54 *Juliana* (2020); page 32: "*That the other branches may have abdicated their responsibility to remediate the problem does not confer on Article III courts, no matter how well-intentioned, the ability to step into their shoes.*"

55 Ibid., dissenting opinion of District Judge Josephine Staton; pages 45–46: "*The majority portrays any relief we can offer as just a drop in the bucket* [...] *In a previous generation, perhaps that characterization would carry the day and we would hold ourselves impotent to address plaintiffs' injuries. But we are perilously close to an overflowing bucket. These final drops matter. A lot. Properly framed, a court order – even one that merely postpones the day when remedial measures become insufficiently effective – would likely have a real impact on preventing the impending cataclysm. Accordingly, I conclude that the court could do something to help the plaintiffs before us. And "something" is all that standing requires. In Massachusetts v. EPA, 549 U.S. 497 (2007), the Supreme Court explicitly held that a non-negligible reduction in emissions – there, by regulating vehicles emissions – satisfied the redressability requirement of Article III standing.*"

would not mean that judicial enforcement of constitutional principles should be barred. Judge Staton argued that in cases of existential threats and constitutional violations, it was time for courts to intervene. Therefore, classic approaches to the separation of powers and the role of courts require re-evaluation. If courts were to adhere to conservative interpretations, they would never step in, she argued.[56]

It appears from *Juliana* that *injury in fact* and *causation*, which the Justices still debated in *Massachusetts v. EPA*, were no longer issues. The court accepted that plaintiffs could establish both prongs. However, it ruled that the plaintiffs did not meet the *redressability* requirement.

Judge Josephine Staton's dissent suggested that some federal judges might reconsider the traditional separation of powers framework, and, notably, the requirements of *Article III* standing, in the context of mitigating climate change. If courts do not adopt a more flexible approach, standing will remain a significant hurdle to obtaining a court decision on the merits.

## 4 Climate Rights and Public Trust Obligations

Since the case was dismissed on standing grounds,[57] there is no final ruling on its merits. Nevertheless, the Oregon District Court's dicta on public trust obligations (Section 4.1) and climate rights (Section 4.2) should be emphasised, as they are essential to climate litigation.

### 4.1 Public Trust

The Due Process Clause of the Fifth Amendment, public trust, and substantial fundamental rights interconnect. The Oregon District Court held that plaintiffs could assert claims against federal defendants for violations of public trust rights before a federal court.[58]

In 2018, the Oregon District Court, ruling on the government's motions for judgment on the pleadings and summary judgment, did not revisit its 2016 ruling on the applicability of the public trust doctrine. It did not identify an error in the previous ruling and, since the defendants did not present new arguments, declined to revisit the decision. The District Court further empha-

56 Ibid., dissenting opinion of District Judge Josephine Staton; pages 63–64: "*To be sure, unless there is a constitutional violation, courts should allow the democratic and political processes to perform their functions. And while all would now readily agree that the 91 years between the Emancipation Proclamation and the decision in Brown v. Board was too long, determining when a court must step in to protect "never"; I say it is now.*"

57 *Juliana* (2020).

58 *Juliana* (2016); pages 36–51.

sised that the public trust question should be addressed later with a full factual record.[59]

### 4.2 Climate Rights

In the *Juliana* case, plaintiffs and defendants concurred on many scientific and factual statements about global warming, including the threat of dangerous climate change. They notably agreed that climate change has already affected life on Earth and that fossil fuel emissions increase the risks posed by global warming. Despite this knowledge and recognition, the federal government has not ceased supporting fossil fuels and continues to authorise or subsidise carbon-based energy, its extraction, consumption, and exportation.[60]

The defendants disagreed with the plaintiffs' claims regarding fundamental rights, arguing that there is no right to a climate system capable of sustaining human life. Such recognition would be unprecedented in the U.S.; although this claim is not new, courts have previously refrained from recognising that right.

In 2016, the Oregon District Court, for the first time, derived such a right from the U.S. federal constitution: "*I have no doubt that the right to a climate system capable of sustaining human life is fundamental to a free and ordered society.*"[61] According to the Court, new judicial interpretations of constitutional rights remain possible even in the absence of precedent. The judicial branch must interpret the Constitution and protect constitutional rights against "*governmental action that is affirmatively and substantially damaging the climate system in a way that will cause human deaths, shorten human lifespans, result in widespread damage to property, threaten human food sources, and dramatically alter the planet's ecosystem.*"[62]

To support its opinion, the Oregon District Court cited Justice Kennedy's Supreme Court opinion in *Obergefell v. Hodges*, which held that the court may assign new meanings to constitutional rights in response to changing exigencies. Therefore, the courts interpret the Constitution and amendments as living instruments.[63] As for substantive due process, the court acknowledged

59 *Juliana* (*2018*); pages 54 & 55.

60 Ibid., pages 5&6.

61 *Juliana* (*2016*), page 32.

62 Ibid., page 33.

63 *Obergefell v. Hodges*, 576 U. S. (2015); United States Supreme Court; 26.06.2015; page 11 & *Juliana* 2016; page 31: "*The nature of injustice is that we may not always see it in our own times. The generations that wrote and ratified the Bill of Rights and the Fourteenth Amendment did not presume to know the extent of freedom in all its dimensions, and so they entrusted to future generations a charter protecting the right of all persons to enjoy liberty*

that such a violation would be exceedingly difficult for the claimants to prove; however, this is not a reason to prevent the claimants from taking the case to trial.

## 5 Rising Support for Youth Cases

*Juliana* and subsequent State-court lawsuits could represent a turning point in U.S. federal courts' engagement with climate protection cases.[64] We will assess the proceedings at the federal-state level (Section 5.1), followed by an examination of the essential state court cases (Section 5.2).

### 5.1 Proceedings at the Federal-State Level

An array of experts, politicians, children's rights advocates, environmental groups, international organisations, and NGOs submitted *amicus curiae* briefs in *Juliana,* arguing that federal courts can indeed provide climate relief and that courts have both the competence and the duty to remedy constitutional grievances. In one of the *amicus curiae* briefs, twenty-four members of Congress argued that the judiciary, as a coequal branch, must ensure that the political branches comply with the constitutional framework, especially concerning the fundamental rights to life, liberty, and property. The brief argued that the fundamental rights of children and future generations are at stake and that courts are neutral and not bound by majoritarian politics. Courts must clearly state the law in cases alleging constitutional violations, and federal courts may order appropriate remedies. Therefore, as the brief claims, federal courts should grant plaintiffs' standing for trial.[65] Other *amicus curiae* briefs exposed what the government could do to redress injuries.

After the Court of Appeals for the Ninth Circuit issued its ruling, the *Juliana* plaintiffs submitted motions to amend their case in the Oregon District Court. By referring to *Brown v. Board of Education,*[66] the *Juliana* plaintiffs sought a declaratory judgment that the U.S. fossil fuel-based energy system is uncon-

---

*as we learn its meaning. When new insight reveals discord between the Constitution's central protections and a received legal stricture, a claim to liberty must be addressed."*

64 Kuh Katrina Fischer; *The Legitimacy of Judicial Climate Engagement*; Ecology Law Quarterly 63 (2019); 43; pages 11–17.

65 *Amicus Curiae* brief by twenty-four members of Congress (8–36082, ID: 11628535, Docket Entry: 179, 03.12.2020); page 6: "*We affirm the duties of the federal judiciary to assess the constitutionality of the conduct of its coequal branches and provide appropriate redress, and the vital role that our system of checks and balances plays in the healthy functioning of our democracy, ensuring each branch respects the fundamental rights of the people.*"

66 *Brown v. Board of Education of Topeka*, 347 U.S. 483 (1954); United States Supreme Court; 17.05.1954; ("*Brown v. Board of Education*").

stitutional. In *Brown v. Board of Education*, the U.S. Supreme Court ruled unanimously that racial segregation in public schools violated the Fourteenth Amendment to the U.S. Constitution and expanded civil rights protections. Judge Ann Aiken acknowledged in a telephonic status conference that all three branches of government needed to collaborate to address the climate crisis. She ordered the parties, the *Juliana* plaintiffs and the Department of Justice (*DOJ*) to engage in settlement discussions.[67] On November 1, 2021, Our Children's Trust announced that settlement discussions had failed to reach a resolution.[68]

On November 18, 2021, thirty-nine members of the House of Representatives wrote to President Biden, expressing their concerns that the Biden administration's stance in *Juliana* contradicted the President's commitments, even though the Oregon District Court recognised that all three branches of government needed to work together to address the climate crisis and ordered the parties (the *Juliana* plaintiffs and the Department of Justice) to engage in settlement discussions.[69]

Also, on November 18, 2021, in a letter to President Biden, nine U.S. Senators referred to the World Leaders' Summit, where President Biden pledged to confront the climate crisis and build a better world for all our children and grandchildren. The Senators urged the President to take climate change mitigation measures: "*We urge you to carefully review any appropriate programmatic and executive options that you have available across your Administration to make progress, and thus further your commitment to 'listen to science – and act,' by using a 'Government-wide approach' to tackling the climate crisis.*"[70]

---

67 Minutes of proceedings; Telephonic Status Conference held before Judge Ann L. Aiken; 13.05.2021.

68 Our Children's Trust press release; 01.11.2021: "*While I* [*Chief legal counsel Julia Olsen of Our Children's Trust*] *am unable to share specifics from these confidential talks, I can say, without reservation, that we came to the table in good faith and sought to participate in a productive discussion on behalf of our young clients, as was requested by Judge Aiken. However, it takes the participation of both sides of the table to have meaningful communication and seek solutions. When and if the Biden administration wants to talk to the youth about their case, they will be ready. Right now, our goal is to get to trial as fast as possible. Our nation is in a climate emergency. And yet emergency falls short in describing the climate situation and its devastating impact on these young Americans. We eagerly await a ruling from Judge Aiken on our amended complaint, which, if favourable, will put us back on track to trial in 2022.*"

69 *U.S. House of Representatives*; letter from thirty-nine members of the House of Representatives to President Biden; 18.11.2021.

70 *U.S. Senate*; letter from nine U.S. Senators to President Biden; 18.11.2021.

Again, on November 18, 2021, 167 environmental organisations sent a letter to the U.S. Department of Justice supporting the *Juliana* plaintiffs. The organisations urged the DOJ to consider President Biden's climate commitments and to pursue settlement negotiations in good faith.[71]

*Our Children's Trust* did not abandon the proceedings, and in 2022, it submitted further filings to the Oregon District Court, citing three recent Supreme Court rulings in support of its case. First, regarding *Dobbs v. Jackson Women's Health Organisation,* Juliana's attorneys argued that courts are competent to determine whether a right is constitutionally protected and whether the state has violated it. Declaratory judgment would qualify as an appropriate remedy. Second, referring to *West Virginia v. EPA,*[72] the plaintiffs emphasised that the EPA must control air pollution within the legal framework set by Congress. It would be an abuse of discretion to allow dangerous levels of GHGs. Third, according to *New York State & Pistol Assoc. v. Bruen,*[73] there would be a constitutional right to protect oneself against potential threats to life and limb. Climate change would not merely represent a potential danger but a real threat.

Ultimately, the defendants successfully prevented the case from proceeding to trial. On December 9, 2024, the Juliana plaintiffs filed a petition for a *writ of certiorari* in the U.S. Supreme Court seeking review of the Ninth Circuit's order dismissing the case. On March 24, 2025, the U.S. Supreme Court denied that petition.[74]

Since *Juliana,* the federal youth-led climate cases appear to have reached a dead end due to unloosened standing requirements, which, in turn, hinder full factual discussion of the right to a sustainable climate and climate-related public trust obligations. Judge Josephine Staton's dissent on the redressability prong of *Article III* standing has not yet had a substantial effect at the federal level.

---

71 167 environmental organisations, letter to the Department of Justice, 18.11.2021: "*We stand with these youth in our dismay with the DOJ's position and tactics in the Juliana litigation. This position flies in the face of the Biden administration's recent executive orders and policies addressing climate injustice and the climate crisis. The DOJ and defendant agencies must honour President Biden's commitments to listen to the science across all agencies and work with the youth to protect their rights and those of future generations. A critical step in fulfilling this commitment is for the DOJ to reverse its legal position, pursue good faith settlement discussions, and if those discussions do not achieve a resolution of the case, allow the youth plaintiffs their day in court.*"

72 *West Virginia v. EPA*, 597 U. S. __ (2022); United States Supreme Court; 30.06.2022.

73 *New York State Rifle & Pistol Assoc. v. Bruen*, 597 U. S. _ (2022); United States Supreme Court; 23.06.2022.

74 *Kelsey Cascadia Rose Juliana et al. v. United States et al.*; docket 24-645; order list 604 U.S.; United States Supreme Court; 24.03.2025; ["*Juliana* (2025)"].

### 5.1.1 *Lighthiser v. Trump*[75]

In *Lighthiser v. Trump*, 22 young people from Montana, Oregon, Hawai'i, California, and Florida filed a constitutional rights lawsuit challenging three Executive Orders (EO) issued by President Trump during his first month in office. These orders, which promote fossil fuels and restrict climate science, would worsen the climate crisis and threaten the youth plaintiffs' climate, health, and safety. The plaintiffs sought both declaratory and injunctive relief. The court should declare the presidential orders ultra vires and prohibit their implementation or enforcement.

The case was dismissed for lack of jurisdiction. As in *Juliana*, the plaintiffs proved both injury in fact and causation by presenting strong evidence that the production and combustion of fossil fuels contribute to global warming and endanger children's health and life. The challenged Executive Orders would lead to an increase in carbon dioxide levels and affect the plaintiffs in tangible ways. While acknowledging the plaintiffs' evidence and the real harms presented by climate change and the impact of the challenged *EO*s on carbon dioxide emissions, the court nevertheless dismissed the case. The court held that it could not provide redress.[76] In other words, the plaintiffs failed to meet the redressability prong.

The court distinguished this case from *Massachusetts v. the EPA* because, in the latter case, the plaintiffs challenged the denial of a rulemaking petition, a procedural right, and the case amounted to a procedural due process review. Additionally, Massachusetts, a sovereign state, would warrant broader standing. In the present case, the court would not grant wider access to trial by relaxing the standing criteria. The court could not provide adequate redress in this case because the relief sought would require it to scrutinise every climate-related agency since January 20, 2025, thereby implicating a broad range of policymaking. This would exceed the court's powers under the separation of powers. It would not only concern the invalidation of three Presidential Orders, but also the invalidation of all policy decisions, regulations, and projects of twelve federal agencies and the Executive Office of the President, which would normally require hundreds of lawsuits, not just one.[77]

On October 20, 2025, the youth plaintiffs appealed the lower court's decision to the United States Court of Appeals for the Ninth Circuit. The case is currently pending.

---

75 *Eva Lighthiser et al v. Donald J. Trump*; United States District Court for the District of Montana; CV 25-54-BU-DLC; 15.10.2025; (*Lighthiser v. Trump*).

76 Ibid; page 10.

77 Ibid; pages 26–28.

If there is no significant progress on redressability at the federal court level, there have been significant developments at the state court level.

### 5.2 Impacts from State Court Youth Cases

Following *Juliana*, youth cases were filed and decided in the state courts, which, in turn, could influence upcoming cases at the federal level. Like in *Juliana*, the state cases concerned climate rights and public trust obligations and hinged on the redressability prong. They sparked discussions about injunctive and declaratory relief. The youth plaintiffs initially faced a series of setbacks, and their cases were dismissed before reaching the trial stage as the courts exercised judicial restraint.

The following cases are examples of youth-led State court cases in which the petitioners were unable to reach the trial stage in their constitutional climate cases.

#### 5.2.1 *Aji P. v. State of Washington*[78]

In this case, opposing the state's fossil fuel-based energy and transportation policies, the plaintiffs argued for the *right to a stable climate system that sustains human life and liberty*. The court restrained itself by declining to hear the case in a 7–2 vote. Chief Justice González and Justice Whitener of the Washington Supreme Court would have granted judicial review.[79]

#### 5.2.2 *Chernaik v. Brown*[80]

In *Chernaik v. Brown*, a public trust case, the youth plaintiffs sought declaratory and injunctive relief against the State of Oregon for its failures to meet its fiduciary obligations to protect natural resources from climate impacts, which would require an expanded view of the public trust doctrine. The petitioners requested an expansion of the trust to encompass the atmosphere and other natural resources and sought a declaration that the State of Oregon is breaching its duty to prevent substantial impairment of the public trust resulting

---

78 *Aji P. v. State of Washington* (No. 80007-8-I; Supreme Court of the State of Washington; 10.06.2021.

79 They wrote in their dissent that this lawsuit would have been "*an opportunity to decide whether Washington's youth have a right to a stable climate system that sustains human life and liberty. We recite that we believe the children are our future, but we continue actions that could leave them a world with an environment on the brink of ruin and no mechanism to assert their rights or the natural world. This is our legacy to them described in the self-congratulatory words of judicial restraint.*"

80 *Chernaik v. Brown*; Docket number: S066564, 367 Or 143 (2020); Supreme Court of the State of Oregon; 22.10.2022.

from GHG emissions. The court held that, in the past, it adapted the trust to new situations and could expand it to cover more natural resources. The court did not want to extend the doctrine at that time and exercised judicial self-restraint. In his dissenting opinion, Justice Walters highlighted that courts must determine what the law requires and that the time would be ripe for an extension of the public trust doctrine.

#### 5.2.3 *Sagoonick v. State of Alaska*[81]

In *Sagoonick v. State of Alaska,* also a public trust and climate rights-based state court case, young Alaskans sought declaratory and injunctive relief concerning the state's energy policy. By failing to reduce GHG emissions, the state would violate the plaintiffs' constitutional rights and the constitutional provisions protecting natural resources. The Alaska Supreme Court exercised judicial self-restraint. Injunctive relief would concern political questions belonging to the political realm and refused declaratory relief, even though these claims did "*not necessarily present non-justiciable political questions*" on prudential grounds. Granting declaratory relief would not meaningfully accomplish the goals petitioners seek or settle the issue. Justices Maassen and Carney wrote a partially dissenting opinion arguing that a declaratory judgment recognising the constitutional right to a liveable climate would matter. The court should have granted the demand for declaratory relief.

#### 5.2.4 *Layla H. v. Commonwealth of Virginia*[82]

In *Layla H. v. Commonwealth of Virginia,* young people challenged the constitutionality of the Virginia Gas and Oil Act. Promoting fossil fuels would infringe on their rights to life and liberty, as well as the state's public trust obligations. The court exercised judicial self-restraint and dismissed the case, citing sovereign immunity, thereby shielding government action from judicial review.

#### 5.2.5 *Natalie R. v. State of Utah*[83]

Young claimants from Utah challenged the state's fossil-fuel-friendly policies and government conduct, arguing that these policies and conduct violated their rights to life and liberty under the Utah Constitution. According to the

81 *Sagoonick v. State of Alaska;* No. S-17297, Opinion No. 7583; Supreme Court of the State of Alaska; 28.01.2022.

82 *Layla H. v. Commonwealth of Virginia;* CL22000632-00; Richmond Circuit Court, Commonwealth of Virginia; 16.09.2022.

83 *Natalie R. v. State of Utah*; Case no. 220901658; Utah, District Court of the Third Judicial District; 09.11.2022 & *Natalie R. v. State of Utah*; 2025 UT 5; Utah, Supreme Court of the State of Utah; 20.03.2025.

court, declaratory relief could not effectively redress the plaintiffs' harms, nor would even an injunctive order. Striking down fossil fuel policies would not be sufficient to meet the redressability criterion, because this would not necessarily change the governmental stance on fossil fuel development. Additionally, it would violate the separation of powers principle, as the case was not based on specific permits but on broad state policies. Hence, the case was dismissed for lack of redressability and justiciability.

Following a series of setbacks, the youth plaintiffs successfully reached the trial stage and even obtained a ruling in their favour in *Held v. Montana*. Despite the federal court's decision on standing in *Juliana*, the Montana court held that the youth plaintiffs met the standing requirements, including the redressability prong.

### 5.2.6 *Held v. Montana*[84]

The Montana court held that the plaintiffs do not need to prove that *"the relief sought is 'substantially likely to redress their injuries."* It held, instead, that the plaintiffs' burden *"is to demonstrate that the redress sought will alleviate, remedy, or prevent harm caused by Defendants."* A court decision declaring that the State Energy Policy and the Climate Change Exception to the Montana Environmental Policy Act (*MEPA*) are unconstitutional would alleviate the harm they cause. The court distinguished between injunctive and declaratory relief. Although it could not order the establishment of a climate recovery plan, as this involved political questions, it could nonetheless grant declaratory relief.[85] Hence, the court allowed the plaintiff's claims for declaratory relief to proceed to trial.

---

84 *Rikki Held, et al. v. State of Montana, et al*, CDV-2020-307; Montana 1st Judicial District Court, Lewis & Clark County, 04.08.2021; ["*Held v. State of Montana (2021)*"] & *Rikki Held, et al. v. State of Montana, et al.*, CDV-2020–307; Montana 1st Judicial District Court, Lewis & Clark County, 14.08.2023; ["*Held v. State of Montana (2023)*"].

85 *Held v. State of Montana (2021)*, pages 21 & 22: Ordering such a remedial plan, and retaining jurisdiction over the plan's development, would require the court to make or evaluate complex policy decision entrusted to the discretion of other governmental branches. See Larson, ¶39, Juliana, 947 F.3d at 1171. In a similar vein, the court also finds that the requested injunctive relief seeking an accounting of GHG emissions violates the political question doctrine. Plaintiffs ask the court to order that Defendants retroactively review and "prepare a complete and accurate accounting of Montana's GHG emissions, including those emissions caused by the consumption of fossil fuels extracted in Montana and consumed out of state, and Montana's embedded emissions." Complaint ¶6 (Mar. 13, 2020). Such an order would require the court to exceed its authority by overseeing analysis and decision-making that should be left to "the wisdom and discretion of the legislative or executive branches." See Juliana, 947 F.3d at 1171. However, Youth Plaintiffs also offer a second argument: the court may grant declaratory

On the merits, the young petitioners challenged a provision of the *MEPA* that prohibits state agents from considering GHG emissions when assessing environmental impacts (the *MEPA limitation*), thereby favouring extractive industries and supporting fossil-based energy sources. Relying on the right to a clean and healthful environment enshrined in the Montana constitution, the court declared the *MEPA limitation* unconstitutional. The state failed to protect the plaintiffs' constitutional rights by authorising projects without comprehensive environmental impact assessments.[86] The court also granted injunctive relief, prohibiting the implementation of the unconstitutional *MEPA* limitation.

The State of Montana appealed to the Montana Supreme Court. While the case was pending, the Montana Supreme Court denied the defendant's motion to stay the trial court's order.[87] On December 18, 2024, the Montana Supreme Court affirmed the District Court's ruling on all points.[88] It held that the plaintiffs had standing to challenge the constitutionality of the *MEPA limitation*. The court affirmed that the right to a clean and healthful environment includes the right to a stable climate system, and it held that the *MEPA limitation* violated that right.[89]

On January 16, 2026, the plaintiffs filed a new case to enforce the Supreme Court's ruling. The young plaintiffs argued that the Montana Legislature had enacted laws that contradict the Supreme Court's order.[90]

---

relief without imposing an injunctive remedy. Courts have "the duty to decide the appropriateness and the merits of the declaratory request irrespective of its conclusion as to the propriety of the issuance of the injunction." Steffel v. Thompson, 415 U.S. 452, 468 (1974). Further, a district court has "power to declare rights, status, and other legal relations whether or not further relief is or could be claimed." Mont. Code Ann. § 27–8-201.

86 *Held v. State of Montana* (2023); pages 99 & 102: "*By enacting and enforcing the MEPA Limitation, the State is failing to meet their affirmative duty to protect Plaintiffs' right to a clean and healthful environment and to protect Montana's natural resources from unreasonable depletion.* [...] *By prohibiting analysis of GHG emissions and corresponding impacts on the climate, as well as how additional GHG emissions will contribute to climate change or be consistent with the Montana Constitution, the MEPA Limitation violates Youth Plaintiffs' right to a clean and healthful environment and is unconstitutional on its face.*"

87 *Rikki Held, et al. v. State of Montana, et al.*, DA 23-0575; Supreme Court of the State of Montana, 16.01.2024; ["*Held v. State of Montana (2024-1)*"].

88 *Rikki Held, et al. v. State of Montana, et al.*, DA 23-0575; Supreme Court of the State of Montana, 18.12.2024; ["*Held v. State of Montana (2024-2)*"].

89 Ibid., points 27 & 28: "In *Montana's living constitution, the right to a clean and healthful environment* is "*forward-looking and preventative.*"

90 *Rikki Held, et al. v. State of Montana, et al.*; Montana 1st Judicial District Court, Lewis & Clark County; (*Held v. State of Montana II*).

CHAPTER 2

# Inadequate GHG Regulation

## Introduction

Following the adoption of national climate protection plans, courts had to adjudicate lawsuits concerning the consistency of the nationally determined GHG reduction targets, their compliance with national and international commitments, the timing and pace of the reductions, the amount of information provided to the public, and even the consistency of the GHG emissions of domestic private companies. This chapter expounds on three of these cases.

Section 1, on *Urgenda,*[1] concerns the state's failure to meet its intermediate GHG reduction targets. These intermediary targets are crucial during the transition to climate neutrality, as they prevent unnecessary delays in decarbonisation.

Section 2 examines the consistency and specificity of climate protection plans. The case *Friends of the Irish Environment*[2] concerns the legality of the climate recovery plan adopted through secondary legislation. In contrast, the German case *Neubauer et al. v. Germany*[3] concerns the constitutionality of the German Climate Protection Law, the *Klimaschutzgesetz* (*KSG*).

These cases provide significant new insights into the exceptional nature and success of judicial review in climate protection. While the Irish Supreme Court did not recognise the potential for the climate recovery plan to violate human rights, the German Constitutional Court did. It even extended the protection of the German Constitution to petitioners from Nepal and Bangladesh.

1 *The State of the Netherlands v. the Urgenda Foundation,* 19/00135, ECLI:NL:HR:2019:2007; Supreme Court (Hoge Raad); 13.01.2020; ("*Urgenda 2020*").

2 *Friends of the Irish Environment CLG v. the Government of Ireland, Ireland and the Attorney General,* [Appeal No: 205/19]; Supreme Court; 31.07.2020; ["*Friends of the Irish Environment* (2020)"].

3 *Neubauer, et al. v. Germany,* ECLI:DE:BVerfG:2021:rs20210324. 1bvr265618; Bundesverfassungsgericht; 24.03.2021; ("*Neubauer*").

 | HTTPS://DOI.ORG/10.1163/9789004771710-006

## Section 1: Failure to Meet GHG Reduction Targets

### *The Urgenda Foundation v. the State of the Netherlands*[4]

### 1 Introduction

In Europe, the *Urgenda* decision is one of the leading cases, if not the leading case, on climate protection, the duty of care, and climate-related human rights. It concerns the state's failure to meet its intermediate GHG reduction targets. The case went through all three judicial instances: first, The Hague District Court (*Rechtbank Den Haag*); second, The Hague Court of Appeal (*Gerechtshof Den Haag*); and third, the Supreme Court (*Hoge Raad*). The government was unsuccessful in all three instances. Since the court rulings are consistent, I will focus on the highest court's decision and highlight significant differences from lower court decisions where necessary.

The *Urgenda* rulings enable us to examine the court's toolkit in climate-related judicial review. Scientific knowledge, international standards, international conventions, and human rights enabled the Dutch courts to issue significant decisions in favour of the plaintiffs despite the governmental authorities' arguments regarding the separation of powers. In the following developments, we will discuss what enabled the judicial branch to order a 25% reduction in Dutch GHG emissions by 2020, as compared to 1990.

### 2 The Petition

On November 12, 2012, the Urgenda Foundation sent a letter to the Dutch Prime Minister, requesting a 40% reduction in Dutch GHG emissions by 2020 compared to 1990 levels. *Urgenda* claimed that the state's GHG emissions are unlawful and violate the human rights enshrined in articles 2 (the right to life) and 8 (the right to home and family life) of the European Convention on Human Rights (ECHR). The Minister for Infrastructure and the Environment responded to *Urgenda*'s petition. On the one hand, Urgenda and the government agreed that the state must reduce GHG emissions. On the other hand, they disagreed about the speed and the amount of those reductions. The

4 *The Urgenda Foundation v. The State of the Netherlands*, C/09/456689 / HA ZA 13-1396, ECLI:NL:RBDHA:2015:7196; the Hague District Court (Rechtbank Den Haag); 24.06.2015; ("*Urgenda 2015*"); *The State of the Netherlands v. the Urgenda Foundation*, C/09/456689 / HA ZA 13-1396, ECLI:NL:GHDHA:2018:2610; the Hague Court of Appeal (Gerechtshof Den Haag); 09.10.2018; ("*Urgenda 2018*") & *The State of the Netherlands v. the Urgenda Foundation*, 19/00135, ECLI:NL:HR:2019:2007; Supreme Court (Hoge Raad); 13.01.2020; ("*Urgenda 2020*").

Dutch state did not want to commit to more than a 20% reduction in GHG emissions by 2020 relative to 1990, which would have been compatible with the agreed-upon EU climate protection policies at the time.

*Urgenda* thereon submitted a complaint to the District Court in The Hague, arguing that even if the state could meet its subsequent reduction targets, the delayed reduction increased the risk of exceeding the available carbon budget. *Urgenda* contended that state reductions should reach at least 25% by the end of 2020, as deemed necessary by climate science and international climate standards.

The Court had to determine whether the Dutch state was legally obliged to reduce its GHG emissions by a greater percentage than it had planned for 2020.

## 3 The Court Rulings

In all three instances, the Dutch courts ruled that the state had a legal obligation to reduce its GHG emissions to a greater extent than it had intended by 2020. All three courts ordered the state to reduce GHG emissions by 25% by 2020 compared to 1990 levels. The Dutch judges determined that the state was required to respect the internationally determined reduction target for developed countries, specifically a reduction from 25% to 40% until 2020, relative to 1990. This target had been set in Cancún by the parties to the Kyoto Protocol.[5] The District Court, affirmed by the Appellate Court and the Supreme Court, held that the state must comply with the lower end of the 25–40% norm. All three courts required the government to reduce its GHG emissions, but left it to the government's discretion to determine how to comply with the court orders.

The three *Urgenda* decisions support the assertion that scientific knowledge underpins international conventions and political standards in climate protection. The importance of scientific knowledge and international standards (Section 3.1), the significance of international commitments (Section 3.2), and the acknowledgement of positive obligations flowing from climate-related human rights (Section 3.3) were essential instruments in the courts' toolbox, either standing alone or in interplay with one another. Given that the separation of powers was a significant concern, Section 3.4 assesses how the courts addressed it.

---

5 Adams Sam; Earth Journalism Network; *A Way Forward: Agreements Reached in Cancun*; 10.12.2010; https://earthjournalism.net/stories/a-way-forward-agreements-reached-in-cancun. <07.01.2024>.

### 3.1 Scientific Knowledge and International Standards

To prevent dangerous climate change, scientists agreed that global warming should not exceed 2°C above pre-industrial levels. The District Court of The Hague ruled that this was the "*starting point for the development of climate policies*" worldwide.[6] More recently, scientific understanding has concluded that 2°C is still too high and that global temperatures should not surpass 1.5°C.

The courts referred to scientific knowledge: The District Court acknowledged that it had no independent knowledge or expertise in climate matters.[7] All three courts extensively referred to the fourth and fifth reports of the IPCC and summarised the legal and political international measures related to climate change.

### 3.2 International Commitments

The courts provided an overview of the relevant international conventions. One hundred and ninety-five (195) states, including the Netherlands, ratified the 1992 United Nations Framework Convention on Climate Change (*UNFCCC*) to prevent dangerous global warming. The *UNFCCC* distinguishes between *Annex I* states, the developed countries, and *Annex II* countries, the developing states. *Annexe I* countries are expected to lead in climate protection. Their GHG reduction targets must be more ambitious than those of *Annex II* countries, and they should provide economic support to developing states. That distinction between developed and developing states persists beyond the scope of that first framework convention. The Climate Change Conferences, also known as the Conferences of the Parties (*COP*), have successively specified the reduction goals. Following the recommendation of the 4th *IPCC* report, at each *COP* (19–21), states systematically reiterated that *Annex I* states should reduce their emissions by at least 25–40% below 1990 levels by 2020. The Netherlands is an *Annex I* country, so its GHG reduction target for 2020 should be at least 25% below 1990 levels.

The European Union (*EU*) aimed to lead the fight against climate change and decided to increase its overall reduction target from 20% to 30% by 2020, compared to 1990, provided that other *Annex I* countries would do the same.

---

6 *Urgenda* (2015); point 4.1.4.

7 Ibid., point 4.3. "*The court does not have independent expertise in this area and will base its assessment on that which the Parties have submitted and the facts admitted between them. This concerns both current scientific knowledge and (other) data the State acknowledges or deems to be correct. Many of these data are available under section 2 of this judgment ("The facts"). An analysis of these data, which are sometimes repeated, will enable the court to determine the severity of the climate change problem. Based on this information, the court will assess the claim and the defence put up against it.*"

The Netherlands decided in 2007 to pursue a 30% reduction target by 2020 compared to 1990. However, from 2011 onwards, it chose to follow the initially set 20% target. It then adjusted its policy objectives downward, despite gaining a greater understanding of the risks posed by climate change. The forecast was that the Netherlands would achieve a 14–17% reduction compared to 1990, thereby falling short of the reduction expectations of an Annex *I* country.

It is insufficient for the state to only achieve medium- to long-term reduction targets; it must also respect short-term targets. Immediate and short-term actions matter given the imminent threat posed by dangerous climate change. Science exposed climate hazards and emphasised that political actors must take the necessary precautions. In *Urgenda*, those precautions resulted in at least a 25% reduction in 2020 compared to 1990.[8] Failing to meet intermediate targets diminishes the available carbon budget and reduces the options for future political leaders, as GHG reductions would have to become more ambitious later.[9] Human rights were essential considerations. We now turn to these.

### 3.3 Applicability of Articles 2 and 8 ECHR and the Duty of Care

*Urgenda* argued that, under Articles 2 (the right to life) and 8 (the right to a home and family life) of the ECHR, the state has a positive obligation to take protective measures to prevent dangerous climate change. Even before the ECtHR had its say on the applicability of Articles 2 and 8 of the ECHR to

---

8 *Urgenda* (*2015*); point 4.73: "*[I]n view of the latest scientific and technical knowledge it is the most efficient to mitigate and it is more cost-effective to take adequate action than to postpone measures in order to prevent hazardous climate change. The court is therefore of the opinion that the State has a duty of care to mitigate as quickly and as much as possible.*"

9 *Urgenda* (*2018*); point 71: "*To summarize, from the foregoing it follows that up till now the State has done too little to prevent a dangerous climate change and is doing too little to catch up, or at least in the short term (up to end-2020). Targets for 2030 and beyond do not take away from the fact that a dangerous situation is imminent, which requires interventions being taken now. In addition to the risks in that context, the social costs also come into play. The later actions are taken to reduce, the quicker the available carbon budget will diminish, which in turn would require taking considerably more ambitious measures at a later stage, as is acknowledged by the State (Statement of Appeal 5.28), to eventually achieve the desired level of 95% reduction by 2050. In this context, the following excerpt from AR5 (cited in legal ground 2.19 of the judgment) is also worth noting: "(...) Delaying mitigation efforts beyond those in place today through 2030 is estimated to substantially increase the difficulty of transition to low-longer-term emissions levels and narrow the range of options consistent with maintaining temperature change below 2 C relative to pre-industrial levels.*"

climate protection cases.[10] The Hoge Raad ruled that the rights to life and to private and family life oblige the Dutch state to protect the climate.[11]

The Dutch Supreme Court did not deem it necessary to ask for an advisory opinion before issuing its decision.[12] It simply assumed that climate change poses a threat that entails real and immediate risks to the population and demands positive state actions to protect the rights to life, home, and family life.[13] It based its findings of positive state obligations on science and internationally accepted standards: "*When giving substance to the positive obligations imposed on the State pursuant to Articles 2 and 8 ECHR, one must consider broadly supported scientific insights and internationally accepted standards. Important in this respect are, among other things, the reports from the IPCC.*"[14]

On April 9, 2024, the ECtHR issued rulings on its first three climate cases: *Carême v. France*,[15] *Duarte Agostinho and Others v. Portugal and 32 Others*,[16]

---

10 *Urgenda* (2020); point 5.6.3; page 27: "*As the State has asserted, the ECtHR has not yet issued any judgments regarding climate change or decided any cases that bear the hallmarks that are particular to issues of climate change. Those hallmarks are, briefly put, the dangers presented by a globally occurring activity – the emission of greenhouse gases all over the world, and not just from Dutch territory – whose consequences will have a worldwide impact, including in the Netherlands. The question is whether the global nature of the emissions and the consequences thereof entail that no protection can be derived from Articles 2 and 8 ECHR, such that those provisions impose no obligation on the State in this case.*"

11 *Urgenda* (2020); point 5.7.1; page 27: "*The answer to the question referred to in 5.6.3 above is in the opinion of the Supreme Court, that, under Articles 2 and 8 ECHR, the Netherlands is obliged to do 'its part' in order to prevent dangerous climate change, even if it is a global problem.*"

12 *Urgenda* (2020); point 5.6.4; page 27: "*The Supreme Court considers the answer to this question to be sufficiently clear. It will therefore give the answer to this question itself and will not submit it to the ECtHR for an advisory opinion, as is possible but not compulsory under Protocol no. 16 to the ECHR, which entered into effect on 1 June 2019. In addition, both parties have asked the Supreme Court to hand down its judgment before the end of 2019, in view of the time to which the District Court's order, upheld by the Court of Appeal, relates, which is the end of 2020.*"

13 Spier Jaap; *The "Strongest" Climate Ruling Yet': The Dutch Supreme Court's Urgenda Judgment; page* 324.

14 *Urgenda* (2020); page 5.

15 *Carême v. France*, application no. 7189/21; ECtHR; 09.04.2024. The ECtHR dismissed the case because Mr. Carême did not meet the victim test as he left the municipality of Grande-Synthe and moved to Brussels to become a member of the EU Parliament. Grande-Synthe's municipality successfully defended its citizens' interests before the French Conseil d'État.

16 *Duarte Agostinho and Others v. Portugal and 32 Others*, application no. 39371/20; *ECtHR*; 09.04.2024. The ECtHR dismissed the *Portuguese youth case* on two grounds. On the one

and *Verein KlimaSeniorinnen Schweiz and Others v. Switzerland.*[17] Only *KlimaSeniorinnen* is a decision on the merits. The ECtHR ruled for the first time on the applicability of Articles 2, 8, and 6 in relation to climate change. Whereas Article 8 would undoubtedly apply to climate change, *"it would be possible to assume that a serious risk of a significant decline in a person's life expectancy owing to climate change ought also to trigger the applicability of Article 2.*[18]

The Court eventually ruled that the Swiss Government had violated Articles 8[19] and 6.[20]

### 3.4 The Separation of Powers

The *Urgenda* rulings can be qualified as activist decisions. This section explores what entitled the courts to order reductions in Dutch GHG emissions and whether the court decisions could be considered violations of the separation of powers.

*Urgenda* claimed that a court order to reduce GHG emissions does not affect the *trias politica*, whereas the state defendants believed it does. The three courts also understood that this case could blur the line of demarcation between the branches of government.

The District Court clarified that it would not interfere with the democratic branches and would carefully weigh legal protection against governmental discretion. Even though the court stated that it did not intend to interfere with the policy-making area, the District Court devoted an entire section to the doctrine of separation of powers, demonstrating that it was walking a tightrope. Each instance dealt with judicial overreach separately; the District Court decision was the most explicit.

---

hand, it did not want to extend its extraterritorial jurisdiction; on the other hand, the claimants failed to exhaust the remedies available in Portugal.

17 *Verein KlimaSeniorinnen Schweiz and Others v. Switzerland*, application no. 53600/20; *ECtHR*; 09.04.2024 (*"KlimaSeniorinnen"*).

18 Ibid., points 513 & 536.

19 *Ibid.*, point 537: *"In conclusion, there were some critical lacunae in the Swiss authorities' process of putting in place the relevant domestic regulatory framework, including a failure by them to quantify, through a carbon budget or otherwise, national GHG emissions limitations. Furthermore, the Court has noted that, as recognized by the relevant authorities, the State had previously failed to meet its past GHG emission reduction targets (see paragraphs 558 to 559 above). By failing to act in good time and in an appropriate and consistent manner regarding the devising, development and implementation of the relevant legislative and administrative framework, the respondent State exceeded its margin of appreciation and failed to comply with its positive obligations in the present context."*

20 Ibid., points 632-639. The domestic court did not seriously engage with the legal actions and disproportionally restricted access to the court.

Through its constitution, laws, and adherence to international conventions, the state provided the framework for the judicial branch to perform its checks on legality. In other words, the state must respect its legal commitments under national and international law. In *Urgenda*, those commitments stemmed, among other things, from signing and adhering to international conventions such as the *UNFCCC* and the Kyoto Protocol. The state explicitly acknowledged its responsibility and obligation to reduce GHG emissions sufficiently to prevent dangerous climate change. Whether the state breached its duty of care by taking insufficient measures to prevent hazardous climate change is a legal issue, not a political one.

The Dutch system is characterised by a balance between state powers, and the judicial branch's role is to settle legal disputes by upholding the rule of law, including actions of its co-powers that are challenged in such disputes.[21] The Supreme Court reaffirmed this.[22]

When reviewing legality, the court applies the law to the facts of the case. However, policymaking, interest balancing, and defining specific reduction goals across sectors such as transport, energy, building, or agriculture are political concerns. They are not, strictly speaking, matters of law.[23] Nevertheless, they are not entirely disconnected from the law. Not all policy considerations are legally acceptable. As discussed above, state conduct must consider scientific insights, international standards, human rights, and the duty of care. The state cannot, for instance, delay its GHG reductions on the grounds that domestic emissions are insignificant compared to global emissions or international GHG reduction efforts.[24]

---

21 *Urgenda* (2015); point 4.95: "*It is worthwhile noting that a judge, although not elected and therefore has no democratic legitimacy, has democratic legitimacy in another – but vital – respect. His authority and ensuing "power" are based on democratically established legislation, whether national or international, which has assigned him the task of settling legal disputes. This task also extends to cases in which citizens, individually or collectively, have turned against government authorities. The task of providing legal protection from government authorities, such as the State, preeminently belong to the domain of a judge. This task is also enshrined in legislation*".

22 *Urgenda* (2020); page 6: "*This mandate to the courts to offer legal protection, even against the government, is an essential component of a democratic state under the rule of law.*" & Ibid., page 40: "*If the government is obliged to do something, it may be ordered to do so by the courts, as anyone may be, at the request of the entitled party* [...]. *This is a fundamental rule of constitutional democracy, which has been enshrined in our legal order.*"

23 *Urgenda* (2015); point 4.95.

24 Ibid., point 4.79.

The court held that it did not enter the political domain in the current case but applied the law to the facts to provide legal protection.[25] After the first injunctive order, it left the state's political branches with complete discretion over how to comply. It did not impose a climate policy nor specify a channel to inform the public about climate change risks.

The court's appreciation that it did not interfere with the political powers is controversial, as it has considerably limited the state's discretion in addressing global warming by prioritising the reduction of GHG emissions over adaptation measures.[26]

## 4 Effects of the *Urgenda* Decisions

The judicial branch considerably limited the political leeway to address global warming by ordering the state to respect its prior commitments. The state could decide on more ambitious GHG reductions, but not on less ambitious ones. Henceforth, the state must meet the intermediary reduction steps to which it has committed itself.

*Urgenda* is referred to in climate cases worldwide and has had a multiplying effect. The UN High Commissioner for Human Rights emphasised in a news release about the Urgenda decision that "*the decision confirms that the Government of the Netherlands and, by implication, other governments have binding legal obligations, based on international human rights law, to undertake strong reductions in emissions of greenhouse gases.*"[27]

---

25 Ibid., page 1: "*With this order, the court has not entered the domain of politics. The court must provide legal protection, also in cases against the government, while respecting the government's scope for policymaking. For these reasons, the court should exercise restraint and has limited therefore the reduction order to 25%, the lower limit of the 25%-40% norm.*"

26 Ibid., point 4.75: "*The court emphasizes that this first and foremost should concern mitigation measures, as adaptation measures will only allow the State to protect its citizens from the consequences of climate change to a limited level. If the current greenhouse gas emissions continue in the same manner, global warming will take such a form that the costs of adaptation will become disproportionately high. Adaptation measures will therefore not be sufficient to protect citizens against the aforementioned consequences in the long term. The only effective remedy against hazardous climate change is to reduce the emission of greenhouse gases. Therefore, the court arrives at the opinion that from the viewpoint of efficient measures available the State has limited options: mitigation is vital for preventing dangerous climate change.*"

27 The United Nations; OHCR; *Bachelet welcomes top court's landmark decision to protect human rights from climate change*; <12.10.2021>.

One essential effect of *Urgenda* is that citizens are entitled to a viable climate through Articles 2 and 8 of the ECHR. The positive obligations arising from those articles inform the duty of care owed by the contracting parties.

Following *Urgenda*'s success, Dutch courts expanded the state's obligations to private companies (Section 4.1). *Urgenda* even gained importance beyond the Dutch state, as citizens worldwide took their governments to court, claiming that national climate protection efforts were insufficient (Section 4.2).

### 4.1 Expanding *Urgenda* in the Netherlands

The Dutch District Court in The Hague expanded GHG reduction obligations to private companies and their emissions outside the EU (Section 4.1.1). It furthermore expanded the Dutch Kingdom's responsibilities to its overseas territories (Section 4.1.2). However, this expansion reached a limit in civil aviation and cross-border flights (Section 4.1.3).

#### 4.1.1 *Milieudefensie Et Al. v. Royal Dutch Shell Plc*[28]

In *Milieudefensie et al. v. Royal Dutch Shell plc*, the District Court in The Hague ruled that Royal Dutch Shell also owes a duty of care to reduce its GHG emissions. The Shell group must cut emissions by at least 45% by 2030, compared to 2019, including emissions from subsequent energy combustion.

The court deduced from the *UN Guiding Principles on Business and Human Rights* and other soft law instruments that companies are also obliged to respect human rights. The Court rejected Shell's arguments that the EU Emissions Trading System (*ETS*) precluded the court from ordering further emission cuts. The court clarified that the *ETS* only covered European emissions, not non-EU emissions, and that the standard of care requires Shell to reduce all global emissions that could harm Dutch citizens, not just those on EU territory.

Shell appealed the decision on July 20, 2020, and the Court of Appeal of the Hague issued its decision on November 11, 2024. It confirmed that private companies, such as Shell, must reduce their GHG emissions. The court carefully assessed the human rights obligations in the context of climate change, including their horizontal effect, drawing on national and international law and case law. The court specifically determined the direct effect of the right to climate protection in private relationships. It held that companies have "*their*

---

28 *Milieudefensie et al. v. Royal Dutch Shell plc*, C/09/571932 / HA ZA 19-379, ECLI:NL:RBDHA:2021:5339; The Hague District Court (Rechtbank Den Haag); 26.05.2021 & *Milieudefensie et al. v. Royal Dutch Shell plc*; 200.302.332/01, ECLI:NL:GHDHA:2024:2100; The Hague Court of Appeal (Gerechtshof Den Haag); 12.11.2024.

*own responsibility in achieving the targets of the Paris Agreement.*"[29] As a major oil company, Shell would bear a special responsibility.[30]

Regarding the specific reduction target set by the court in the first instance, the Court of Appeal stated that the overall reduction target could not be imposed on Shell. Referring to *KlimaSeniorinnen*, it reiterated that States have limited discretion regarding their commitment to reduce GHG emissions but enjoy broad discretion in deciding how to reach climate goals, which requires policy choices. In *KlimaSeniorinnen*, the ECtHR concerns about the separation of powers principle by holding that its action would complement the democratic processes. Pointing to the principle of subsidiarity, the Court acknowledged that the states are entitled to a large but not unlimited margin of appreciation. It ruled on the questions of law but refrained from intervening in policy or political choices. The Court ruled that the Swiss Government had violated Articles 8 and 6, emphasising that its rulings are essentially declaratory and that the state parties remain responsible for determining how to effectively implement the court decision, which is subject to the supervision of the Committee of Ministers.

So far, the Dutch legislator has not imposed specific reduction targets on individual companies, so the court cannot hold Shell accountable for the average global reduction rate.[31]

### 4.1.2 *Greenpeace Netherlands and Eight Citizens of Bonaire v. State of the Netherlands*[32]

In this case, the petitioners claimed, among other points, that the state failed to adequately protect the citizens of Bonaire, a Caribbean island belonging to the Dutch Kingdom, against the dangers posed by climate change. The court concluded that the state breached the positive obligations under Article 8

---

29 *Milieudefensie et al. v. Royal Dutch Shell plc;* 200.302.332/01, ECLI:NL:GHDHA:2024:2100; The Hague Court of Appeal (Gerechtshof Den Haag); 12.11.2024; English translation; point 7.27.

30 Ibid., point 7.79.

31 *Milieudefensie et al. v. Royal Dutch Shell plc;* 200.302.332/01, ECLI:NL:GHDHA:2024:2100; The Hague Court of Appeal (Gerechtshof Den Haag); 12.11.2024; English translation; point 7.81: "*The court has taken into account the fact that Shell is a major player in its decision that there is a legal obligation for Shell to reduce its emissions." However, given that there are different reduction pathways for different sectors in different countries, this fact does not mean that Shell can be held to the average global reduction rate.*"

32 *Greenpeace Netherlands and eight citizens of Bonaire v. State of the Netherlands;* C/09/659832 / HA ZA 24-53 (ENG); the Hague District Court (Rechtbank Den Haag); 28.01.2026.

ECHR, as well as Article 14 ECHR and Article 1 of Protocol 12 to the ECHR on discrimination.

By considering the latest scientific knowledge and applying relevant international climate law provisions (i.e. the UN climate framework), and referencing the ECtHR decision in *Klimaseniorinnen*, the ICJ advisory opinion on the obligations of States in respect of climate change, and the *Urgenda* ruling, the court identified several shortcomings related to climate adaptation,[33] climate mitigation,[34] and procedural safeguards[35] (obligations that I consider to be democratic participatory rights).

Being a particularly vulnerable territory, Bonaire faces greater climate risks than the European Netherlands. The Bonaire population is already experiencing adverse consequences. By being more proactive in addressing climate adaptation on its European territory, the Kingdom violated Article 14 of the ECtHR in conjunction with Article 8 of the ECHR.[36]

The court issued declaratory and injunctive relief. In accordance with international obligations, the Dutch state must address the shortcomings identified by the court. Some deficiencies concern the Kingdom as a whole; others relate specifically to Bonaire. The state must comply with its international obligations, including respecting the specific timeframes. As in *Urgenda*, the court left the question of how to comply to the political branches of government.

This ruling extended the *Urgenda* decision to the Kingdom's overseas territories.

### 4.1.3 *Greenpeace Netherlands v. State of the Netherlands*[37]

Greenpeace Netherlands, in a petition to the District Court of The Hague, demanded that the state impose $CO_2$ reduction obligations on KLM. The court rejected such an order because transboundary GHG emissions fall within the competence of the International Civil Aviation Organization (*ICAO*) rather than the Dutch state.

In other words, transboundary GHG emissions from air carriers do not impact the national reduction targets; therefore, neither the Dutch government nor KLM has a duty of care towards Greenpeace Netherlands in that transnational policy area.

---

33 Ibid, pages 43–47.
34 Ibid, pages 47–52.
35 Ibid, pages 52–53.
36 Ibid, pages 53–55.
37 *Greenpeace Netherlands v. State of the Netherlands*, C/09/600364 / KG ZA 20-933, ECLI: NL:RBDHA:2020:12440; The Hague District Court; 12.09.2020.

### 4.2 Effects beyond the Dutch State

The *Urgenda* decisions are frequently cited and quoted by courts around the world. In what follows, we will highlight the Belgian decision *ZW Klimaatzaak v. Kingdom of Belgium and Others* as one of the more recent decisions that underscore the significance of *Urgenda.*

The NGO "*ASBL Klimaatzaak*" and 58,000 citizens filed a lawsuit[38] against the Belgian State, the Walloon Region, the Flemish Region, and the Brussels-Capital Region for the lack of consistent climate protection measures. The state entities would infringe upon the general duty of care imposed by the Belgian Civil Code and the human rights obligations set out in Articles 2 and 8 of the European Convention on Human Rights (ECHR). Petitioners argued that the law required the Belgian government to reduce GHG emissions more ambitiously than it had. They asked the court to impose the GHG reduction targets set by the Belgian Expert Group on Climate and Sustainable Development. The targets should be 40% by 2020, 48% or at least 42% by 2025, 65% or at least 55% by 2030, and climate neutrality by 2050.

Before making a decision, the court provided a 36-page review of background information on climate protection from 1988 to 2021, including scientific insights (i.e., IPCC reports), international conventions, COP decisions, European policies, and Belgian climate protection measures.

As in *Urgenda*, the Belgian court determined that the federal state and the three regions, jointly and individually, breached their duty of care by failing to implement the necessary measures to prevent dangerous climate change. Even after repeated warnings from the European Union, Belgium continued to fall short in effective climate governance, and the complex cooperation between the federal government and the federated entities led to shortcomings in climate mitigation.

#### 4.2.1 First Court Stage

According to the court, considering the state entities' knowledge about dangerous climate change, federal and federated entities should have acted with greater prudence and diligence by taking adequate measures to prevent it, which is in tension with the general duty of care of the Belgian Civil Code and articles 2 and 8 of the ECHR.[39]

---

38 *Klimaatzaak* (*2021*); page 66 of the English translation.

39 Ibid., page 83 of the English translation: "*Holds that, in pursuing their climate policy, the defendants do not behave as normally prudent and diligent authorities, which constitutes a fault within the meaning of Article 1382 of the Civil Code;* [*h*]*olds that, in pursuing their climate policy, the defendants infringe the fundamental rights of the plaintiffs, and more*

With direct reference to *Urgenda*, the court held that the global nature of climate change does not exempt state entities from their obligations under Articles 2 and 8 of the ECHR.[40] However, unlike Urgenda, the court held that Belgium must not reduce its GHG emissions from 25% to 40% by 2020 compared to 1990, because that target would not be considered compulsory. The only binding target would be the 20% reduction target set by the amended Kyoto Protocol (Doha Amendment). Most developed states aimed to achieve a 20% reduction, which would, therefore, be the only binding target for Belgium.

The court found fault with the Belgian authorities but declined to impose the reduction targets demanded by the petitioners.[41] As long as the political branches do not convert the reduction targets set by the Belgian Expert Group on Climate and Sustainable Development into binding legal instruments, the court cannot intervene. In other words, if state entities fail to take consistent mitigation measures, the court can hold them responsible for abusing discretion. However, it cannot set reduction targets up front.

#### 4.2.2 Appeal Stage

The petitioners appealed the judgment of the first instance. They again requested a court injunction imposing the specific reduction targets. The general duty of care and human rights obligations would require the state to respect those more stringent reduction targets.

On November 30, 2023, the Court of Appeal of Brussels[42] confirmed that the Belgian state, the Flemish Region and the Brussels-Capital Region had violated articles 2 and 8 of the ECHR and committed faults under articles 1382 and 1383 of the Civil Code concerning the climate policy they pursued for the periods from 2013 to 2020 and from 2021 onwards. Considering Articles 13 of the ECHR and 9.4 of the Aarhus Convention, the court should end human rights violations, prevent harm, and provide remedies. The court relaxed the Walloon Region and ordered:

---

*specifically Articles 2 and 8 of the ECHR, by failing to take all necessary measures to prevent the effects of climate change on the plaintiffs' life and privacy."*

40 Ibid., page 61 of the English translation.

41 Ibid., page 80 of the English translation: "*In other words, if the judiciary is competent to establish the fault committed by the public authority, even in the exercise of its discretionary power, it cannot, on this occasion, deprive the latter of its political freedom nor substitute itself for it – The judiciary cannot assess the appropriateness of the action of the public authority when the latter is exercising its competence nor exercise itself the discretionary power which belongs to this public authority.*"

42 *Klimaatzaak* (2023).

> the Belgian State, the Flemish Region and the Brussels-Capital Region to take, in consultation with the Walloon Region, the appropriate measures to do their part in reducing the overall volume of annual GHG emissions from Belgian territory by at least 55% in 2030 compared with 1990 [the relevant EU reduction target].[43]

## 5 Conclusion

*Urgenda* has significantly impacted climate-based judicial review worldwide and is notable for the court's enforcement of the state's duty to limit GHG emissions to a specific target in order to protect the climate.[44] Imposing such a GHG threshold on the Dutch state was possible because of binding international obligations. The end of the GHG reduction period drew closer, and the numbers indicated a failure to meet the target. Moreover, the government stated that it did not intend to reduce GHG emissions by more than 20% by 2020, relative to 1990 levels. Even if the *Urgenda* ruling was a progressive decision, it was grounded on existing legal dispositions and principles.[45]

In *Milieudefensie et al. v. Royal Dutch Shell plc*, the Dutch court expanded the obligation to reduce GHGs to Dutch companies, but ultimately did not set a mandatory GHG reduction target. Although the Court of Appeal in The Hague highlighted in *Milieudefensie et al. v. Royal Dutch Shell plc* that private companies must also reduce their own GHG emissions, they are not automatically subjected to the global reduction rate. The Dutch State enjoys broad discretion in deciding how to reach its climate goals. The Dutch legislator could impose specific targets for specific sectors. In *Greenpeace Netherlands and eight citizens of Bonaire v. State of the Netherlands,* the court reaffirmed the state's obligation to comply with international climate law obligations and extended that protection to the Kingdom's overseas territories. The court highlighted their particular vulnerability and stressed the need for timely and effective adaptation measures.

---

43 *Klimaatzaak* (2023), page 158 of the English translation.

44 Colby Heather, Ana Stella Ebbersmeyer, Lisa Marie Heim, and Marthe Kielland Røssaak; *Judging Climate Change: The Role of the Judiciary in the Fight Against Climate Change;* Oslo Law Review 7, No. 3 (17 December 2020); 168–85.

45 Geel Oliver; *Urgenda and Beyond: The past, present and future of climate change public interest litigation,* Maastricht University Journal of Sustainability Studies, Vol. 3 (01.07.2017); page 65 with reference to Heringa, A.W. (2016). Rechter en politiek: verzaakt de politiek/wetgever of dient de rechter juist het belang van de wetgever? Milieu en Recht. 3(34), pages 203–206.

In *VZW Klimaatzaak v. Kingdom of Belgium and Others,* the first instance court upheld the duty of care and the protection of human rights under Articles 2 and 8 of the ECHR, similar to *Urgenda*. However, the Belgian decision also demonstrated that arguments based on scientific insights have their limitations. Because the political branches did not translate the scientifically determined reduction targets into binding legal instruments, the Belgian Court held that it could not order respect for those targets. It could not interfere with the political branches of government that are solely competent to implement climate policies.

The Court could, in turn, assess whether the state entities implemented their climate change policies with prudence and diligence, in conformity with their state responsibilities, including the protection of human rights. On appeal, the court held that GHG emission reductions from Belgian territory must meet the European Union's 2030 target of at least 55% relative to 1990.

## Section 2: Adequacy and Specificity of the Climate Protection Plan

### Introduction

Lawsuits concerning the adequacy of climate protection plans raise concerns about constitutional, human, and participatory rights. The consistency, precision, foreseeability, and effects of the projected governmental mitigation measures on people's rights and liberties are a significant concern in these cases.

We will first discuss the *Friends of the Irish Environment v. Ireland* lawsuit (I), which concerns the consistency of the GHG reduction trajectory set by the government's Climate Protection Plan. The Irish Supreme Court did not perceive any constitutional rights risks from the recovery plan aimed at reducing the state's GHG emissions. However, it quashed the plan for lack of precision, thereby promoting participatory rights.

Then, we will turn to *Neubauer v. Germany* (II), a case about the consistency of the GHG emission reduction trajectory set by the German Climate Protection Law (*Klimaschutzgesetz*, hereafter *KSG*). In 2021, the German Federal Constitutional Court, the *Bundesverfassungsgericht*, addressed four constitutional complaints regarding the constitutionality of the federal Climate Protection Act. Unlike the Irish Supreme Court, the German court could perceive the constitutional risks associated with climate protection, provided guidance, and refrained from quashing the law.

### I) *Friends of the Irish Environment v. Ireland*[46]

#### Introduction

*The Friends of the Irish Environment* lawsuit shows that climate litigation is extraordinary because the Irish Supreme Court accepted the case directly, thereby bypassing the appeal stage. Such a *leapfrog appeal* is permitted only in exceptional circumstances. The Supreme Court acknowledged the exceptional circumstances posed the threat of dangerous climate change, which the parties agreed upon, and, notably, the scientific evidence calling for urgent

46 *Friends of the Irish Environment CLG v. the Government of Ireland, Ireland and the attorney general,* [2017 No. 793 JR]; High Court, 19.09.2019; ["*Friends of the Irish Environment* (2019)"] & *Friends of the Irish Environment CLG v. the Government of Ireland, Ireland and the attorney general,* [Appeal No: 205/19]; Supreme Court; 31.07.2020; ["*Friends of the Irish Environment* (2020)"].

climate protection efforts. The Supreme Court decision is also significant because it strengthened public participation by imposing precision and transparency requirements for the governmental climate mitigation plan.

The lawsuit highlights the challenges courts face in handling quasi-political cases. The court had to address arguments on justiciability, standing, and the separation of powers. The High Court ruled that the government's climate mitigation plan was beyond its reach and that, given the executive branch's discretion, it should not intervene. The Supreme Court overturned the High Court's decision and the mitigation plan. It ruled that the mitigation plan may have been policy at one point, but became law after approval.

## 1 Background of the Case

The Irish legislator, the *Oireachtas*, enacted the Climate Action and Low Carbon Development Act (*CALCDA*) in 2015, which defined a National Transition Objective (*NTO*) for an environmentally sustainable Irish economy by 2050. It also stipulated the need to adopt a GHG mitigation plan. The government adopted and approved the National Mitigation Plan (*NMP*), published on July 19, 2017. The Advisory Council, also established by the *CALCDA*, expressed its concerns in its 2018 annual report because, in 2016, GHG emissions were increasing instead of decreasing. In its 2017 periodic review, the Advisory Council projected that Ireland would miss its 2020 intermediate reduction targets.[47]

In 2017, the Friends of the Irish Environment (*FIE*), an environmental non-governmental organisation, initiated a lawsuit against the Irish government, the Attorney General, and the Minister for Public Expenditure and Reform, asking the court to quash the *NMP* and to order the adoption of a plan consistent with the *CALCDA* and the *NTO*. FIE argued that the adopted and approved Plan does not conform to *CALCDA* and is therefore *ultra vires*. The court should enforce the *CALCDA* and order the government to adopt a compliant mitigation plan consistent with international GHG reduction targets.

*FIE* neither challenged the constitutionality of *CALCDA* nor the NTO as defined. The lawsuit concerned the *NMP*, which was adopted and approved by the government. *FIE* claimed that the state must immediately reduce GHG emissions. Focusing solely on long-term reduction targets would lead to the early depletion of carbon budgets. According to projections, argued *FIE*, Ire-

47 *Friends of the Irish Environment* (2020); point 6.42.

land would miss both the internationally set target for developed countries and the EU target.[48]

*FIE* contended that the governmental mitigation plan should be void because it failed to achieve sufficient short-term reductions in GHG emissions. It also argued that GHG emissions should not increase before they begin to decrease.[49] Insufficient GHG emission reductions in the short- to medium-term would contribute to dangerous climate change. In contrast, the state would have to safeguard an appropriate carbon budget and a viable climate for current and future generations. *FIE* argued that the *NMP* would violate the rights under *CALCDA*, the Constitution, and the ECHR. *FIE* argued that it did not seek to impose a policy or become involved in balancing considerations; it would merely request judicial review and annulment of unlawful state action. They would leave the policy decisions to the political branches.

## 2 The Court Rulings

The following paragraphs outline the main issues arising from the lawsuit and the parties' respective positions. After that, we present, in an integrated approach, how the High Court and the Supreme Court addressed the justiciability of the government's climate recovery plan, including its lack of immediate GHG reductions and its consistency with fundamental or constitutional rights.

The High Court held that *FIE*, as a corporate entity rather than a natural person, did not have the right to life, bodily integrity, or an unenumerated right to an environment consistent with human dignity. For the sake of argument and because the ECtHR adopts a more flexible approach, the court was willing to assume *FIE* had standing. In the Court's view, even if the applicant possessed such rights, they could not possibly be infringed by the *NMP* because the mitigation plan aimed to reduce GHG emissions.[50] It was undisputed that

48 *Friends of the Irish Environment* (2019); point 24.

49 *Ibid.*, points 12, 24 & 64.

50 *Ibid*; point 132: "*The constitutional rights which are stated to be infringed are the rights to life, the right to bodily integrity and the right to an environment consistent with human dignity. Even if I were to accept that these rights are in some way engaged, which I do for the purposes of this case, the difficulty which I perceive in the applicant's claim is that it is seeking to have the court declare that it is the Plan which is impacting upon those constitutional rights. I am not satisfied that it has been established that the making or approval of the Plan by the respondent has the effect of breaching those rights. Accepting, for the purposes of this case, that there is an unenumerated right to an environment consistent with human dignity, in my view, it cannot be concluded that it is the plan which places these rights at risk. As I previously stated, I could not reasonably conclude that the Plan resiles*

*FIE* enjoyed standing to challenge the legality of the mitigation plan. The courts had to decide whether to uphold or quash the *NMP*.

The High Court held that it had the power and the duty to review whether the government had violated constitutional rights. It could, however, not exercise executive powers on behalf of the government, meaning it should not intervene in policymaking, as this would infringe on the principle of the separation of powers. In other words, the court could determine whether governmental policies comply with the law or the Constitution, but not replace the policy decisions of the elected branches.

#### The *NMP* Is *Intra Vires*

Even if it considered itself entitled to review the *NMP*, the High Court granted the executive branch considerable discretion. It emphasised that it did not intend to second-guess the government's decision. Moreover, it interpreted the *NMP* as a living instrument that did not foreclose immediate reduction efforts. The Court concluded that the *NMP* was not *ultra vires* the *CALCDA* because the act would not impose immediate reductions. The government had acted within its margin of discretion, and the *NMP* would constitute a first step, subject to recurrent adaptations as a living instrument. The court reiterated that the applicants did not challenge the constitutionality of the *CALCDA* itself.

#### The *NMP* Is *Ultra Vires*

Notwithstanding the High Court's ruling, the Supreme Court stated that once the government approved the *NMP*, it ceased to be a policy and became secondary legislation. Law and legal questions fall within the judicial branch's competence: "*It may have been the policy of a particular government to introduce the legislation in question, but once that legislation is passed, it then becomes law and not policy.*"[51] The Supreme Court emphasised that even if the mitigation plan is grounded on policy decisions, secondary legislation must comply with primary legislation. The *NMP* was *ultra vires* because it did not sufficiently explain to the public how it would achieve the *NTO* as

*from the national transition objective as specified in the legislation, nor could I reasonably conclude that the plan runs contrary to the national policy on climate change. The Plan is but one, albeit extremely important, piece of the jigsaw."*

51 *Friends of the Irish Environment* (2020); point 6.25. and point 8.15: "*As noted in the section on ultra vires, what might well have been a non-justiciable question of policy clearly became justiciable because both a policy (the NTO) and the need to specify how that policy was to be achieved became matters of law by virtue of the 2015 Act.*"

set out by the *CALCDA*."[52] Considering the lack of specificity and transparency, the Supreme Court quashed the *NMP*. Protection measures must be *"specified not only for the first five years but for the full length of the period then unexpired up to 2050."*

The court increased public pressure on the government by strengthening citizens' participatory rights. The informed public can intervene at the polls, express discontent on the streets, or pursue legal action. The Supreme Court imposed this pressure on the political branches without overly interfering with the elected branches: Considering the longer-term targets, the court's intervention was minimal. Courts, as shown in the case at bar, can step in if near-term political delays in measures disproportionally burden younger generations, affecting the reduction trajectory but not the long-term goal. It limits the political branches' possibilities to achieve that goal. The reduction trajectory must respect human rights. Therefore, it is no longer acceptable to adopt an ostrich policy, delay action, and force future political representatives to decide on harsh measures. The need to inform the public adequately about the projected mitigation measures and the need for planning security disqualifies obscure policy positions, consequently narrowing political discretion.

## 3 Effects of the Court Ruling

This 2021 Climate Action Plan has replaced the 2019 National Mitigation Plan. It is more resolute than the 2019 plan.[53] By 2030, there should be a 51% reduction in GHG emissions, and by 2050, Ireland should achieve climate neutrality. The government complemented climate protection measures with additional measures to meet the 2030 targets. The new Plan set more ambitious sectoral reduction targets.[54] The plan provides reduction ranges for each sector of the economy and must be updated annually.

---

52 Ibid., point 6.47: *"But the public is entitled to know what current thinking is and, indeed, form a judgment both on whether the Plan is realistic and whether the types of technology considered in the Plan are appropriate and likely to be effective. In my view, a reasonable and interested observer would not really have a sufficient view of just how it is currently hoped that such measures might contribute towards achieving the NTO to form a considered judgment."*

53 Ireland; Department of the Environment, Climate and Communications; (Department of the Taoiseach); climate action plan 2021;, https://www.gov.ie/en/publication/6223e-climate-action-plan-2021/; publication on the website. *"This Plan makes Ireland one of the most ambitious countries in the world on climate."*

54 Ireland; Department of the Environment, Climate and Communications; (*Department of the Taoiseach*); *Climate action plan 2021*; page 16; https://www.gov.ie/en/publication/6223e-climate-action-plan-2021/.

*Friends II*[55]

On June 2, 2023, the Friends of the Irish Environment challenged the Irish government's 2023 Climate Action Plan and sought an order to quash it, arguing that it was insufficiently specific. The High Court, however, did not invalidate the plan because *"the applicant hasn't discharged the onus of proof to show that a reasonable person would be unable to evaluate whether the plan is realistic."*[56]

The court, nonetheless, cautioned the government and provided complementary precision about the suitability of a climate mitigation plan. It stated that, under the amended *CALCDA*, the government must quantify GHG emissions, and these quantifications must comply with the carbon budget and sectoral ceilings.[57]

Other courts, such as the German Constitutional Court (Bundesverfassungsgericht) in *Neubauer*, have cited the Irish Supreme Court ruling and its emphasis on strengthening public participation. We will now turn to this ruling.

∴

55 *Friends of the Irish Environment v. the Minister for the Environment, Climate and Communications, the Government of Ireland, Ireland and the Attorney General,* [2025] IEHC 61, [H.JR.2023.0000627]; High Court, 07.02.2025; [*"Friends II"*].

56 Ibid., pages 24 & 26: *"Ultimately, the complaint that the figures aren't justified doesn't get off the ground when the applicant hasn't made any real attempt to engage with the material that the plan does contain. Yes in one sense I can see the argument that even if the numbers add up, a reasonable person would need to have some reasonable sense of the justification for the numbers in order to know whether the plan is realistic. But that complaint needs to be firmly situated in the context of detailed engagement with the totality of information that is there, not just whining that the plan could contain more."*

57 Ibid., pages 25 & 26 *"That is just a decision on these facts, on these pleadings, and on these arguments – but I emphasise the point made above that the applicant is ultimately correct as to the need for quantification and for a demonstration of the consistency of this with the overall budget and sectoral ceilings. What this judgment most certainly is not is a finding that Ireland's climate ambitions are on track. The reports highlighted by the applicant are consistent with the view that delivery of necessary measures is well off-course, and inferentially that urgent and significant additional action is required, given the dynamically narrowing nature of the margin of appreciation in the carbon budgeting process. But this isn't a case pleaded or argued in a way that would permit the court to grant any relief based on such a situation."* The court held that the amended CALCDA *"demands considerably more than a merely reasonable plan – it must be a plan that ensures compliance with carbon budgets and sectoral ceilings. That involves qualifications, balancing the no-policy-change baseline projected forward with the impact of new policy measures projected forward. This may involve estimation but it can't involve a purely narrative, qualitative effort for any element of the budget. A budget ultimately is meaningless without a bottom line."*

## II) *Neubauer v. Germany*[58]

### Introduction

*Neubauer* focuses on the consistency of the GHG-emission-reduction trajectory established by the German Climate Protection Law. In 2021, the German Federal Constitutional Court addressed four constitutional complaints regarding the constitutionality of the federal Climate Protection Act (*KSG*), dated December 12, 2019. The *KSG* is a framework law related to the systematic GHG reductions outlined in the climate protection plan, "*Klimaschutzplan.*"

We will present the content of the four complaints comprehensively and mainly analyse what entitled the Federal Constitutional Court to intervene. *Neubauer* combines the participatory rights aspects highlighted in *Friends of the Irish Environment* with substantive human rights considerations. The lawsuit is also significant because the German Constitutional Court accepted petitions from Bangladesh and Nepal, allowing foreign petitioners to challenge the constitutionality of the *KSG*.

### 1 Background of the Constitutional Complaints

The plaintiffs, some of whom were very young, claimed that the state had violated their fundamental rights because it lacked an adequate short-term strategy to mitigate climate change. The state would fail to sufficiently reduce GHG emissions in the short term, leading to disproportionate restrictions on the petitioners' rights and liberties in the future. They would be unevenly affected by governmental climate protection measures. Altogether, the projected reductions would be insufficient, and current GHG emissions would be twice the level allowed to meet the 1.5 degrees goal set by the Paris Agreement.[59] The state would, therefore, be in breach of its duty of care. They based their claim on constitutional and human rights.[60]

According to the petitioners, the *KSG* would irreversibly postpone high-emission-reduction burdens until after 2030. If GHG emissions were too high, options and liberties would be limited in the future. Moreover, Germany's cur-

---

58 *Neubauer, et al. v. Germany,* ECLI:DE:BVerfG:2021:rs20210324, 1bvr265618; Bundesverfassungsgericht; 24.03.2021 ("*Neubauer*").

59 *Neubauer;* page 35.

60 Notably the right to life, the right to physical integrity, the right to property, human dignity, the right to an ecological subsistence minimum (*ökologisches Existenzminimum*), article 20a of the fundamental law Basic Law for the Federal Republic of Germany, articles 2 and 8 of the European Convention on Human Rights.

rent measures would not even be sufficient to meet the unsatisfactory 2030 target, namely a 55% reduction compared to 1990.

Petitioners from Bangladesh and Nepal, two of the most vulnerable countries to the dangers of climate change, argued that Germany would also jeopardise their property and health rights. They claimed that the duty of care extends to petitioners from abroad, as the German climate protection policy would contribute to catastrophic global warming and harm.[61]

## 2 The Court Ruling

The court referred at length to international conventions (notably the Paris Agreement and the *UNFCCC*) and scientific evidence (notably the reports of the IPCC and the German Expert Council for Climate Questions) to expose the effects of dangerous climate change and to inform the duty of care. The Constitutional Court also referred to European law and foreign court rulings, notably, *Urgenda* and *Friends of the Irish Environment*.

We will hereafter discuss how the court addressed standing and admissibility (Section 2.1), Germany's short-term climate protection strategy (Section 2.2), its long-term strategy (Section 2.3), and participatory rights (Section 2.4).

### 2.1 Standing and Admissibility

The Constitutional Court held that the constitutional complaints, to the extent they concern the legal dispositions of the *KSG* and its constitutionality, are admissible. The court held that natural persons, including those from Bangladesh and Nepal, are entitled to submit their constitutional complaint to defend their rights to life, bodily integrity, and property, on the grounds that the measures of the *KSG* could be unsuitable for tackling dangerous climate change. The petitioners living in Germany could also claim that the undue postponement of reduction measures in the future affected their freedoms and liberties.[62]

### 2.2 Germany's Short-Term GHG Emission Strategy (until 2030)

The court held that Article 20a of the fundamental law[63] is a justiciable constitutional provision that obliges the state to take climate action, even though

---

61 *Neubauer;* pages 46–47.

62 Ibid., page 49.

63 Federal Ministry of Justice and the Federal Office of Justice; Basic Law for the Federal Republic of Germany, https://www.gesetze-im-internet.de/englisch_gg/englisch_gg.pdf): Article 20a of the fundamental law Basic Law for the Federal Republic of Germany: "*Mindful also of its responsibility towards future generations, the state shall*

Germany is not the sole contributor to global warming. Those climate measures must protect the rights and liberties of the younger generations.[64]

The court stated that the required GHG reductions after 2030 could be considerable. However, whether these reductions will be so drastic that, from today's perspective, they would constitute unreasonable impairments of fundamental rights cannot yet be determined. The government's mitigation measures for the period after 2030 must respect fundamental rights. Achieving carbon neutrality by 2050 without undue harm to human rights must remain a feasible and attainable goal. The state must initiate the transition to climate neutrality in good time to minimise the risk of future severe burdens. The Constitutional Court held that if the postponement of short-term GHG reduction measures beyond 2030 depletes the carbon budget and a smooth transition and transformation to carbon neutrality are no longer feasible, this would indeed infringe the duty of care and necessitate drastic GHG reductions that seriously affect fundamental rights and liberties.[65] Political branches must fulfil their responsibilities towards younger generations, who will be particularly affected by climate change and climate mitigation measures, and evenly distribute the climate burden.

### 2.3 Long-Term GHG Emissions Strategy (from 2030 Onwards)

By referring to the jurisprudence of the ECtHR, the German Federal Constitutional Court held that the right to life and bodily integrity encompasses protection against environmental damage, including climate change. Although Germany cannot halt climate change, it must mitigate global warming, and the ultimate goal is to establish a zero-net carbon society. The *KSG* would not obstruct achieving this goal by 2050, and the 2030 targets are an intermediate step toward carbon neutrality.

While it was clear that the long-term reduction objective is to achieve carbon neutrality by 2050, it remained unclear how much GHG emissions the state was entitled to emit during the transition to that zero-net-carbon society. The Constitutional Court had to assess whether the state should aim for the 1.5 degrees objective as an absolute limit, or for the Paris Agreement's objective of an average global temperature rise well below 2 degrees, preferably limited to 1.5 degrees. The court analysed the IPCC reports and held that they were not

---

*protect the natural foundations of life and animals by legislation and, in accordance with law and justice, by executive and judicial action, all within the framework of the constitutional order."*

64 *Neubauer*; page 83.

65 Ibid., pages 64, 65 & page 82.

normative. The targets the state must achieve to protect life and body integrity must be clarified. Those of the Paris Agreement, pursued by the political representatives, could be enough to protect the mentioned fundamental rights.[66] The legislator would need to consider scientific quantifications of the available carbon budget, even if those calculations remained uncertain.[67]

### 2.4 The Need to Know

At an early stage, the state must transparently formulate GHG reduction targets to guide the necessary development and implementation processes while ensuring adequate planning security. On the one hand, it is constitutionally essential that the state determines further reduction measures in good time beyond 2030 and sufficiently far into the future. On the other hand, the state must establish annual emission quantities and reduction measures that are adequately specified, providing clear direction.

The political branches must inform the public about the measures they plan to take beyond 2030 and far into the future to provide planning security. The Constitutional Court referred explicitly to the Irish Supreme Court judgment in *Friends of the Irish Environment.*

The state must define the annual emission allowances promptly and sufficiently far in advance to facilitate planning and preparation. According to the *KSG, t*he 2030 emission allowances will be defined in 2025, leaving only 5 years of planning, which is insufficient. The legislator should promptly and well in advance define the reduction plan or instruct the executive branch to do so.[68]

## 3 Conclusion

The Federal Constitutional Court ruled in favour of the youth petitioners. It was grounded on the duty of care for constitutional rights and liberties (the positive obligation of the state to take precautionary measures to protect human rights) and intergenerational justice. The Constitutional Court did not perceive that the federal state's GHG mitigation strategy had already violated fundamental rights or that the legislator had missed its constitutional discretion. However, the court held that such violations could still occur in the future. The branches of government must fairly distribute the burdens of climate change among current and future generations. The state should not allow current actors to deplete the carbon budget to the detriment of the

---

66 Ibid., page 70.

67 Ibid., page 96.

68 Ibid., page 2.

rights and liberties of future generations. If the state postpones GHG reduction measures in the future, this could result in disproportionate and severe restrictions on people's fundamental rights. Therefore, the short-term strategy must protect fundamental rights and liberties. The state could unduly infringe upon liberties if it were to drastically reduce its GHG emissions after 2030. A violation of future generations' rights to life and bodily integrity could also occur if the state fails to meet its 2030 climate change objectives because its GHG emissions before 2030 are too high.[69]

According to the *Neubauer* ruling, the German state is required to implement adequate mitigation measures during its transition to carbon neutrality. The impact on the rights and principles of current and future generations must be proportionate, meaning the state should mitigate fundamental rights risks arising from overly harsh GHG reductions beyond 2031. The state must develop a consistent plan, define a compliant GHG-reduction trajectory with adequate interim targets, and provide on-time information on sector emissions to ensure development and planning security.

At the latest, the legislature must define the reduction targets from 2031 onward by 31 December 2022. The political branches need to respect the constitutional proportionality principle. The legislator ordering the necessary GHG reductions must do so with foresight so that future liberties and restrictions remain reasonably safeguarded despite increasing climate protection obligations. The state should not distribute the burden of reductions une qually over time and across generations, to the detriment of future generations. In other words, the state should not allow current generations to deplete the carbon budget to the detriment of future generations' liberties. The KSG should not impose unfair burdens on future generations.[70]

The Federal Constitutional Court strengthened rights and liberties without excessively encroaching on the political branches' domain. It did not set overall or specific reduction targets, but it outlined the risks to fundamental rights and liberties, offered guidance, and set a time frame. The Federal Constitutional Court left the branches of government with the discretion to define interim targets for the state and the various sectors through regular democratic procedures.

69 Ibid., page 81.
70 Ibid., page 105.

## 4 Effects

The Federal State announced it would adjust its *KSG* in light of the court's ruling.[71] The Federal Government, in its proposal, intended to tighten climate protection measures to achieve Germany's climate neutrality by 2045.[72] The amended law passed by the Bundestag on June 24, 2021, revised the short-term target for 2030. The state must reduce GHG emissions by 65% from 1990 levels, rather than the previous 55%. By 2040, the reduction target should be 88%, constituting a new interim target.[73]

The amended *KSG* redefined emission allowances for the six sectors (energy, industry, buildings, transport, agriculture, and waste management) for the period from 2023 to 2030 and established cross-sectoral annual reduction targets for the period from 2031 to 2040. By 2032, the federal government should submit a new legislative proposal to set annual reduction targets from 2040 until climate neutrality is achieved in 2045. By 2024, the state must define the specific sectoral targets from 2031 to 2040. By 2034, for the period from 2041 to 2045.

Strengthening participatory rights may be seen as a continuation of the *Friends of the Irish Environment* ruling. The German Federal Constitutional Court introduced new elements. It held that the state's climate change policy must not disproportionately harm the rights and liberties of younger generations, thereby further limiting the political branches' discretion. Another new element is planning security. The state must clearly define sectoral targets in the short and long term to ensure planning security for the different economic sectors.

By holding that the people of Nepal and Bangladesh have standing and could challenge the KSG to defend their rights to life, bodily integrity, and property, because the measures of the KSG would be unsuitable for tackling dangerous climate change, we might even question traditional aspects of state sovereignty, as we shall point out in the next chapter.

71 AP News; *Germany pledges to adjust climate law after the court verdict;* 30.04.2021; https://apnews.com/article/germany-europe-climate-climate-change-environment-and-nature-191b8ffca5ba6994ebd402b04432e6c8.

72 Deutscher Bundestag; Gesetzentwurf der Bundesregierung, Entwurf eines Ersten Gesetzes zur Änderung des Bundes-Klimaschutzgesetzes; Drucksache 19/30230; 02.06.2021; https://dserver.bundestag.de/btd/19/302/1930230.pdf.

73 Deutscher Bundestag, Amendment KSG; Drucksache 30949; 22.06.2021; https://dserver.bundestag.de/btd/19/309/1930949.pdf.

CHAPTER 3

# Overall Analysis and Intermediary Conclusions

## Introduction

Our study of climate-related judicial review reveals the emergence of a new type of lawsuit alongside judicial petitions challenging specific climate-related government decisions. The number of quasi-political climate protection cases is likely to increase in the coming years, mainly due to the further development of scientific evidence and the more pronounced adverse effects of global warming.

More ambitious protection measures and targets challenge people's rights, freedoms, and lifestyles today. Even temporary restrictions on these aspects can potentially lead to social unrest. During my research, the world was in the midst of the COVID-19 pandemic. People expressed concerns about governmental health measures and expressed their disapproval on the streets. This could foreshadow what is to come in terms of civil disobedience and legal action against stricter government climate policies. Later, the war in Ukraine greatly affected the global economy, especially by pushing up energy prices, prompting calls for state intervention and solidarity. Governments again beg an subsidising fossil fuels. Individual interests and economic and energy needs might be prioritised over climate protection efforts.

Conversely, delayed mitigation measures could disproportionately impact the rights and freedoms of future generations. Currently, lawsuits mainly address the inadequacy of short-term climate protection efforts, which may ultimately affect the rights and freedoms of younger generations. Present generations do not yet face severe restrictions, but this situation will change as we transition towards climate neutrality. Judicial review can advance climate protection even if it takes the form of a declaratory judgment. Following court rulings in *Friends of the Irish Environment* and *Neubauer*, political bodies have increased their efforts to protect the climate. This emerging form of litigation relates to the complex politico-legal framework for climate protection and adaptation, involving a range of policy decisions that require balancing interests and prioritising actions, roles typically reserved for the political sphere. Court intervention in such matters raises concerns about the separation of powers and the judiciary's role.

Throughout the world, courts must handle cases they would typically dismiss, often citing political discretion or their inability to provide redress. The

 | HTTPS://DOI.ORG/10.1163/9789004771710-007

shift in the nature of climate-related cases brought before courts, along with the courts' stance, might influence our understanding of how judges approach politically charged questions. The courts' posture may have shifted from a strict separation of powers approach to a more flexible one, fostering what I call the cooperation of powers.

Climate protection and the respectworthiness of our democratic systems might require a shift away from the conservative judicial approach. In the first U.S. federal climate protection cases, the standard approach was for courts to declare themselves incompetent or hold that the petitioners would not meet standing requirements, primarily because they could not establish a particularised interest or because a court could allegedly not provide the demanded redress. The courts typically deferred to political representatives or to the polls to effect political change. In recent climate protection and public trust cases, we have observed that, although the courts' approach was rather cautious, they rendered decisions that could be labelled activist.

Our study of climate-related judicial review cases allows us to draw some preliminary conclusions about the court's toolkit (1), the role of the judicial branch in a democratic system (2), and the separation of powers (3).

## Section 1: Overall Analysis

### 1 The Court's Toolbox

In the cases we analysed, several tools enabled courts to justify their intervention in climate matters and to avoid manifestly overstepping the role typically attributed to the judicial branch. Scientific knowledge may be one of the most significant tools in court proceedings on climate matters (Section 1.1), alongside the state's legal and constitutional framework and the rule of law (Section 1.2). The reference to foreign jurisprudence has also been significant in climate protection cases (Section 1.3).

### 1.1 Scientific Knowledge and International Commitments

Science first guides political authorities in their legislative and executive duties. Then, it provides the necessary substance for courts to assess the extent of political discretion and the political obligations. In the cases we analysed, the courts relied on scientific knowledge to determine the state's duties, the impacts on human rights, and the consistency of the adopted measures. They even summarised scientific insights as part of their decisions because science provided the background facts against which courts assessed the reasonableness of state (in)action.[1]

It is not new for courts to consider scientific insights in climate-related lawsuits when making their decisions. However, the significance appears to have grown. The further back in time one looks, the more uncertain the knowledge becomes and the louder the call for governmental discretion and judicial self-restraint. In more recent cases, the litigating parties generally agreed that states must mitigate global warming and that decarbonisation is necessary. They disagreed, however, about the discretion conferred on the political branches, the intermediate targets the state must achieve, their policy-balancing priorities (such as balancing ecological needs against energy needs and economic growth), or the speed and extent of the near-term reductions. Respondents in climate-related lawsuits, typically ministries and public

---

1 See, for instance, the judicial decisions in *Massachusetts v. EPA*, *Urgenda*, *Neubauer*, *Friends of the Irish Environment*, *Minors Oposa* (*Minors Oposa v. Sec'y of the Dep't of Envt'l & Natural Res., G.R. No. 101083, 33 I.L.M. 173;* the Philippines Supreme Court; 30.07.1993), *People v. Arctic Oil* (*Greenpeace Nordic Ass'n and Natur og Ungdom v. Ministry of Petroleum and Energy*, 20-051052SIV-HRET; Norway Supreme Court; 22.12.2020), or the *Thabametsi Power Project* case (*Earthlife Africa Johannesburg v. Minister of Environmental Affairs and others*, Case no. 65662/16 (2017); South Africa, High Court in Pretoria; 06.02.2017 &19.11.2020).

administrations, advance scientific uncertainties to defend their political decisions and justify discretionary actions.

U.S. federal courts have granted greater deference to the political branches in cases involving scientific uncertainty.[2] In *EPA v. Massachusetts*, the Court began its ruling by citing evidence on climate change. The majority and the dissenters interpreted scientific evidence differently. The former highlighted scientific facts, whereas the latter pointed to scientific uncertainties. In *Held v. State of Montana*, the court relied on expert testimony and scientific evidence to verify whether the plaintiffs met the standing requirements.

Scientific knowledge alone might not be sufficient. It can help inform the duty of care and verify standing requirements; however, a court can only enforce scientifically determined reduction targets when they are part of binding legal instruments, such as the UN Framework Convention on Climate Change, the Kyoto Protocol, or the Paris Agreement. In the cases we studied, European courts relied on those international commitments. In *Urgenda*, scientific knowledge helped the Dutch courts to determine the minimum GHG reduction targets. Scientific knowledge has shown that the internationally determined standards are minimum requirements, especially considering the *emission gap*.[3] The courts eventually relied on international conventions to determine that, as a developed state, the Dutch state must, by 2020, achieve at least a 25% GHG reduction compared to 1990. The court used this international commitment to reject the domestically determined political target.

Even if we did not examine climate cases from courts in developing states, my overall research on judicial review indicates that those courts appear more activist and are driving the development of international environmental law. We can, for instance, refer to decisions of the Supreme Court of the Philippines, the Lahore High Court in Pakistan, and the Supreme Court in India. Those courts have been actively developing international environmental law

---

2 Glicksman Robert, Daniel Kim, and Keziah Groth-Tuft; *Judicial Review of Scientific Uncertainty in Climate Change Lawsuits: Deferential and Nondeferential Evaluation of Agency Factual and Policy Determinations;* 2022; page 1.

3 *Urgenda* (2015); points 2.29 and 2.30: "*The gap is the difference between the desired emissions level in a certain year and the level of emissions anticipated for that year based on the reduction goals pledged by the countries concerned.* [...] *The "executive summary" of the Emissions Gap Report 2013 includes the following: "(...) This report confirms and strengthens the conclusions of the three previous analyses that current pledges and commitments fall short of that goal. It further says that, as emissions of greenhouse gases continue to rise rather than decline, it becomes less and less likely that emissions will be low enough by 2020 to be on a least-cost pathway towards meeting the 2 C target. As a result, after 2020, the world will have to rely on more difficult, costlier, and riskier means of meeting the target – the further from the least-cost level in 2020, the higher these costs and the greater the risks will be.*"

rights and principles, such as intergenerational justice, intergenerational equity, the environmental rule of law, the principle in *dubio pro natura*, environmental justice, the precautionary principle, the sustainable development principle, the right to a healthy environment, and the right to a viable climate.

*Asghar Leghari v. the Federation of Pakistan*[4] could be one of the most progressive rulings on climate protection. The Lahore High Court ordered several ministries, departments, and authorities to appoint a 'climate change focal person' to ensure the implementation of the National Climate Change Policy and to assist the court. It then instituted a Climate Change Commission (*CCC*) to ensure that the competent authorities take their climate change responsibilities. After its exemplary service, the court dissolved the *CCC* and constituted a Standing Committee on Climate Change (*SCCC*) as an intermediary between the Court and the government. If necessary, the *SCCC* could *"approach th[e] Court for appropriate order to enforce the people's fundamental rights in the context of climate change, if and when required. If any such application is filed, the case shall be revived and fixed before any Green Bench as per the Case Management Plan."*

## 1.2 Human Rights and Constitutional Essentials

We commonly accept that courts should protect human rights and constitutional essentials against manifest abuses of discretion by holding the branches of government accountable for the duty of care they owe to the people and, perhaps, even to the environment. Some authors claim that the development and protection of human rights should be the courts' primary concern in climate protection cases. As guardians of the law, courts should take an active posture and stimulate the introduction of GHG reduction targets.[5]

Despite the controversy surrounding their climate dimension, there appears to be an upward trend in the receptiveness of human rights, constitutional rights, and public trust arguments in climate-based judicial review. Court protection of climate essentials undoubtedly played a crucial role in the cases we analysed. According to Davide Castagno, three conditions must be met for successful climate change litigation: *"First, the national basic law must include the protection of nature as a fundamental right* [...] *Second, the mechanism of constitutional review has to be directly open to individuals* [...].

4 *Asghar Leghari v. the Federation of Pakistan*, W.P. No. 25501/2015, Lahore High Court; 25.01.2018.

5 See, for instance, Colby Heather et al., *Judging Climate Change: The Role of the Judiciary in the Fight Against Climate Change.*

*Finally, since a regulation concerning climate change must be challenged, such regulation needs to have been previously promulgated by a legislator* [...]."[6] The cases we studied in chapters 1 and two seem to confirm this. In the U.S., climate rights are still subject to debate at the federal level. Youth-led cases were successful before state courts that explicitly protect climate rights, such as those of the State of Montana[7] and the State of Hawaii.[8]

In Europe, the ECtHR recognised the applicability of articles 2, 6 and 8 to climate litigation, thereby binding E.U states, as all of them are also parties to the ECHR. Even before the ECtHR ruled on the applicability of Articles 2 and 8 to climate protection matters, member state courts, such as the Dutch Supreme Court in *Urgenda* and the Court of Appeal of Brussels in *Klimaatzaak*, had already ruled that Articles 2 and 8 entail a climate dimension and that the state would violate it. Sometimes conventions, such as the ECHR, are considered living instruments that are interpreted by the court. Other International human rights actors also provided insights on that subject. For instance, the UN Human Rights Committee has held that the right to life, enshrined in Article 6 of the International Covenant on Civil and Political Rights (*ICCPR*), imposes positive obligations on states to protect the climate. Furthermore, the UN Committee on the Rights of the Child (*UNCRC*) has announced its commitment to children's rights and the Environment, with a focus on climate change. On August 22, 2023, the *UNCRC* published General Comment No. 26 to guide states that have ratified the Convention on the Rights of the Child and to provide impetus for climate action. The United Nations International Children's Emergency Fund (*UNICEF*) has been engaging youth to receive their views on climate change.

The three dimensions of a human right give rise to different state obligations. The negative aspect obliges states to refrain from violating the right, providing vertical protection against the state (the rule of law). The positive dimension obliges states to take proactive measures to protect the right, and the procedural aspect requires states to render the right effective, for instance, by informing citizens of the risks and the proposed measures, granting public participation, and providing access to courts, including judicial remedies.

---

6 See also Castagno Davide; *Challenging Legal Standing in Climate Change Litigation: A Comparative Approach to the Italian Case 'Giudizio Universale*; International Journal of Procedural Law 14, No 1 (5 September 2024); 47–72; page 52.

7 *Rikki Held, et al. v. State of Montana, et al*, CDV-2020-307; Montana 1st Judicial District Court, Lewis & Clark County, 04.08.2021; & *Rikki Held, et al. v. State of Montana, et al.*, CDV-2020-307; Montana 1st Judicial District Court, Lewis & Clark County, 14.08.2023.

8 *Navahine F. v. Hawai'i Department of Transportation*, 1CCV-22-0000631; First Circuit Court of the State of Hawai'i; 06.04.2023 & *Navahine F. v. Hawai'i Electric Light Company*, Inc., CIVIL NO. 1CCV-22-0000631; Circuit Court of the First Circuit, State of Hawai'i; 20.06.2024.

In climate protection cases, courts must focus on the more contentious positive dimension, because concrete harms and potential violations may lie in the future and be uncertain, raising questions about the extent of the precautionary measures a state must take to meet its positive obligation under the rights to life and family life.

Constitutional provisions also played a pivotal role in the cases we discussed. Debates have arisen around the justiciability of specific environmental provisions, such as Article 20a of the German Constitution, which pertains to the protection of the natural foundations of life and animals, as discussed in *Neubauer.*[9] In the U.S., the question of a federal constitutional right to a climate system capable of sustaining human life, declared by the Oregon District Court in *Juliana*, remains controversial and has not been settled.

### 1.3 Foreign Jurisprudence

In climate protection matters, parties and courts cited pivotal foreign court decisions to support their arguments. The court in *Friends of the Irish Environment* referred to *Urgenda,* and the German court in *Neubauer* referred to both *Urgenda* and *Friends of the Irish Environment.* This lends judicial decisions greater credibility, showing that they are not isolated. Since climate protection is a shared goal and the international climate framework is common, comparing court decisions and referring to other courts makes sense.

Courts outside Europe also referenced pivotal climate-based court rulings from other countries. For instance, in *Sheikh Asim Farooq v. Federation of Pakistan,*[10] a case we did not discuss, the Lahore High Court justified its intervention by pointing to Indian jurisprudence. It was revealed that foreign courts also recognised the environmental principles of *dubio pro natura* and the precautionary principle. In South Africa, in the *Thabametsi Power Project case,*[11] the High Court in Pretoria relied on U.S. case law to rule that the Minister must consider all environmental effects, including climate impacts, before

9 Federal Ministry of Justice and the Federal Office of Justice; Basic Law for the Federal Republic of Germany, https://www.gesetze-im-internet.de/englisch_gg/englisch_gg.pdf; Article 20a: "*Mindful also of its responsibility towards future generations, the state shall protect the natural foundations of life and animals by legislation and, in accordance with law and justice, by executive and judicial action, all within the framework of the constitutional order.*"

10 *Sheikh Asim Farooq v. Federation of Pakistan*, W.P. No. 192069 of 2018; Lahore High Court; 03.08.2019.

11 *Earthlife Africa Johannesburg v. Minister of Environmental Affairs and others*, Case no. 65662/16 (2017); South Africa High Court in Pretoria; 06.02.2017 &19.11.2020; "*Thabametsi Power Project case*".

authorising the construction of a coal-fired power station. Foreign court decisions were less frequently cited in the U.S., where courts tended to rely on their extensive national case law.

## 2 The Role of the Judicial Branch in a Democratic System

In a democratic system, courts are undeniably competent to scrutinise legal questions that can be distinguished from political ones. In *Juliana*, Judge Aiken held that the judiciary, as a coequal branch, must protect constitutional rights. Whether the state violated a constitutional right is a legal question within the judiciary's field of competence. In *Friends of the Irish Environment*, the Supreme Court distinguished between policy and law by holding that a climate recovery plan remains policy, submitted to political discourse, until the political branches approve it. From its passage into law onwards, it becomes subject to judicial scrutiny.

Conversely, courts should not assume the roles of the legislature or the executive. They should refrain from balancing and prioritising interests. The political branches must balance interests and decide on the prioritisation of rival interests. The separation of powers is, however, not absolute. Courts can and perhaps must intervene in cases of manifest abuses of discretion, which promotes the rule of law and the respectworthiness of the democratic process. We will address this in more detail in Part 2.

In the past, environmental cases involving a climate dimension were primarily administrative law issues requiring proper administrative decision-making. These lawsuits primarily concerned the review of precise administrative decisions, which were less controversial because the judicial review approach was essentially procedural, aimed at ensuring well-informed decision-making. Courts considered whether the decision-maker had correctly assessed the ecological impacts before reaching their final decision. U.S. courts review whether administrative decisions are based on proper environmental impact assessments. It is not enough if impacts have been assessed de facto; such assessments must be consistent. The decision must not be *arbitrary, capricious, or otherwise inconsistent with the law*.[12]

The right to public information, participation, and access to justice are essential participatory rights. After the competent administration issued its decision, the initial appeal was, in principle, directed to the political authority

12 See, for instance, *Wildearth Guardians v. U.S. BLM et al.*, D.C. No. 2:13-CV-00042-ABJ, the United States Court of Appeals, 10th Circuit; 15.09.2017.

above. The courts intervened *ex post* to the final decision of the competent minister as a sort of last-resort authority. This promotes good governance and holds political decision-makers accountable to the public. For instance, in the South African *Thabametsi Power Project case*, the High Court in Pretoria refrained from reviewing whether the executive had correctly balanced the different interests. However, the court inquired whether all relevant factors had been adequately assessed and considered before the political decision-maker issued the environmental authorisation.

This brings us to U.S. case law, where courts have established the "*arbitrary and capricious standard*" for reviewing administrative decisions. In administrative law cases, courts examine whether the decision-maker has thoughtfully and sufficiently assessed and considered all environmental impacts, whether the decision is based on the proper evaluation of all relevant factors, and whether all options have been considered, including the "*no-action alternative*." We saw this, for example, in *Massachusetts v. EPA*. The Supreme Court could set aside the administrative decision because it was "*arbitrary, capricious, an abuse of discretion or otherwise not in accordance with the law*."[13]

In Germany (*Neubauer*) and Ireland (*Friends of the Irish Environment*), the courts clarified that the public has the right to know with sufficient detail how the state plans to mitigate climate change over time, allowing interested observers to foresee how the climate measures will, over time, affect their way of life, their rights, and liberties. An adequate level of specificity should also provide economic sectors with planning security. Participatory rights promote public engagement beyond Election Day. Overall, the procedural stance of judicial review poses less interference with political discretion. If political actors preserve the people's participatory rights and base their decisions on sound information, they retain political discretion.

As we will discuss later, procedural review may not always be sufficient. Constitutional essentials might require judicial protection beyond merely procedural checks on political action. In *Friends of the Irish Environment*, constitutional rights were of lesser concern than in *Neubauer*, where the German Constitutional Court outlined potential risks to substantive constitutional provisions. In the latter case, the court explained that if it could not yet perceive a violation, the state must nonetheless refrain from depleting the available carbon budget to the detriment of the rights and liberties of future generations. Therefore, the government must ensure that achieving carbon neutrality remains possible without imposing disproportionate and

13 See also, Ballotpedia; *Arbitrary-or-Capricious Test;* https://ballotpedia.org/Arbitrary-or-capricious_test; <29092021>.

severe restraints on people's fundamental rights. Hence, delaying GHG reductions could result in violations of rights.

The limits of the judicial branch and new developments in the judiciary become apparent in court decisions through dissents and divided courts. In several national and international court systems, including those in the United States, the Philippines, and the ECtHR, concurring and dissenting opinions are made publicly available. Those dissenting opinions might perturb, pointing out weaknesses in the Court's majority opinion and can become very important in subsequent proceedings or future cases. They provide arguments to claimants in later litigation and help raise public awareness.

Sometimes, claimants know from the beginning that their chances of winning the lawsuit are meagre. Nonetheless, unsuccessful environmental litigation still helps raise public awareness, participation, and political pressure. NGOs effectively diffuse achievements and failures through social media and mailing lists. They hold conferences to give the plaintiffs a voice, invite the public to follow judicial proceedings, and discuss court decisions. They share experiences and raise funds through donations. In the U.S., judges are personalised, quoted, and sometimes even portrayed as champions of environmental protection. They are drawn from the bench to the public, from the back office to the centre of attention, which puts pressure on courts and political bodies.

Although this may be rather exceptional, in *Massachusetts v. EPA* (2005), all three circuit judges disagreed with one another. All three interpreted the facts differently, and only because one of the Circuit Judges was willing to join the opinion closest to his could the court eventually issue an opinion. The case shows that dissenting opinions matter. Circuit Judge Tatel's dissent convinced the Supreme Court Justices and paved the way for new judicial developments.

The experience of judges from the same court instance disagreeing with one another is remarkable to continental Europeans, who are accustomed to thinking of court judgments as coherent and unified decisions. Disagreements or incoherences become apparent when a higher court quashes a lower court's decision. The judicial branch is the only branch that is accountable to itself. Higher courts review lower court decisions, ensuring consistency within the judicial system. One could acknowledge that dissenting opinions provide precious insights.

When reading climate-related court decisions, including the various individual opinions, one might wonder what motivates judges to depart from traditional interpretations of the law, adopt a living instrument approach, and change their stance in climate protection cases. The answer could involve a combination of various factors. If too much time passes, especially if no time is left and the political branches remain inactive despite explicit and undisputable scientific evidence, this could amount to a manifest abuse of discretion. Aside from the passage of time, suffering is another consideration. When parties establish suffering and damages linked to political (in)activity, courts may consider the need for a push to shield constitutional essentials from political impairment. The ripeness of the decision could be a third element. If the court can foresee that political actors, market forces, and civil society will endorse a new interpretation, courts would promote an already accepted reality, which would arguably be less of an encroachment onto the political sphere. Courts need to know whether the political branches or the people are ready to implement the new ruling. In *Massachusetts v. EPA*, we held that the EPA was willing to regulate GHG, but the political branches barred it from doing so. One could argue that the Supreme Court foresaw the EPA complying with its decision.

## 3 Separation of Powers Concerns

Participatory cases typically involve fewer counter-majoritarian difficulties than lawsuits about the state's climate protection plans, the existence of climate rights, or public trust obligations. The elaborate rules and tests that courts have developed to avoid undue interference in the political realm are characteristic of cases involving participation.

Justiciability concerns the court's competence to hear the case and the petitioners' capacity (standing) to bring it before the court. Courts must determine whether a question or a constitutional provision is justiciable. If a matter is non-justiciable or the petitioners fail to establish standing, the court lacks the authority to decide the case and will not examine its merits.

We will address the questions of justiciability and political discretion (Section 3.1) before turning to standing (Section 3.2).

### 3.1 Justiciability and Political Discretion

#### 3.1.1 Justiciability of the Lawsuit

In the U.S., federal courts developed the political question doctrine. It is one of the doctrines of justiciability that courts use to avoid addressing a case's merits by invoking the separation of powers.[14] The political questions doctrine

14 See Tushnet Mark in Mourtada-Sabbah Nada; *The Political Question Doctrine and the Supreme Court of the United States;* (Lanham, Lexington Books, 2007); page 48.

distinguishes between legal questions that fall within the courts' competence and political questions that courts should not review but instead refer to the political branches.[15] However, not every politically coloured question is non-justiciable.[16] The idea is that courts are incompetent to make policy decisions. The political question doctrine concerns the six criteria the Supreme Court outlined in *Baker*.[17] Those criteria indicate whether the case at bar may involve a political question that the court should not address.

In *Massachusetts v. EPA* (2005), Circuit Judge Sentelle, in his partial dissent, held that global warming is a question of general interest. Legislatures and presidents should deal with it, not the judicial branch. Notwithstanding, the

15 *Native Village of Kivalina v. ExxonMobil Corporation*, 663 F. Supp. 2d 863 (N.D. Cal. 2009); California District Court; 30.09.2009, page 6: "*The political question doctrine is a species of the separation of powers doctrine and provides that certain questions are political as opposed to legal, and thus, must be resolved by the political branches rather than by the judiciary.*"

See also Smith Thurman; *Supreme Damage: Rescuing Representative Government from Judicial Overreach;* (Smithurmann Publishing, 2020); page 143: "*The Supreme Court has held that certain allegations of unconstitutional government conduct should not be ruled on by federal courts, even though all jurisdictional and other justiciability requirements are met. The Court has said that constitutional interpretations in these areas should be left to the politically accountable branches of government: the President and Congress. In other words, the term "political questions doctrine" refers to the subject matter that the Court deems inappropriate for judicial review.*"

16 *Connecticut v. American Electric Power Co*, 05-5104-cv, 05-5119-cv; United States Court of Appeals 2nd Circuit; 21.09.2009; pages 17–19: "*However, not all cases touching upon constitutional issues that may also raise "an issue of great importance to the political branches" and have "motivated partisan and sectional debate," present non-justiciable political questions. In Montana, the Supreme Court wrote that, in invoking the political question doctrine, a court acknowledges the possibility that a constitutional provision may not be judicially enforceable. Such a decision is very different from determining that specific congressional action does not violate the Constitution. That determination is a decision on the merits that reflects the exercise of judicial review rather than the abstention from judicial review that would be appropriate in a case of a true political question. The second – and more frequently litigated – area where cases "might pose special questions concerning the judiciary's proper role [is] when adjudication might have implications in the conduct of this nation's foreign relations. In sum, [t]he political question doctrine excludes from judicial review those controversies which revolve around policy choices and value determinations constitutionally committed for resolution to the halls of Congress or the confines of the Executive Branch. The Judiciary is particularly ill-suited to make such decisions, as 'courts are fundamentally underequipped to formulate national policies or develop standards for matters not legal in nature. Nevertheless,[t]he political question doctrine must be cautiously invoked [...] and simply because an issue may have political implications does not make it non-justiciable. [...] [t]he doctrine "is one of 'political questions,' not one of 'political cases.*"

17 *Baker v. Carr*, 369 U.S. 186 (1962); United States, Supreme Court; *26.03.1962; "Baker".*

Supreme Court addressed the question and provided redress. A common criticism is that judicial review would be a piecemeal approach to climate change compared to the political branches' wisdom. Courts resolve disputes between parties. In principle, they should not make decisions that entail *erga omnes* effects, whereas the political branches should and can enact primary and secondary legislation with general effects. Courts should enforce those *prima facie* valid norms rather than creating or replacing them. Judicial review is limited to assessing the case's legal and factual situation, and the court cannot consider other possible facts or interests.[18] Climate protection litigation, however, probably always entails *erga omnes* effects.

In *Juliana*, after thoroughly assessing the *Baker* criteria, the Oregon District Court concluded that the case does not involve a non-justiciable political question. The essence of the case was whether the state defendants violated the claimants' constitutional rights, a legal question within the judiciary's field of competence.

In *Aji P. v. Washington*, the Court of Appeals of the State of Washington held that it was incompetent to address the youth petitioners' claims because implementing and monitoring a climate action plan would involve political questions reserved for the executive and legislative branches.

In *Urgenda*, the Dutch courts determined what the law required of the political branches. The State had to reduce its GHG emissions by 25% by 2020 compared to 1990. The court left the political decision-makers with complete discretion regarding the policy decisions to reach the legal GHG reduction target. However, it imposed on them the duty to take adequate measures. The political branches should make these policy decisions.[19]

In *Minors Oposa v. Factoran*,[20] a significant case from the Philippines that we did not study, the state defendants argued that the petition involved a political question (i.e., whether logging should be forbidden) for which the court lacked competence. However, the Supreme Court noted that the polit-

18 See, for instance, Habermas Jürgen; *Between Facts and Norms: Contributions to a Discourse Theory of Law and Democracy;* New Edition (Cambridge, Blackwell Publishers, 1997); page 243.

19 *Urgenda* (2015); point 4.95: "*The court does not enter the political domain with the associated considerations and choices. Separate from any political agenda, the court has to limit itself to its own domain, which is the application of law. Depending on the issues and claims submitted to it, the court will review them with more or less caution. Great restraint or even abstinence is required when it concerns policy-related considerations of ranging interests, which impact the structure or organization of society. The court has to be aware that it only plays one of the roles in a legal dispute between two or more parties.*"

20 *Minors Oposa v. Sec'y of the Dep't of Envt'l & Natural Res.*, G.R. No. 101083, 33 I.L.M. 173; the Philippines, Supreme Court; 30.07.1993; ("*Minors Oposa v. Factoran*").

ical question doctrine is not absolute and that it can review whether political branches have acted legally and with due care for the people's rights. This would be a legal question that falls within the court's competence. The elected branches should not be entirely shielded from judicial inquiry.

### 3.1.2 Justiciability of Constitutional Provisions

The question of justiciability also arose in the context of constitutional provisions. Some courts had to determine whether environmental constitutional provisions confer rights and obligations or serve as objectives guiding the state's policies and are therefore not justiciable in court.

Constitutional objectives might nonetheless matter in climate-based judicial review. Even if the petitioners cannot invoke them as enforceable rights, courts can use those provisions to assess whether the state branches duly considered them and exercised due care. Depending on the court's stance, this could, on the one hand, mean that as long as the state does not take actions that run counter to the objective, it is compliant. On the other hand, it could also mean that the state needs to take sufficient proactive measures towards reaching the constitutional objective. The former posture grants more discretion to the political arms than the latter.

In *Neubauer*, the German Constitutional Court needed to decide whether Article 20a of the Basic Law (Grundgesetz) was a justiciable constitutional provision. Likewise, in *Minors Oposa v. Factoran,* the Supreme Court of the Philippines had to decide whether the constitutional right to a balanced and healthful ecology is justiciable, and it answered in the affirmative. It would be as justiciable, self-enforcing, inalienable, and crucial as any civil or political right enshrined in the Bill of Rights.

### 3.1.3 Discretionary Leeway

The question of how much discretion courts must grant to the political branches is crucial in climate-related cases.

The Supreme Court of Norway distinguished between two situations in *People v. Arctic Oil,*[21] a recent climate-relevant case we did not study. First, where the executive acted without the legislature's express consent; and second, where the legislature was involved. In the latter situation, discretion would be higher than in the former. In other words, if both political branches

---

21 *Greenpeace Nordic Ass'n and Natur og Ungdom v. Ministry of Petroleum and Energy*, 20-051052SIV-HRET; Norway, Supreme Court; 22.12.2020; ("*People v. Arctic Oil*").

have decided on an action or inaction, the threshold to a possible violation would be higher, and the political discretion to balance interests and to set priorities must also be higher. The higher the margin of discretion, the less appropriate it would be for a court to intervene. However, in cases of manifest abuse of discretion, court intervention could serve as an exceptional "*safety valve.*" States and their political branches can exercise discretion to balance climate interests with economic interests (or energy interests, as seen in the South African *Thabametsi Power Project* case).

Courts generally did not accept the argument that no single state can stop climate change as a valid reason for not sufficiently reducing the state's domestic GHG emissions. Despite political discretion and state sovereignty, courts held the branches of government accountable for their failure to implement adequate climate mitigation measures. National and international commitments, human rights, and scientific insights limit political discretion.

In *Neubauer*, the Court granted greater discretion regarding longer-term targets given the higher level of uncertainty. It was more apparent that the near-term political delay in implementing measures disproportionally burdened younger generations.

In *Massachusetts v. EPA*, the Supreme Court distinguished between an agency's decision not to pursue enforcement and its denial of a rulemaking petition. The court granted more discretion to the former than to the latter. As the Supreme Court has held, the EPA must provide sufficient reasons for denying a rulemaking petition. The Court limited the EPA's options to three. The first option is to conclude that the pollutant endangers public health or public welfare (make an endangerment finding), in which case the EPA must regulate. The second option is to conclude that the pollutant poses no threat to public health or welfare, so there is no need to regulate it. The third and final option is to provide sufficient reasons explaining why the EPA chose not to regulate at that time.

In *Urgenda*, the Court granted discretion to the political branches of government on how to reach, by 2020, the GHG target of 25% (compared to 1990). From the outset of its ruling, the court stated that it did not wish to enter the political domain.

## 3.2 Standing and Redressability

According to Ran Hirschl, standing is, among other things, a protection against the misuse of judicial review by political oppositions for their policy purposes. Judicial review should not be an instrument for the political minority to alter the outcome of the political process and advance their policy preferences against the will of the political majority. Strict standing requirements limit the number of cases concerning non-justiciable political questions, thereby reducing the court's caseload. It also reduces the risk of abuse resulting from wrongful claims by petitioners who lack a genuine interest in the court decision.[22]

Judicial review also entails elements of political participation and protects against potential abuse by the political majority. In the latter case, the merits of the lawsuit are relevant to judicial review. If the standing criteria are strict, it is not easy to reach the trial stage. If a court dismisses a case on standing grounds, it will not issue a decision on the case's merits. A potentially illegal activity or decision might persist if a court denies standing.

Additionally, the courts' role is to resolve specific cases, not to serve as a forum for policy debates. In *Gloucester Resources Limited v. Minister for Planning,*[23] a case we did not address, the Australian Land and Environment Court ruled that it could not encroach on the elected branches of government by adopting general policies or prohibitions, such as a general prohibition on approving coal mines. Therefore, it could only examine the validity of the governmental approval of the coal mine of the concrete case at bar.

In the U.S. federal court system, the U.S. Constitution confers jurisdiction on federal courts to hear "*Cases*" and "*Controversies*." It has been difficult for young people and NGOs to prove standing in climate protection cases. In our discussion of *EPA v. Massachusetts* and *Juliana,* we highlighted the three criteria that plaintiffs must meet to establish standing. They must demonstrate their interest in the lawsuit by showing that the political decision is causing them a concrete and particularised injury. Next, they must demonstrate a connection between the harmful situation and the political action. Thirdly, the lawsuit must provide redress for the alleged problem.

Until the Supreme Court ruling in *Massachusetts v. EPA*, it was difficult for federated states to meet the federal court standing requirements. In *Massachusetts v. EPA* (2005), Circuit Judge Sentelle, in his partial dissent, argued that climate change would not qualify for *Article III* standing because it would not cause particularised harm but rather cause damage to humanity at large.[24] In addition, Chief Justice Roberts stated in his dissent that causation could not be established in climate protection cases because the carbon cycle is highly complex: over time and space, actors emit GHGs, which remain active in the

22 Hirschl Ran; *Towards Juristocracy: The Origins and Consequences of the New Constitutionalism;* (Cambridge London, Harvard University Press, 2007); page 200.

23 *Gloucester Resources Limited v. Minister for Planning,* NSWLEC 7; Australia, Land and Environment Court; 08.02.2019.

24 *Massachusetts v. EPA* (2005); Judge Sentelle's opinion (dissenting in part and concurring in the judgment); page 3.

atmosphere, contributing to global warming. Therefore, it is impossible to establish a clear causal link between a given state action or inaction and the harm suffered at a specific moment. Additionally, these harms would not qualify as a particularised injury but would be common to humanity.

Circuit Judge Tatel stated in his dissent that the projected injuries would not be the same for everyone, even if each person were somehow affected by global warming. The U.S. Supreme Court, taking up Judge Tatel's dissent, softened the standing requirements for the U.S. federated states. As quasi-sovereign entities, they would merit exceptional standing.

Redressability has since been the most significant hurdle. A common defence argument was that no single state could provide redress for climate change. If State A reduces its emissions and State B increases its emissions, the overall result would remain the same. This conception is arguably very narrow, as each GHG reduction mitigates dangerous climate change. If State A does not reduce its emissions and State B increases its emissions, the net result will still be worse than if State A decreases its emissions, as simple mathematics shows. The trend was that courts did not accept that argument. Reducing GHG emissions would mitigate the harmful effects of climate change, and partial redress would be sufficient to meet the redressability criterion, according to Judge Tatel's dissenting opinion in *Massachusetts v. EPA* (2005).

Climate redressability also falls within the political sphere, so a court ruling could not offer such redress. The Court of Appeals dismissed *Juliana* because the petitioners did not meet the redressability prong. According to the Court, the youth's claim would require it to order far-reaching policy decisions that fundamentally reform the U.S. energy system, and such redress would exceed the competence of an Article III court. Judge Staton dissented, writing, similarly to *Massachusetts v. EPA*, that redress need not be complete to meet *Article III* standing requirements and that partial redress would suffice. She argued that in *Massachusetts v. EPA*, partial redress was also sufficient to satisfy the redressability requirement.

In *Aji P. v. Washington*, the Court of Appeals of the State of Washington, like *Juliana*, concluded that courts are incompetent to order, design, supervise, or implement a climate change remedial plan. The judicial branch would, therefore, be unable to provide the redress that youth plaintiffs seek, and only the political branches would be competent to do so.

*Held v. State of Montana*, among other things, centred on whether declaratory relief is sufficient to satisfy the redressability prong. The court eventually held that the plaintiffs met the three standing criteria.

Standing was an issue not only in the U.S. but also in other states. Human rights arguments are complex, and NGOs might not fall under their scope of protection. In *Friends of the Irish Environment* (*FIE*), for example, the High Court held that the *FIE*, as a corporate entity, does not enjoy a right to life, bodily integrity, or an unenumerated right to an environment consistent with human dignity. The High Court adopted a more flexible approach in line with the ECtHR by assuming that *FIE* had standing. The Supreme Court of the Philippines, in *Minors Oposa v. Factoran*, even recognised the petitioners' standing to represent future generations.

## 3.3 Sovereignty

The claim that states can dispose of their resources as they please is inadequate because it considers states solely as rights holders, neglecting their role as obligation bearers. Public trust limits a state's internal sovereignty and may become essential in a court's climate protection toolkit. Mary Christina Wood described the public trust doctrine as an "*ancient and enduring legal principle*" traceable to Roman law. Of concern is the idea that some resources are so essential that they belong to the public and are inalienable.[25] This principle expressly came up in *Juliana*. The Oregon District Court stated clearly that the state cannot legislate those obligations away.[26] Public trust obligations associated with intergenerational justice require the state to protect natural resources for present and future generations of citizens,[27] limiting available political choices and imposing positive obligations upon the sovereign. Some courts have developed and enforced nature's trust obligations in common law systems without requiring legislative enactments. In the U.S., there is an attempt to expand those trust obligations to the atmosphere and GHG concentrations through judicial review. Young people formulated this demand to enforce state obligations to protect the "Atmospheric Trust" in their judicial review petitions.[28]

---

25 Wood Mary Christina; *Nature's Trust: Environmental Law For A New Ecological Age*; pages 14 & 53. & Wood, Mary Christina; *On the Eve of Destruction: Courts Confronting the Climate Emergency*; Indiana Law Journal: Vol. 97: Iss. 1, Article 5. (Winter 2022); page 245.

26 *Juliana 2016*, page 49: "*Public trust claims are unique because they concern inherent attributes of sovereignty. The public trust imposes on the government an obligation to protect the res of the trust. A defining feature of that obligation is that it cannot be legislated away. Because of the nature of public trust claims, a displacement analysis simply does not apply.*"

27 See Blumm Michael and Wood Mary Christina; *The Public Trust Doctrine in Environmental and Natural Resources Law;* 3rd edition (Durham, Carolina Academic Press, 2021).

28 See, for instance, the following youth-led cases: *Chernaik v. Brown* [docket number S066564, 367 Or 143 (2020); Supreme Court of the State of Oregon; 22.10.2022]; *Sagoonick v. State of Alaska* [*No. S-17297, Opinion No. 7583;* Supreme Court of the State of Alaska;

The question of sovereignty may not always be explicitly addressed in a court decision. However, it is invariably at stake, albeit implicitly, when conceptions of the separation of powers and political discretion are in question. In judicial review, on the one hand, courts grant the branches of government varying degrees of discretionary freedom, and this margin of appreciation derives from the internal aspect of sovereignty. On the other hand, judicial review petitioners often advance international commitments and scientific evidence. Henceforth, we will argue that our understanding of state sovereignty may be changing due to climate-based judicial review.

Considerations of state sovereignty have had a significant impact on climate-relevant judicial review. On the one side, it might entail specific rights. Being a sovereign entitles a U.S. state to privileged federal court standing (see *Massachusetts v. EPA*). On the other hand, it might entail obligations, such as preserving natural resources for current and future generations (public trust obligations).

State parties tended to argue that courts must consider only the adverse domestic effects, not those abroad. For example, in *People v. Arctic Oil*, only domestic GHG emissions were considered, not the downstream emissions of exported oil in other countries. In some states, there might still be a perception that what happens elsewhere is less critical when crafting national policies.

In *Neubauer*, Germany's Federal Constitutional Court ruled that even people from Bangladesh and Nepal have the right to submit a constitutional complaint to defend their rights to life, bodily integrity, and property because the measures of the KSG would be unsuitable for tackling the dangers of climate change. In climate protection matters, political and court decisions have an impact beyond the domestic state, meaning that every citizen from every part of the World is entitled to challenge climate-related decisions of the German political branches by calling for the protection of the German Grundgesetz. However, the Federal Constitutional Court held that Germany's duty of care for claimants from abroad would be limited. Foreign states are sovereign entities, and a German court could not take or order adaptation measures abroad. Nonetheless, it could help and support those states in doing so. Germany can protect the rights and liberties of people in Bangladesh and Nepal by reducing its national GHG emissions and gradually establishing a zero-net-carbon society. The disastrous effects of climate change in Bangladesh and

28.01.2022], or *Navahine F. v. Hawai'i Department of Transportation* [1CCV-22-0000631; First Circuit Court of the State of Hawai'i; 06.04.2023].

Nepal could not be attributed to the German KSG because there would be no direct causation.[29]

Another example is the *Huaraz* case;[30] the Oberlandesgericht Hamm (Germany) accepted the lawsuit of the Peruvian plaintiff Saúl Luciano Lliuya against the German energy company RWE for its share in global GHG emissions. RWE would be partly responsible for melting a glacier that could cause flooding on his property in the Andean city of Huaraz, Peru. According to the claimant, RWE should, in proportion to its share of worldwide GHG emissions (0.47%), contribute to the costs of the precautionary measures necessary to protect Saúl Luciano Lliuya's property from flooding. The Oberlandesgericht in Hamm let the case enter the evidentiary phase and gathered evidence in Huaraz. Meanwhile, an independent scientific study by researchers from Oxford and Washington universities concluded that the melting of glaciers in the region above Huaraz is attributed to anthropogenic GHG emissions. According to the Huaraz proceedings, a court could hold a national company liable for its share of global GHG emissions.

According to the court, RWE, a large greenhouse gas emitter, could, under German law, indeed be held liable for damages caused by its contributions to climate change, even if the damages occur in the long term, over a great distance, and even though the GHG emissions are not illegal. Hence, the Peruvian plaintiff could ask the court to hold RWE liable to pay damages in proportion to its contribution to the harm. The court held that RWE's contributions of 0.38% to industrial carbon emissions and 0.24% to total emissions were significant, and that the potential damage was foreseeable since the 1960s.[31] However, the experts appointed by the court determined that the probability of a glacial lake outburst flood occurring within the next 30 years was 1%, which was considered insufficient to pose a threat to the plaintiff's property.[32]

Even if the case was not decided in favour of the plaintiff, it could serve as a blueprint for similar lawsuits to pressure the main GHG emitters.

Sovereignty is also in transition due to the creation of international institutions, which limit internal discretion. In *Greenpeace Netherlands v. the Netherlands*, the court held that the state could not regulate its national air carriers' GHG emissions, as this falls under the competence of the International Civil Aviation Organization (*ICAO*).[33]

---

29 *Neubauer*, page 48.

30 *Luciano Lliuya v. RWE*, No. 2 O 285/15; Germany; Oberlandesgericht Hamm; 28.05.2025.

31 Ibid, pages 34 & 35.

32 Ibid, page 75.

33 *Greenpeace Netherlands v. State of the Netherlands*, C/09/600364 / KG ZA 20-933, ECLI: NL:RBDHA:2020:12440; The Hague District Court; 12.09.2020.

The European Union has become a crucial supranational actor in climate protection, as member states have conferred sovereign rights. The EU's climate stance and relevant legal dispositions limit the discretion available to its member states. The Court of Justice of the European Union has the authority to interpret EU law and also considers the Union's Charter of Fundamental Rights.

In addition, regional human rights conventions and courts also affect the internal affairs of their member states. In Europe, for instance, the European Court of Human Rights reviews petitions from states against other states and from individuals against states.[34]

The ECtHR establishes autonomous notions and considers the ECHR as a living instrument. With its ruling in *KlimaSeniorinnen,* the ECtHR increased pressure on member states and their courts to effectively integrate the climate dimensions of Articles 2, 6, and 8 into their domestic law, considering the global targets set in the Paris Agreement and scientific evidence.[35]

The International Criminal Court (*ICC*) in The Hague is another significant institution that could affect political discretion. The harmful deforestation of the Amazonian Forest in Brazil exposed that the state might disrespect the environmental concerns of their indigenous populations. As there was no adequate remedy at the domestic level, the indigenous community leaders filed a complaint to the ICC in Den Haag. They asked that the court initiate investigations against former Brazilian President Jair Bolsonaro for crimes against humanity.

The UN General Assembly, in its resolution 77/276 of 29 March 2023, asked the *ICJ* to render an advisory opinion on the responsibility of States in respect of climate change. The court had to identify the obligations of States in respect of GHG-intensive activities and determine the legal consequences arising from breaches of these obligations.[36]

The *ICJ* issued its opinion on July 25, 2025.[37] It stated that, under the most relevant applicable law,[38] states have an obligation to prevent significant environmental harm, such as climate change, and a duty to cooperate to pro-

---

34 Grimm Dieter and Cooper Belinda; *Sovereignty: The Origin and Future of a Political and Legal Concept;* pages 85 & 87.

35 Žatková Sandra, Paľuchová Petra; *ECtHR: Verein KlimaSeniorinnen Schweiz and Others v. Switzerland (Application No. 53600/20, 9 April 2024): Insufficient Measures to Combat Climate Change Resulting in Violation of Human Rights*; Bratislava Law Review 8, Nr. 1 (7 July 2024); 227–244; page 238.

36 Ibid, page 40.

37 International Court of Justice; *Advisory Opinion on the obligations of States in respect of Climate Change*; General List No. 187; 23.07.2025.

38 Ibid, page 58: "[…]*the Court is of the view that the most directly relevant applicable law consists of the Charter of the United Nations, the UNFCCC, the Kyoto Protocol, the Paris*

tect the environment. States must act with "*due diligence*."[39] The various legal sources inform one another.[40] Some duties are obligations of result (e.g., the duty to communicate information to the COP); others are obligations of conduct, such as the duty to implement climate mitigation measures or to cooperate. Non-compliance with reduction commitments could constitute an internationally wrongful act.[41] The states' discretion regarding their nationally determined contributions is limited. Those NDCs must be capable of achieving the objectives of the Paris Agreement.[42] The states must make "*good efforts*" to attain their NDCs.[43] A state's international responsibility can be engaged in the context of climate obligations.[44]

## 3.4 The Counter-Majoritarian Difficulty

Judges acknowledge that climate-related judicial review could interfere with the political branches, causing counter-majoritarian difficulties. The thoughts on the possibility of constitutional essentials related to environmental and climate protection are relatively novel. Sustainability, the right to a clean environment, and a climate system capable of sustaining human life are considered third-generation rights, also known as collective rights. They are cost-intensive because they can significantly impact the state's economic setup, and what is economically sustainable may not be environmentally sustainable. We are comparing two very different things: Short-term profits and medium- to long-term climate protection requirements. Climate protection

*Agreement, UNCLOS, the ozone layer treaties, the Biodiversity Convention, the Desertification Convention, the customary duty to prevent significant harm to the environment and the duty to co-operate for the protection of the environment, and international human rights law, as well as certain guiding principles for the interpretation of various applicable rules and principles (sustainable development, common but differentiated responsibilities and respective capabilities, equity, intergenerational equity, and the precautionary approach or principle)."*

39 Ibid, pages 130 & 131.

40 Ibid, page 115.

41 Ibid, page 72.

42 Ibid, page 79.

43 Ibid, page 80.

44 Ibid, page 126: "*It is well established that every internationally wrongful act of a State entails the international responsibility of that State. In the present context, the internationally wrongful act may range from breaches of treaty obligations, such as the procedural obligation of a State to prepare, communicate or implement NDCs under Article 4 of the Paris Agreement, to breaches of obligations under customary international law, such as the failure of a State to regulate emissions of GHGs under its duty to exercise due diligence to prevent significant harm, or its failure to conduct EIAs.*"

costs are imminent, whereas the benefits and the effects of those expensive protection measures lie in the distant future. Those benefits primarily accrue to developing states, as they appear to be more vulnerable to the dangers of climate change, whereas wealthy states would bear most of the costs.

Courts addressed concerns about the separation of powers in their rulings by providing extensive explanations for their decisions. Some judges expressed strong criticism and observations about judicial activism in their opinions. In the cases we analysed, the branches of government responded positively to the climate rulings. In *Massachusetts v. EPA*, the EPA issued an endangerment finding and began regulating GHGs. Congress and the Executive let the EPA proceed with regulating GHG emissions from new cars and stationary sources. In *Neubauer* and *Friends of the Irish Environment*, the political branches accepted the court's reasoning. They increased climate mitigation efforts by amending the climate protection law in the former case and adopting an amended government plan in the latter. They increased their mitigation targets, provided more information to the public, and enhanced security in economic sector planning.

We can argue that courts established a suitable way to intervene without disproportionately impairing the separation of powers. Instead of making fierce and assertive decisions, courts limited themselves to determining the law; they respected political discretion and fostered political discourse, perhaps leading to cooperation among powers to protect the climate and the underlying rights. Courts utilised the tools at their disposal to legitimise and explain their rulings, and they did not directly impose their position on the other branches of government. Courts identified risks, offered guidance on what the political branches should and should not do, and set a time frame.

Eventually, political representatives decided how much weight to assign to a specific interest and elaborated a policy based on the judicial branch's marking criteria. Those considerations did not emerge out of nowhere; courts derived them from the legal framework.

## Section 2: Preliminary Conclusions

Our climate-based judicial review study enables us to draw some preliminary conclusions and findings that Parts 2 and 3 will address in more detail to propose a benchmark for legitimate and respectworthy climate-based judicial review.

Climate protection petitions, predominantly driven by or in the name of young and future generations, have increasingly put the government under pressure and placed the courts in a delicate situation (1). Taking global warming seriously might require more audacious climate protection measures and, allegedly, the cooperative support of the three branches of government, which could lead to a more flexible understanding of the separation of powers (2).

### 1 Pressurising the Political Branches

Children might be the most accepted and legitimate driving force behind climate-related judicial review. Children and youth activists have gathered worldwide to take their governments to court, demanding that they take global warming seriously and honour their public trust obligations. They demanded that states establish a consistent climate remedial plan and reduce their GHG emissions swiftly to prevent climate-related harm. National courts and international or regional courts scrutinise state actions.

Young people are also exerting considerable pressure on governments through demonstrations, speeches, publications, and media exposure. They are forming climate protection movements such as *Fridays for Future* and *Youth for Climate*. These actions have taken place within and beyond their climate-related lawsuits. Greta Thunberg spoke before the UN General Assembly and filed a complaint to demand protection from the devastating impacts of climate change. The United Nations Committee on the Rights of the Child should act in accordance with the UN Convention on the Rights of the Child. Following up on the complaint, an Intergovernmental Declaration on Children, Youth, and Climate Action was signed at the 25th Conference of the Parties in Madrid. The governments of the 196 UN Member States have also been invited to do so. *UNICEF*, the custodian of children's rights, works with governments to support the subsequent implementation of the declaration. The growing support for children's cases could be pivotal to the adoption of consistent climate protection measures. Youth cases have already created dissent among judges and members of the political branches. We have seen that courts have adjusted standing requirements and engaged in new developments regarding substantive constitutional essentials.

In *Juliana*, members of all three branches of government called for judicial remedies to prevent dangerous climate change. The Oregon District Court recognised the existence of a right to a climate system capable of sustaining human life. At the appeal stage, Judge Staton issued a strong dissent, urging the court to intervene to prevent or delay the climate catastrophe. Every effort would matter to prevent the day when remedial measures are no longer possible. After the failed settlement discussions with the *DOJ*, Congressmen and Senators urged President Biden and his administration to respect their climate justice commitments and provide redress to the plaintiffs. In *Aji P. v. Washington*, former King County Superior Court Judge Hollis Hill took a stand in an article in *The Seattle Times* on behalf of youth petitioners. Chief Justice González and Justice Whitener of the Washington Supreme Court called for judicial intervention in a dissenting opinion. The court should not hide behind "*self-congratulatory words of judicial restraint.*"[45] Dissenting opinions favouring court intervention have become recurrent in U.S. climate protection cases. If more judges dissent from the typical judicial solutions, the minority position may eventually become the majority opinion. We may see this happening with regard to standing, public trust, and the right to a sustainable climate.

In *Neubauer*, the German Federal Constitutional Court ruled that the Federal Climate Protection Law could infringe upon constitutional rights. This ruling prompted the political branches to adopt a firmer stance on climate protection, thereby safeguarding the rights of younger generations.

The threat of dangerous climate change has been eligible for expedited judicial proceedings, which have increased pressure on the government. For example, the Irish Supreme Court granted a fast-track proceeding to deal directly with the case (*a leapfrog appeal*); without this, it would have had to pass through the usual appeal stage. Likewise, in the initial pre-trial proceedings of *Duarte Agostinho and Others v. Portugal and Others*, the ECtHR took extraordinary measures by directly accepting the case and allowing it to bypass the national court proceedings. This decision of the Fourth Section of the ECtHR remains significant, even though the Grand Chamber later dismissed the case,

45 *Aji P. v. State of Washington*, No. 80007-8-I; United States; Supreme Court of the State of Washington,; 10.06.2021: Chief Justice González and Justice Whitener wrote in their dissenting opinion (page 2) that this lawsuit would have been "an *opportunity to decide whether Washington's youth have a right to a stable climate system that sustains human life and liberty. We recite that we believe the children are our future, but we continue actions that could leave them a world with an environment on the brink of ruin and no mechanism to assert their rights or the rights of the natural world. This is our legacy to them described in the self-congratulatory words of judicial restraint.*"

as it shows that the Fourth Section was willing to innovate at that time. It posed a series of questions to 33 states to collect evidence for the trial proceedings.[46]

In the U.S., climate protection lawsuits also focused on the positive state obligation to preserve natural resources, including the atmosphere. These cases turned on whether the public trust doctrine encompasses the atmosphere, and the courts left the question unanswered. In their partially dissenting opinion in *Sagoonick v. State of Alaska*, Justices Maassen and Carney emphasised that it was not necessary to extend the public trust doctrine to cover the atmosphere or other natural resources, as global warming already harms traditionally protected natural resources.[47] Likewise, the United States First Circuit Court of the State of Hawai'i held that it was unnecessary to decide whether the climate falls within the public trust because global warming affects all natural resources. It rejected the argument that the state could not protect public trust resources, as people emit GHG globally.[48]

## 2 From the Separation to the Cooperation of Powers?

Climate protection might require shifting from stricter to more flexible approaches to the separation of powers. Preserving a sustainable and healthy environment allegedly requires the support and cooperation of all three

---

46 ECtHR, Fourth Section, *Duarte Agostinho and Others v. Portugal and Others*, Application no. 39371/20; 13.11.2020.

47 *Sagoonick v. State of Alaska*, No. S-17297, Opinion No. 7583; Supreme Court of the State of Alaska; 28.01.2022; page 46: "*Because the various aspects of our ecosystem are interdependent, "[a]llegations that the State has breached its duties with regard to the management of" individual resources "such as water, shorelines, wildlife, and fish" – which we have already recognized as subject to the public trust doctrine – "do not depend on a declaratory judgment about the atmosphere.[…] Simply put, the public trust doctrine is implicated by allegations that a particular State action exacerbates the climate crisis and thereby harms "water, shorelines, wildlife, and fish"* – as *the plaintiffs have alleged here."*

48 *Navahine F. v. Hawai'i Department of Transportation*, 1CCV-22-0000631; First Circuit Court of the State of Hawai'i; 06.04.2023; page 3: "*As a threshold issue, Defendants argue the public trust doctrine does not apply to the climate, because the climate is not air, water, land, minerals, energy resource or some other "localized" natural resource. The court need not decide whether "the climate" is a trust resource or "property," because Plaintiffs argue that deteriorating climate change impacts our natural resources. "[…] Defendants' argument is that it is not required to do anything because the problem is just too big and the State's efforts will have no impact. Putting aside that negative thinking will not solve the problem, the law requires that as trustee, the State/HDOT must take steps to maintain their assets to keep them from falling into disrepair. It is "elementary trust law' that trust property not be permitted to "fall into ruin on [the trustee's] watch."*

branches of state government, each utilising the tools at its disposal. The judicial branch could become a conversation partner actively supporting the development of consistent policies and red-carding manifest abuses of discretion. In the other cases, the court could nonetheless promote discourse by pointing out the risks, as the *Bundesverfassungsgericht* did in *Neubauer*. A court could highlight procedural or substantive issues through declaratory relief and return the ball to the government, which retains sufficient discretion to stay in charge.

In *Juliana* and in *Aji P. v. Washington*, the idea resurfaced that the three branches of government must cooperate to effectively protect the climate. Each branch has its own domain, while the courts can monitor and guide the other branches' efforts. Hollis Hill, a former King County Superior Court judge, published an article in The Seattle Times urging the Washington Supreme Court to allow the 13 youth plaintiffs in *Aji P. v. Washington* to proceed to trial. All three branches should work together to address the climate change crisis: "*As a former judge, I know it is critical that all three branches of government use every tool at their disposal to turn the tide. An incremental approach will not remedy the current crisis or protect future generations.*"[49] Despite this call, the Washington Supreme Court restrained itself by declining to hear the case in a seven-votes against two-votes decision. Chief Justice González and Justice Whitener of the Washington Supreme Court would have granted judicial review.[50]

When discussing cooperation among powers, it is worth noting that *the* Lahore High Court promoted cooperation through "*writs of ongoing mandamus*" in *Sheikh Asim Farooq v. Federation of Pakistan*.[51] It closely monitored the implementation of political action over a considerable period, providing support in a successive manner. The Lahore High Court issued "*writs of ongoing mandamus*" with great success in the context of forestation. Under court dir-

49 The Seattle Times; Hollis Hill; *Let Youth Have Day in Court over Climate Change*; https://www.seattletimes.com/opinion/let-youth-have-day-in-court-over-climate-change <01.10.2021>.

50 United States; Court of Appeals of the State of Washington, *Aji P. v. State of Washington*, No. 80007-8-I, 08.02.2021; dissenting opinion of Chief Justice González and Justice Whitener; page 2: They wrote in their dissent that this lawsuit would have been "*an opportunity to decide whether Washington's youth have a right to a stable climate system that sustains human life and liberty. We recite that we believe the children are our future, but we continue actions that could leave them a world with an environment on the brink of ruin and no mechanism to assert their rights or the rights of the natural world. This is our legacy to them described in the self-congratulatory words of judicial restraint.*"

51 *Sheikh Asim Farooq v. Federation of Pakistan*, W.P. No. 192069 of 2018; Pakistan, Lahore High Court; 03.08.2019.

ection, this led to the adoption of an Urban Trees Plantation Policy, resulting in massive tree plantings. Through ongoing, respectful dialogue among the branches of government, they pulled in the same direction. The positive results in Punjab demonstrated that this ongoing cooperation was highly fruitful. The court appeared to be a dialogue partner actively supporting the development of consistent policies.

Given the inherent dangers to democracy, climate protection could serve as a common objective for cooperation among the three branches of state government within the state and across states internationally. I will later argue that through weak-form judicial review, courts can promote democracy, climate protection, and the respectworthiness of the democratic system as a whole. Courts could perhaps create a disturbance through declaratory judgments that might lead to further democratic discourse and more efficient climate protection.

So far, courts involved in climate protection lawsuits have avoided making complex political decisions by deferring to the legislative and executive branches. Their assessments typically focus on establishing the law (the obligations) and identifying risks to constitutional and human rights.

The following two parts elaborate on the framework of weak-form judicial review. We will argue that dynamic forms of judicial review, starting with a court taking a weak-form judicial-review posture, could permit addressing climate protection deficits in a respectful manner and alleviate counter-majoritarian concerns.

# PART 2

# The Caveats for Democracy

"I have followed the climate issue closely for 40 years now. I have never been as frightened for my grandchildren as I am now, both because of the late hour to try to stop the onslaught of dangers and because of the disturbing disregard for science and the rights of young people and all future generations."[1]

"Washington State's greenhouse gas emissions have increased despite the claims of Olympia politicians that progress is being made. The political branches of government are simply unable to address this crisis on their own. And who can blame them? The climate crisis is incredibly complex – exactly why we need the impartial scrutiny of the judiciary to do its part. Politicians change, and with them, policies can change as well. A court order declaring the constitutional rights of Washingtonians can endure the tides of political change. This may be the only way to protect children – the most vulnerable demographic with the least political power."[2]

1 Speth, James Gustave; *They Knew: The Federal Government's Fifty-Year Role in Causing the Climate Crisis*; page 135.Gustave Speth, regarding the first Trump Administration.

2 The Seattle Times; Hollis Hill; *Let Youth Have Day in Court over Climate Change*; https://www.seattletimes.com/opinion/let-youth-have-day-in-court-over-climate-change <01.10.2021>.

 | HTTPS://DOI.ORG/10.1163/9789004771710-008

# Introduction

The specimens of pivotal cases analysed in Part 1 show that courts have become increasingly involved in climate protection matters. These cases may already have affected our understanding of judicial review, state sovereignty, the separation of powers, and liberal democracy. Similar cases are pending on court dockets worldwide.

Part 2 builds upon the findings of Part 1 and assesses the impact of climate-related judicial review on essential aspects of (liberal) democracy. Should courts intervene, as EU member state courts have done, or dismiss climate protection cases at the pre-trial stage, as U.S. federal courts typically do? Given the ideal of self-government by the people, one might argue that political representatives should decide on climate policies for the people rather than a panel of unaccountable judges. Courts, however, did not always exercise judicial self-restraint by dismissing cases involving political questions. They increasingly went ahead with decisions on the merits, even though they mostly adopted what one might call a rather weak-form judicial posture. Climate-based judicial review petitions and active judicial intervention have become a reality of our time.

This part begins the endeavour to bring judicial review practice, constitutional theory, and political philosophy together, arriving, in Part 3, at a concept for climate-based judicial review that can be squared with basic principles of democracy. Our angle is foremost that of a liberal democracy based on an entrenched constitution. One of the key questions in this part is whether the new form of climate protection judicial review poses a threat to democracy, and notably to the democratic ideal of self-government by the people. Climate protection lawsuits pose challenges and threats to existing understandings of democracy, placing judges in an uneasy situation.

Chapter 4 explains why people seek judicial review rather than pursuing the usual political channels. As we can see from climate-related judicial review petitions and subsequent court decisions, the inherent difficulties of making resolute decisions in democratic government systems are a significant concern. The broad scope of political discretion in environmental matters that governments derive from state sovereignty is not unproblematic. Sovereignty confers broad discretion to the political authorities to define climate policies. Hence, they are free to decide whether to be a party to a binding treaty, refrain from curtailing GHG emissions, or market their natural resources (including

 | HTTPS://DOI.ORG/10.1163/9789004771710-009

carbon sinks, such as forests).[3] The unsatisfactory climate protection records resulting from governmental discretion drive the turn to judicial review for effective remedies. Given this development, a demand that sovereignty must come to play a different role is becoming increasingly evident and persuasive. Instead of simply exercising the freedom to govern, it is increasingly expected to honour the unavoidable responsibility for adequate environmental protection measures, concomitant with the electorate's trust in it. In other words, the freedom to govern could and should be understood as irreducibly subject to a duty of care regarding climate protection.

Chapter 5 discusses the respectworthiness of the politico-legal system, referring to John Rawls' conception of political liberalism in general and Frank Michelman's further developments on it in particular.

We will continue to unpack the constitutional paradox that emerges in discussions of the respectworthiness of politico-legal systems. Two rival ideals of democracy inform these discussions. The first is self-government by the laws of the people, according to which substantive judicial review of majoritarian decisions represents an undue interference with the proper functioning of democracy. The second is that of government bound by law, according to which substantive constitutional essentials also deserve judicial protection. Political noncompliance with substantive constitutional essentials could delegitimise majoritarian decisions. This second ideal leads to judicial review caveats that conflict with majoritarian democratic decision-making and might lead to the so-called counter-majoritarian difficulty, mainly because of the controversial polycentric questions that raise their head in climate protection cases: when petitioners ask the court to order the adoption and implementation of climate protection plans, this involves interest balancing and prioritisation. A court issuing such an order might require the political branches to fundamentally transform society across various economic sectors, including energy, construction, industry, transportation, and waste management. This impacts the economy, the people's way of life, and their rights and liberties.

Michelman's thoughts on the justiciability of socioeconomic rights will be essential to alleviating separation of powers concerns that arise when courts

3 Let us recall that the states primarily concerned with climate protection are indeed developed states and liberal democracies. The latter are responsible for the largest share of current atmospheric GHG concentrations and have the resources and technology to do more. Developing states must adapt to climate change more urgently as global warming affects them disproportionately. This, however, does not mean that developing states do not bear responsibility for climate mitigation, as was highlighted in *Asghar Leghari v. Federation of Pakistan*.

issue rulings on the existence of specific climate rights by interpreting a legal text in light of changing exigencies. Following Michelman's cue, I will question whether climate rights could constitute enforceable constitutional essentials.

CHAPTER 4

# The Emergence of Climate-Based Judicial Review

## Introduction

Given the particular nature of climate protection questions, we wonder why they often end up in court as lawsuits. On the one hand, climate change entails risks to our rights, liberties, and the state economy. Those dangers might be less tangible for some states and more apparent for others. On the other hand, climate protection entails costly political decisions that affect our rights and liberties. Those climate protection effects, however, are directly measurable.

Global warming and our mitigation efforts have already affected what Frank Michelman would probably call the respectworthiness of the democratic system or the idea of the "*at least reasonable.*" The climate emergency threatens (liberal) democracies' state structures, that is, states with entrenched constitutions that institute three separate branches of government, one of which is an independent system of courts exercising judicial review.

Section 1 points out the inherent difficulties that burden urgent or resolute climate-based decision-making in liberal democracies, among which slowness is a significant concern. The democratic process takes much more time than autocratic or dictatorial decision-making. The pluralistic composition of contemporary societies aggravates this problem. The more pluralist and diverse a society, the more time-consuming liberal democratic decision-making becomes.[1] Hence, there is a slowness in liberal democratic responses to climate change and a tendency to turn to the courts to expedite them.

Section 2 focuses on the shallow climate protection records of developed states. In this regard, the U.S., as the world's largest and perhaps most influential liberal democracy, is of fundamental interest. It has a long history of judicial review, and structurally, it has the exact profile of the kind of state we are focusing on in this scholarly work. It has an old and entrenched constitution that pivots on the ideals of the separation of powers and independent judicial review. Moreover, its Supreme Court has a record of responding to changing historical exigencies, including public interest litigation. Furthermore, the

1 Michelman Frank; *Dilemmas of Belonging: Moral Truth, Human Rights, and Why We Might Not Want a Representative Judiciary; page* 1224.

 | HTTPS://DOI.ORG/10.1163/9789004771710-010

U.S. is among the most significant GHG emitters, so its stance on climate protection matters.[2]

∴

2 Geel Oliver; *Urgenda and Beyond: The past, present and future of climate change public interest litigation; page* 60.

## Section 1: A Time-Consuming Process

Majoritarian decision-making is complex and time-consuming, whereas addressing dangerous climate change requires immediate action, particularly urgent and profound structural policy and legal reforms. The liberal democratic process inevitably results in compromises that not everyone approves of, especially for cost-intensive climate protection measures. While climate reality is broadly accepted, the impact of national climate protection measures on global GHG emissions remains subject to debate, especially regarding their adverse effects on people's way of life, rights, and liberties.

In other words, there is a deep tension between the concept of liberal democracy and the need for urgent and profound law reforms, as structural multi-sector reforms can take considerable time. The democratic state must open a discourse to gather the positions and interests of all affected stakeholders, ranging from business leaders to trade unions and civil society interest groups. Dissent is essential and inevitable in this ongoing debate. Whatever decision is taken at any specific moment always underlines the rifts between the prevailing majorities and dissenting minorities. It gives rise to internal processes of reflection in which everyone begins to decide whether the majority's decision is reasonable and worthy of their respect.[3] In the negative, the dissenter decides whether to oppose it and, if so, how. Should they resist in a "*civilised*" and "*democratically acceptable way*", such as protesting in the streets, introducing a rulemaking petition, or filing a judicial review petition? Or should they turn to more transgressive or revolutionary manifestations of resistance? To encourage the former and discourage the latter, political representatives should sufficiently involve the people in decision-making processes and provide clear explanations. All decisions should be made as transparently as possible, which, of course, is time-consuming. The duty of civility and tolerance is always a complex matter. If the majority abuses its discretion, it could precipitate a revolutionary moment that endangers the democratic project.

Filing a petition for judicial review of the legality of governmental action thus means challenging the outcome of the political process. This challenge turns on the idea that not every act of political representatives is valid. The lawsuits show that the petitioners did not consider a policy or an act to be

---

3 See, among others, Michelman Frank; *IDA's Way: Constructing the Respect-Worthy Governmental System;* 72 Fordham Law Review (2003), 345; Michelman Frank; *Legitimacy, The Social Turn and Constitutional Review: What Political Liberalism Suggests;* Michelman Frank; *Constitutional Essentials: On the Constitutional Theory of Political Liberalism.* We will develop the requirements of respectworthiness and reasonableness, with reference to Frank Michelman, in Chapter 5.

respectworthy, or *at least reasonable*. At this moment, the counter-majoritarian difficulty raises its head.

Climate protection introduces an additional layer to this already complex legal discourse, as it impacts the competing interests of current and future generations. Today's climate policies may have a significantly greater impact on the lives of future generations than they currently have on us.[4] Hence, the idea that we should include the interests of those who will succeed us in the political debate. The intergenerational approach is relatively novel and limits the available political options. State powers must preserve the environment not only for the current electorate but also for future generations. Our contemporary political representatives primarily care about current interests, and as elected officials, they obviously seek the support of today's electorates.

Although international law instruments have introduced the principles of intergenerational justice and intergenerational equity, young people and future generations are underrepresented in political decision-making. There is inertia among political decision-makers, as well as reluctance and resistance from parts of the population. Until now, predominantly young people or their representatives (perhaps the *KlimaSeniorinnen* case is a notable exception) have engaged with the political branches through rule-making or judicial-review petitions on behalf of young and future generations. Most individuals would likely respond affirmatively when asked whether they support measures to alleviate global warming. However, public support may wane when the state takes this into concrete political and legal action, requiring personal sacrifices.

People may oppose governmental measures, especially if they are prolonged. We observed this trend in Luxembourg as oil prices rose due to the ongoing conflict in Ukraine. Electric cars are more expensive and less comfortable than thermal cars in terms of autonomy and convenience, which makes people hesitate when switching from fossil-fuelled cars to fully electric ones. Suddenly, the demand for electric vehicles increased. This shift from thermal cars to electric cars is more closely tied to economic interests than to concerns about climate change. For now, the government subsidises electric vehicles, and charging costs are lower than fuel costs, but this may change. Another example of prioritising economic interests is the additional subsidisation of

---

4 See, for instance, Speth James Gustave; *They Knew: The Federal Government's Fifty-Year Role in Causing the Climate Crisis*; page 29; Spentzou Danai; Climate Change Litigation as a means to address Intergenerational Equity and Climate Change; Queen Mary Law Journal 2 (2021); DOI: 10.26494/QMLJ3944; & *Rikki Held, et al. v. State of Montana, et al.*, CDV-2020-307; Montana 1st Judicial District Court, Lewis & Clark County, 14.08.2023; ["*Held v. State of Montana* (2023)"].

fossil fuels to mitigate the price increase resulting from the Ukraine conflict. Climate mitigation imperatives are subjected to short-term economic state interests. Many citizens support this policy because their own economic interests are also at stake.

In addition, if the people are not yet experiencing ecological harm, they might favour immediate benefits over long-term needs. Against this background, political branches and the courts in judicial review must consider state obligations and measures. The potential for parts of the population to reject liberty-intrusive state measures is relatively high. We observed this fierce opposition from minorities due to the government's sanitary measures during the COVID-19 pandemic.

The more apparent the adverse effects of climate change, the more urgent the need for mitigation and adaptation measures seems to us. In the words of Al Gore: "*The most dangerous threat to our global environment may not be the strategic threats themselves but rather our perception of them, for most people do not yet accept the fact that the crisis is extremely grave.*"[5]

Jared Diamond studied why societies collapsed and argued that governments often prioritised short-term interests over long-term goals, leading decision-makers to delay responses to threats until they became imminent. Then, it might already be too late: "*Governments, too, regularly operate on short-term focus: they feel overwhelmed by imminent disasters and pay attention only to problems that are on the verge of explosion.*"[6] Others feared democracy might not endure a life-threatening crisis: "*If life ends,* democracy *ends.*"[7]

The climate protection "*time lag*" creates further controversies. The GHG we curb today will benefit people in the future, while the costs of climate protection are imminent. It is challenging for the electorate and political representatives to fully commit to climate protection and accept the economic costs associated with decarbonisation.

Instead of telling the People the hard truth and making hard policy choices, politicians used distraction and delay tactics to avoid making resolute decisions on climate protection: "*And since the substance of politics is hard choices, it is precisely the hard choices that are excluded wherever possible. They are hidden, neglected, postponed and ignored. And the voters are distracted with all manner of clever and extremely powerful manufactured messages. Means*

5 Gore Albert; *Earth in the Balance: Forging a New Common Purpose*; page 36.

6 Diamond Jared; *Collapse: How Societies Choose to Fail or Survive* (New York, Penguin Books, 2011); page 434.

7 Runciman David; *How Democracy Ends* (Profile Books, 2019); pages 7 & 83.

*become ends. Tactics prevail over principles. Too often, principles themselves become tactics, to be changed as the circumstances warrant."*[8]

Despite the latest scientific knowledge, climate protection measures remain largely insufficient, and states have delayed their efforts to mitigate climate change. In an op-ed article penned for the *Washington Post*, Mr Guterres described the sixth IPCC report as *"a litany of broken climate promises,'* which revealed a *'yawning gap between climate pledges and reality."*[9]

The political disagreement on climate action is nourished by the question of whether climate neutrality is an unrealistic goal. It would be disproportionate and too costly. According to some economists, we should pledge our trust in innovation rather than setting limits on human activity. According to Prof Bjorn Lomborg,[10] states should prioritise adapting to climate change over achieving climate neutrality. Both approaches, wait-and-see and aiming for carbon neutrality, would be incorrect. He argued that GHG emissions should indeed decrease, but not too drastically. He questions whether the global political target for addressing climate change is realistic. Those targets would be disproportionate, thereby rendering the underlying policies ineffective. If climate protection became too expensive, Lomborg argued, people would stop supporting those policies. He pointed to the need for affordable energy. While writing these lines, the ongoing Ukrainian war has significantly impacted energy prices, prompting states to intervene by capping costs despite climate protection requirements. The economic impact of high energy costs on industry and households could be substantial. Alternative energy sources are not yet sufficient to meet the tremendous power demands. Despite global warming considerations, political leaders were willing to reconsider the use of coal and coal-fired power stations.

Professor Lomborg is not the sole thinker arguing from that standpoint. Ted Nordhaus and Michael Shellenberger argued that an 80% decrease in overall GHG emissions would be impossible without investing in new technologies, such as clean energy. Innovations must play a significant role. The world needs technologies that enable economic growth without adverse environ-

---

8 Gore Albert; *Earth in the Balance: Forging a New Common Purpose;* page 168.

9 The United Nations; UN Climate Report: *It's 'Now or Never' to Limit Global Warming to 1.5 Degrees*; https://news.un.org/en/story/2022/04/1115452; <04.04.2022>.

10 Lomborg Bjorn; *False Alarm: How Climate Change Panic Costs Us Trillions, Hurts the Poor, and Fails to Fix the Planet;* Reprint Edition (New York, Basic Books, 2021); pages 12 & 27.

mental impacts. It would be wrong to focus extensively on limiting human activities.[11]

Conversely, the IPCC tells another story. It released its sixth report on March 20, 2023, emphasising that since the conclusion of the Paris Climate Agreement, states have not done enough to protect the climate. To stop that "*ticking climate time bomb,*" the developed states would need to decarbonise their societies by 2040 and developing countries by 2050: The "*1.5-degree limit is achievable ... But it will take a quantum leap in climate action,*" said UN Secretary-General Antonio Guterres in his video message for the press conference. "*In short, our world needs climate action on all fronts – everything, everywhere, all at once.*"[12]

Aware of the difficulties that burden unpopular decisions in times of present or imminent crisis, especially if constitutional rights are at stake, states sometimes resort to instruments that allow them to circumvent normal decision-making processes, such as "*states of exception*" or "*états de crise.*" These instruments enable quick, flexible responses to changing situations. States typically introduced these exceptional decision-making processes in response to terrorism, calamities, or public health crises, which, for instance, have proven effective in flattening the curve at the beginning of the *COVID-19* pandemic. The state could organise itself and introduce science-based sanitary measures, including restrictions on freedoms, rights, and liberties. Liberal democratic states, nevertheless, always act under the constraint of returning to regular democratic proceedings as soon as possible.

However, climate change currently strikes one as a timeless or long-term challenge. It confronts governments with a permanent or temporally indefinite crisis. If they were to resort continuously to "*states of exception*" or similar instruments, they would sound the death knell of liberal democratic government. However critical and urgent, climate protection measures must continue to pass through time-consuming, ordinary decision-making processes. The longer it takes to act on climate change, the greater the potential need for harsh measures.

The critical junction between crisis and regularity underlines the importance and predicament of judicial review. Courts are necessary to ensure that the political branches of government respect the constitutional essentials and

---

11 Shellenberger Michael and Nordhaus Ted; *Break Through: From the Death of Environmentalism to the Politics of Possibility;* First Printing Edition (Houghton Mifflin Harcourt, 2007); page 15.

12 The United Nations; Secretary-General Calls on States to Tackle Climate Change 'Time Bomb' through New Solidarity Pact, Acceleration Agenda, at Launch of Intergovernmental Panel Report.

refrain from abusing their discretion. Nevertheless, the very act of doing so creates institutional disturbances. Declaring an act of government unconstitutional casts a shadow on the legitimacy of the government responsible for it.

## Section: 2 Inadequate Climate Preservation Records

The international climate setting's background is that developed states have a more carbon-intensive past than developing states. The former would, in theory, have the technical means and the money to reduce their anthropogenic GHG emissions more significantly. Therefore, their international climate protection obligations are considerably higher than those of developing states. The main question is whether phasing out fossil fuels and transitioning to renewables in due time is politically feasible.[13]

There are subsequent or underlying questions to the previous ones, such as: Will political representatives dare to do what climate protection requires, in line with updated scientific knowledge? Will people accept changing their way of life and make concessions to strive for a climate that supports life? Will the states strive for intergenerational and climate justice, or will they protect their short- to medium-term interests behind impenetrable, solid walls of state sovereignty? Will people maintain their commitment to democracy and still regard it as worthy of their respect, or will climate change cause the democratic process as we know it to collapse? Hence, the question is whether judicial review could help address the state's shortcomings in climate protection without damaging the reasonableness and respectability of the democratic project.

So far, liberal democracies, despite their carbon-intensive ecological footprint, have allegedly failed to protect the climate on time. The complex, discursive decision-making process and the balancing of conflicting interests led to inconsequential climate protection records in the past. States have continued to promote fossil fuel activities. Authors such as Gustave Speth, Al Gore, and Mary Christina Wood have stressed the inadequacy of climate protection measures. These "*political failures*" are increasingly subject to lawsuits. Petitioners challenged the continuation of GHG-intensive activities and the lack of climate protection plans. The transition to low-carbon societies is challenging. Developed states may be unwilling to meet the internationally settled GHG reduction targets (see, for instance, *Urgenda*). The continued promotion of fossil fuels and reliance on carbon-based energy sources delays decarbonisation.

U.S. case law exemplifies, in a striking manner, the challenges associated with making long-term decisions on climate protection. During the proceed-

---

13 See Sumudu Atapattu and Schapper Andrea. *Human rights and the environment: key issues*, key issues in environment and sustainability (New York, Routledge, 2019); page 207.

ings in *Juliana*, James Gustave Speth testified on behalf of the youth petitioners. In his book *They Knew: The Federal Government's Fifty-Year Role in Causing the Climate Crisis*, he shows how each administration contributed to the development of dangerous climate change, from Johnson to Trump (President Trump's first term). In the U.S., every president except Donald Trump has publicly acknowledged the dangers of global warming and the need for climate protection. Ultimately, all allegedly failed to take science-consistent actions, despite promising climate protection measures during their campaigns and at the outset of their mandates. In 1981, at the end of the Carter administration, public authorities were aware of the dangers of climate change associated with burning fossil fuels.[14] At that time, experts had already recommended an energy transition away from carbonised energy: "*During the Carter Administration, the federal government's awareness of climate science and the link between fossil fuel use and dangerous global warming and climate change became well established.*"[15] Instead of engaging in such a transition, the United States continued promoting its national fossil-based system.[16]

Climate protection and climate adaptation require short-, medium- and long-term measures, which presuppose a consistent climate protection plan. Given the complexity of these matters, the need for stability is not straightforward in a two-party system where both parties disagree on climate change. In the United States, significant policy rollbacks depend on whether Republicans or Democrats hold the majority in Congress. President Trump rolled back some of the environmental progress made by the Obama administration. The Biden administration again engaged with the International Community to mitigate climate change and re-entered the Paris Agreement.[17] Beyond presidential orders, significant legislation cannot pass through the two houses of Congress.

States and environmental associations united to challenge President Trump's rollback efforts on environmental protection in court. Courts might need to provide continuity in the state's climate protection approach by upholding the rule of law. President Trump's climate-related presidential orders have led to *Lighthiser v. Trump*, a lawsuit we briefly discussed in Part 1. Also, the withdrawal of the EPA's endangerment finding for carbon dioxide

14 During the Carter administration, James Gustave Speth served as Chairman of the U.S. Council on Environmental Quality.

15 Speth James Gustave; *They Knew: The Federal Government's Fifty-Year Role in Causing the Climate Crisis*; page 15.

16 Ibid, page 3.

17 Ibid, pages 94 & 148–149.

under the Clean Air Act has prompted a youth-led judicial petition to overturn that decision.[18]

We can conclude that delays and inadequacies in climate protection actions have led people to turn to the courts, bringing climate-related questions to the forefront. Courts are less exposed to political pressures and can promote intergenerational interests through constitutional rights and obligations of public trust. If courts sidestep climate protection cases, carbon-intensive activities remain unchecked to the detriment of the younger generations.[19]

This is also true when courts avoid the legal questions by dismissing climate protection lawsuits at the pre-trial stage: The U.S. Court of Appeals for the Ninth Circuit recognised in *Juliana* that the evidence for climate reality and the climate emergency is substantial, yet dismissed the case for lack of standing.[20] This court posture has compelled the *Juliana* plaintiffs to continue litigating, as the court has not addressed the legal questions.

Should courts intervene in this context or instead defer those political questions to the elected political actors so that they can make those difficult decisions with due consideration of all the interests at stake? It is to that question we now turn.

---

18 Our Children's Trust; *Venner v. EPA*; https://www.ourchildrenstrust.org/venner-v-epa <26.02.2026>.

19 Kuh Katrina Fischer; *The Legitimacy of Judicial Climate Engagement*; pages 24–26.

20 *Juliana 2020*; page 14: "*The record leaves little basis for denying that climate change is occurring at an increasingly rapid pace. It documents that since the dawn of the Industrial Age, atmospheric carbon dioxide has skyrocketed to levels not seen for almost three million years. For hundreds of thousands of years, average carbon concentration fluctuated between 180 and 280 parts per million. Today, it is over 410 parts per million and climbing. Although carbon levels rose gradually after the last Ice Age, the most recent surge has occurred more than 100 times faster; half of that increase has come in the last forty years. Copious expert evidence establishes that this unprecedented rise stems from fossil fuel combustion and will wreak havoc on the Earth's climate if unchecked.*"

CHAPTER 5

# The Respectworthiness of the Politico-legal System

## Introduction

Given the particularities of climate protection questions, this chapter lays the foundation for proposing a benchmark for climate-related judicial review that is consistent with (liberal) democracy.

Section 1 distinguishes between two rival ideals of democracy that clash in judicial review – the ideal of self-government by laws of the people and the ideal of government bound by law.[1] The constitution lays down the procedures to govern the state validly (the procedural part) and sets out a list of protected fundamental rights and a bill of rights (the substantive part).[2] This gives rise to a constitutional paradox. What should courts consider in judicial review: the former, the latter, or both? The clash of ideals is even more problematic in the case of an entrenched constitution, as judicial review of climate rights might require a court to respond to changing exigencies – a living-instrument approach – thereby opening the door to court activism.

Courts must resolve this clash of ideals stemming from their double function. On the one hand, the judge must enforce the law, thereby backing the political branches. On the other hand, he must shield the constitutional essentials against political abuse when majoritarian law and the rule of law conflict. Upholding legislation can undermine the ideal of the rule of law and lend legitimacy to wrongful political acts, whereas substituting majoritarian legislation through court orders can undermine political legitimacy and raise counter-majoritarian concerns.

We will discuss the two ideals and explore the possibility of a workable compromise, aiming to establish a benchmark for climate-based judicial review that can alleviate counter-majoritarian tensions and enhance the respectworthiness of the democratic project.

Section 2 takes up Frank Michelman's insights on constitutionalism and the protection of socioeconomic rights to assess whether this framework is trans-

1 My research addresses this paradox with reference to Frank Michelman. See, for instance, Michelman Frank; *Brennan and Democracy;* Revised Edition (Princeton University Press, 2005); pages 4–11.

2 This substantive part is sometimes referred to as political or constitutional morality. See, for instance, Michelman Frank; *Constitutional Legitimation for Political Acts;* The Modern Law Review 66 (2003) 16; page 2.

HTTPS://DOI.ORG/10.1163/9789004771710-011

posable to climate protection. Suffice it, for now, to argue that socioeconomic and environmental rights are similarly problematic because their judicial recognition could, in a liberal democratic state, affect core aspects of the political realm.

## Section 1: Two Clashing Democratic Ideals

Our discussion of political discretion, state sovereignty, and the separation of powers shows that courts exercise a degree of deference to the political branches. This section will study the two rival democratic ideals that clash in judicial review. We will begin with the ideal of self-government by laws of the people (1) and then proceed to that of government bound by law (2).[3] The aim is to determine whether the two ideals can be reconciled (3).

### 1 Self-Government by the Laws of the People

According to the democratic ideal of *self-government by laws of the people*, it is an essential feature of democracy that the people choose who should govern them. The electors cast their votes according to their political agendas. Hence, the idea is that courts should not invalidate procedurally valid decisions of political majorities that derive their authority from the electorate and the Constitution. Therefore, courts should only review whether the political branches acted in the due democratic process. In other words, have the political branches done their job according to the procedural constitutional rules? Participatory rights, such as access to public information and the right to participate, may be essential in answering this question.

The ideal of self-government through laws of the people does not necessarily ensure the substantive rule of law. A court prioritising this ideal would typically uphold a political decision if it respects the constitutional process. It would defer to the political branches or the polls when confronted with potential political questions. The counter-majoritarian potential of judicial review flows from the ideal of self-government by the laws of the people. If courts uphold the legislation, this is not counter-majoritarian as it legitimates political decisions.[4] The difficulty arises when courts invalidate or even replace majoritarian decisions.

Judicial review is often considered "*undemocratic*" because judges are independent and not accountable to the public or the political branches. If courts were to grant judicial review and order the remedies petitioners may seek in complex climate protection cases, this could require a strong judiciary to interfere in the political realm, thereby encroaching on political powers and disrupting the democratic process. Courts would sanction and override deci-

---

3 See, for instance, Michelman Frank; *Brennan and Democracy;* pages 4–11.

4 See, for instance, Bickel Alexander; *The Least Dangerous Branch: The Supreme Court at the Bar of Politics;* page 29.

sions that are prima facie procedurally valid and issued by legitimately elected political majorities. The separation of powers would be at stake. According to Ran Hirschl, delegating political power to courts could lead to undesirable outcomes, including a shift from democracy to *juristocracy*.[5]

The literature on the counter-majoritarian difficulty and on arguments for and against different forms of judicial review is extensive, particularly within the U.S. system with a strong Supreme Court at the federal level. According to the ideal of government by the laws of the people, if the political representatives enact a law in a constitutionally valid manner, courts should uphold it. Otherwise, the judicial decision risks allowing a political minority (the petitioners) to take control of the prevailing political majority through the judicial branch.[6] The least democratic branch of government would have the final say in how the people should govern themselves. According to judicial activism opponents, the court's powers must be limited. They ask for "*the protection of majoritarian democracy against overreach by headstrong courts.*"[7] Petitioners could bypass the normal political process by addressing their concerns directly to the judge rather than through political representatives.

Ran Hirschl's research on the "*judicialisation of politics*" concerns the expansion of judicial powers into the political sphere.[8] He distinguishes three different forms of *judicialisation*: first, the spread of legal discourse, jargon, rules, and procedures into the political sphere, policy-making forums, and processes. Second, judicialisation through "*ordinary*" administrative and judicial review. Third, the judicialisation of "*pure politics*" or "*mega politics*." It reviews the essential political matters and the questions that "*define* (*and often divide*)" society. This review goes beyond procedural aspects. It concerns significant substantive controversies.[9]

The first two forms of judicialisation appear relatively unproblematic, given the ideal of self-government by laws of the people; however, judicial review of

5 See, for instance, Hirschl Ran; *Towards Juristocracy: The Origins and Consequences of the New Constitutionalism;* page 15. & Grimm Dieter, *Verfassungsgerichtsbarkeit,* (Berlin, Suhrkamp Verlag, 2021); page 83.

6 Bickel Alexander; *The Least Dangerous Branch: The Supreme Court at the Bar of Politics;* page 16 & see also Pulliam Mark; *Unleashing The "Least Dangerous" Branch: Quis Custodiet Ipsos Custodes?;* Texas Review of Law & Politics, vol. 22, no. 3, 2018; pages 423–468.

7 See, for instance, Michelman Frank; Constitutional Essentials: On the Constitutional Theory of Political Liberalism; page 160.

8 Boyd David; *The environmental rights revolution: a global study of constitutions, human rights, and the environment;* Law and Society series (Vancouver, UBC Press, 2012); page 5.

9 Hirschl Ran; *The New Constitution and the Judicialization of Pure Politics Worldwide; Fordham Law Review* Vol. 75, Issue 2, Article 14 (2006); 36; pages 722–728.

"pure politics" could promote the transition from democracy to *juristocracy*. According to Hirschl, this tendency would primarily be a political issue rather than a judicial one. Political representatives would struggle to address contentious issues. They would long for the electorate's support and might postpone difficult decisions, thereby risking a lack of political responsibility.

We could categorise climate protection under the second and third categories of judicialisation. The cases concerning state authorisations of climate-intensive activities concern specific administrative decisions and primarily involve procedural due-process judicial review. For instance, in the *Thabametsi Power Project case*, the High Court in Pretoria conducted a procedural due process review of the administrative decisions, examining whether the decision-makers adequately assessed and considered all environmental impacts before making their decisions.

The "*pure politics*" cases concern climate protection policies and mitigation plans, specifically the court review of the state's climate strategies. These cases raise polycentric political questions that pose counter-majoritarian difficulties and affect the legitimacy of the democratic system, including the decisions of the three branches of government. Political representatives could disregard their responsibilities and pass the hot potatoes to the judicial branch, as the judiciary is not subject to the same electorate pressures as the political branches.

Courts ordering climate protection measures through judicial review when elected representatives hesitate[10] would allow politicians to bypass political gridlocks and address democratic shortcomings indirectly through the cloak of court orders.[11] It may be especially problematic if courts limit political responsibility. Courts should hold political branches accountable and avoid exempting them from their duty to make difficult decisions.

## 2 Government Bound by Law

Leaving behind the ideal of government by the laws of the people, this partition turns to the rival democratic ideal of government bound by law.

The constitutionalisation of rights, especially after World War II, and the institution of independent courts with review powers empowered judges to

10 Rosenberg Gerald; *The Hollow Hope: Can Courts Bring About Social Change?* (Chicago, University of Chicago Press, 1991); page 30.

11 Hirschl Ran; *The New Constitution and the Judicialization of Pure Politics Worldwide;* pages 744–746.

interfere with majoritarian political decision-making.[12] Democracies, as we know, are systems of limited government. The constitution, on the one hand, confers power to legislators, executives, and the judiciary, but on the other hand, it also constrains these state branches. The ideal of government bound by law means that the State, through its representatives, must respect its commitments and obligations.

Hirschl emphasised that having a list of rights provides the court with essential tools to monitor the political branches and protect citizens. Judicial review of legislative or executive actions is a powerful instrument against political oppression.[13] Courts can hinder political encroachment on constitutional rights by reviewing the constitutionality of an act beyond the threshold of procedural due process. The constitution, as we know, is the highest national source of law and confers validity on lower norms. The latter must conform to the former.[14]

The ideal of government bound by law permits sanctioning majoritarian norms that violate the substantive constitutional kernel. By applying the substantive rule of law, courts uphold the balance of powers and protect the people from political abuse of discretion. Especially in the United States, the so-called "*threshold doctrines*" have made it difficult for climate protection cases to proceed to the trial stage.[15] Those judicial self-restraint rules hinder discovery and the court's assessment of the merits in climate protection cases. This undermines the ideal of government bound by law in favour of self-government by the people, as courts sidestep significant climate protection questions and fail to explore the legal implications of global warming. This could mean courts privilege traditional separation of powers doctrines over concerns about climate protection and climate-related rights.

People generally accept that minorities need protection against majoritarian abuse and that some constraints on majoritarian government are necessary.[16] This protection hinges on the constitutionalisation of rights and judi-

12 Hirschl Ran; *Towards Juristocracy: The Origins and Consequences of the New Constitutionalism;* page 125.

13 Tate Neal and Vallinder Torbjorn; *The Global Expansion of Judicial Power;* New Edition (New York, New York University Press, 1997); pages 15 & 18.

14 Michelman Frank; *Constitutional Authorship by the People; Notre Dame Law Review* 74 (o. J.); 27; page 1618.

15 See Kuh Katrina Fischer; The Legitimacy of Judicial Climate Engagement; page 2: "*To date, courts have almost uniformly invoked threshold doctrines like standing, the political question doctrine, and displacement or preemption to avoid reaching the merits of common law and constitutional claims.*"

16 Ely John Hart; *Democracy and Distrust: A Theory of Judicial Review* (Cambridge, Harvard Univ. Press, 1980); pages 5–9.

cial review. The possibility of addressing unconstitutional behaviour is vital to preserve the respectability of the politico-legal system.

An entrenched constitution provides stability to the legal system and protects constitutional essentials against majoritarian abuse. However, framers and legislators cannot foresee all potential rights issues that may arise over time. The people should be able to bring those issues to public attention through judicial review.[17] Courts could play an important role in enforcing rights when the political branches are inert or face legal "*blind spots*."[18]

The ideal of government bound by law offers protection against political abuse; it depends on judicial intervention. However, a poor court decision could also weaken trust in the judiciary and undermine the legitimacy of the democratic system.

## 3 The Possibility of a Compromise

How should courts deal with cases involving climate protection questions? This question is relevant because the climate crisis is increasing the number of polycentric political cases entering the court's dockets. I will argue that in climate protection, all three branches matter and that judicial review could promote cooperation between powers by taking a weak form, thereby strengthening democracy.

Recalling that, according to the ideal of self-government by the people, courts should principally intervene as a protector of the democratic principle of equality, meaning that every citizen can participate on equal footing in the democratic process (procedural review) and that substantive judicial review would promote the ideal of government bound by law and would thereby considerably limit political discretion, which is an inherent requirement of the ideal of self-government by laws of the people. How is it then, on the one hand, possible to think of effective climate-based judicial review when, on the other hand, courts refrain or should refrain from interfering with majoritarian decisions to avoid disturbing the proper democratic process?

Considering the potential delegitimising effect of substantive judicial review, courts may be inclined to leave the issue to the ordinary political pro-

---

17 Waldron Jeremy; *The Core of the Case against Judicial Review; page* 1370: Jeremy Waldron accepted that argument for the sake of weak-form judicial review only. Suffice it, for now, to say that the form of judicial review might matter. I will address the forms of judicial review in Part 3.

18 Dixon Rosalind; *Creating Dialogue about Socioeconomic Rights: Strong-Form versus Weak-Form Judicial Review Revisited;* International Journal of Constitutional Law 5, No. 3 (2007); 391–418; page 391.

cess. However, as discussed, proper political discourse is time-consuming, whereas unconstitutional political activity and the threats posed by climate change may require urgent redress. If the political branches fail to provide an adequate response, there is a potential risk of compromising political legitimacy and credibility.

In the past, counter-majoritarian judicial interference happened occasionally. For instance, throughout its history, the U.S. Supreme Court has certainly upheld federal laws far more often than it has invalidated them. From 1791 until 2011, the U.S. Supreme Court upheld federal law in three-quarters of the cases.[19] This record nevertheless demands a plausible response to the fact that one in four cases reviewed was struck down. In other words, the U.S. Supreme Court invalidated majoritarian legislation quite regularly. This record is quite questionable from the perspective of the principle of the separation of powers. Adherence to this principle demands stricter deference to laws passed by a constitutionally legitimate legislature. There are cases in which everyone agrees that the courts should intervene. Courts generally consider the seriousness of the alleged mistake. Was it a manifest "*clear mistake*" or a minor, reasonable one? If the challenged political decision is not unreasonable, the court may limit its review to procedural due process concerns, thereby strengthening participatory rights and promoting sound, informed political decision-making. This court posture predominantly encourages the ideal of government by the laws of the people.

Mere procedural judicial review may be insufficient for climate protection cases in which substantial constitutional rights are at stake. Courts could honour both ideals, that is, the rule of law and government by the people, in those cases by intervening with a relatively weak stance, as in *Neubauer*. They might, for instance, limit themselves to determining whether primary or secondary legislation, or its implementation, is compatible with the constitutional essentials, and outline the potential risks. In *Friends of the Irish Environment*, the Irish Supreme Court distinguished between the three branches of state power and emphasised that each branch must respect the core competencies of the others. The judiciary is competent to protect litigants' constitutional rights against encroachments by the political branches.[20]

19 Whittington Keith; *Repugnant Laws: Judicial Review of Acts of Congress from the Founding to the Present*; pages 25–26.

20 *Friends of the Irish Environment* (2019); point 88: "*It is fundamental to the separation of powers that no one of the three organs of Government is paramount in the exercise of State power. Each must respect the powers and functions of the other. The court's jurisdiction can only be exercised in deciding on justiciable matters and the courts have no general supervisory or investigatory functions. The doctrine of separation of powers has nothing to do*

The debate over climate rights and whether courts can derive them from entrenched constitutions could raise significant concerns about the separation of powers. For this reason, we now turn to Michelman's *experimentalist* model of judicial review proposed in the context of socioeconomic rights.

Michelman's arguments, we shall see, point to how the tension between political discretion and the substantive rule of law can be resolved, or at least alleviated.

∴

*with the merits or otherwise of the separate question of whether it is desirable that the provision in question should be made. The Government, and the Government, alone may exercise the executive powers of Government. The courts have the right and duty to interfere with the activities of the Executive in order to protect or secure the constitutional rights of individual litigants where such rights have been, or are being, invaded by those activities; or where activities of the executive threaten an invasion of such rights."*

## Section 2: The Case of Socioeconomic Rights

Judicial review of socioeconomic rights has generated a substantial body of doctrinal literature. Reflecting on the recognition of socioeconomic rights and the respectworthy constitution, Frank Michelman argues that those rights could represent a condition for social peace and civility, "*a minimal condition for the expectation of loyalty*."[21] However, if a state acknowledges that social rights are constitutional essentials, judicialisation could raise concerns because the resulting costs might significantly impact the state's economic policies. Judicial recognition of socioeconomic rights could compel the state to guarantee a social minimum of access to basic needs, thereby increasing the number of lawsuits challenging the state's socioeconomic measures, again putting the courts in a difficult position.

A satisfactory judicial approach to socioeconomic rights might instructively guide the climate rights debate. The caveats that courts must consider are the same in both cases. Both types of rights could significantly affect a state's economic policies and raise broader systemic concerns. According to the counter-majoritarian difficulty and the principle of separation of powers, courts should not interfere in political matters because they lack the legitimacy and capacity to do so.

Capacity and legitimacy are among the most frequently discussed arguments against judicial review in doctrinal literature. Judges have no particular qualification, experience, or democratic legitimacy to issue political decisions. Adopting a policy or a programme and deciding how to implement it are core functions of the Executive. Additionally, courts have no authority over the state budget; instead, the legislature defines and oversees the budget, considering all relevant interests. A judicial decision that interferes in the political sphere may entail costs. Climate protection has a profound impact on all economic sectors.[22]

---

21 Michelman Frank; *Legitimacy, The Social Turn and Constitutional Review: What Political Liberalism Suggests*; pages 190 & 192.

22 See, for instance, Bickel Alexander; *The Least Dangerous Branch: The Supreme Court at the Bar of Politics;* 2nd Edition (New Haven, Yale Univ. Press, 1986); Waldron Jeremy; *The Core of the Case against Judicial Review;* The Yale Law Journal 115, No. 6 (2006); 1346–1406; https://doi.org/10.2307/20455656; Friedman Barry; *The History of the Counter-majoritarian Difficulty, Part One; The Road to Judicial Supremacy*; NYU Law Review 73, Number 2 (Mai 1998); 333–433 &. Whittington Keith; *Repugnant Laws: Judicial Review of Acts of Congress from the Founding to the Present*; Illustrated Edition (Kansas, Univ. Press of Kansas, 2019).

Given the courts' limited capacity and legitimacy, they should avoid exceeding the law's assessment. Therefore, it is helpful to distinguish between injunctive court relief and declaratory court relief, as declaring the law falls within a court's realm, whereas changing the content of the law interferes with the political branches. It demands balancing and prioritising interests.[23] The high courts of many countries have consistently emphasised that judges should not second-guess the decisions of political branches.[24] Therefore, courts, in principle, refrain from intervening when confronted with political questions and refer the matter to the political branches.[25]

This leads us to the question of whether courts should address issues of socioeconomic or climate rights, or exercise judicial self-restraint and defer to the political branches. The judicial posture matters, especially when the constitution is rigid, and its content may need to be adapted to changing realities to remain worthy of respect in the eyes of the people. Otherwise, state branches could not address today's needs because prior political representatives had validly adopted constitutional norms in different exigencies years ago. The constitution's content or interpretation may need to bridge the gaps between past, present, and future needs so that the people can safeguard their faith in the constitutional framework. The climate crisis and climate protection are intrinsically intergenerational challenges, and their urgency poses a threat to liberal democracy.

---

23 See, for instance, *Friends of the Irish Environment* (*2019*); point 92: "*I must accept that a consequence of the separation of powers doctrine is that the court should avoid interfering with the exercise of discretion by the legislature or executive when its aim is the pursuit of policy. Courts are and should be reluctant to review decisions involving utilitarian calculations of social, economic and political preference, the latter being identifiable by the fact that they are not capable of being impugned by objective criteria that a court could apply.*"

24 See, for instance, *Juliana* (*2016*), page 10: the court posed the question "*whether adjudicating a claim would require the Judicial Branch to second-guess decisions committed exclusively to another branch of government*" – see, likewise, *Greenpeace Nordic Ass'n and Natur og Ungdom v. Ministry of Petroleum and Energy*, 20-051052SIV-HRET; Supreme Court; 22.12.2020 ("*People v. Arctic Oil*").

25 *American Electric Power Co. v. Connecticut*; 04 Civ. 5669, 04 Civ. 5670; District Court of New York (southern district); 19.09.2005, page 14: "*In this case, balancing those interests, together with the other interests involved, is impossible without an "initial policy determination" first having been made by the elected branches to which our system commits such policy decisions, viz., Congress and the President.*"

Michelman argues that constitutionalising socioeconomic rights could take the court beyond what would be widely accepted as a law court's field of competence. Socioeconomic rights are complex and not well received by liberals, which has led to controversy. What posture should a court take when ruling on socioeconomic rights? Michelman proposes an "*experimentalist*" model of judicial review. The court should refrain from defining the exact contours of socioeconomic rights and, instead, establish a reasonably broad standard to promote public discourse. The political endorsement of that benchmark could lead to more potent forms of judicial review in later cases. It is a multi-step, discursive, case-by-case approach.[26] According to Oliver Gerstenberg, the *experimentalist* mode of judicial review opens up a "*conceptual space for the gradual constitutionalisation of socioeconomic rights.*"[27]

Courts need to review, from time to time, whether the state's actions meet the minimum requirements for socioeconomic essentials. A prima facie weak court posture could alleviate the resistance to recognising socioeconomic rights as constitutional essentials[28] and promote the discourse between the three state branches, leading to what I call the *cooperation of powers*. Starting with a relatively weak posture does not mean the court cannot take a stronger stance in a future case when branches of government refuse to endorse the judicial decision and inaction becomes unreasonable.

---

26 Michelman Frank; *Constitutional Essentials: On the Constitutional Theory of Political Liberalism;* page 150: "*The court acts in the first instance as instigator and non-dictatorial overseer of engagements among stakeholders very broadly defined – governments of course included – in an ongoing process of interpretative clarification of what a constitutionally declared right of (say) 'access to health care services' consists of in substance. The court engages the parties over what sorts of steps by what classes of actors are concretely (in the current conditions of society, economy, and so on) now in order toward the achievement of due and adequate service to everyone's core interest – a process of successively clarified 'benchmarking' as it is sometimes called. As the discursive benchmarking moves along and the emerging answers gain public recognition and authorization, the court turns up the heat on deployment of its powers of review. At a relatively early stage, what the court presumes to dictate will be agendas of questions to be addressed and answered by one or another stakeholder group or class. At later stages, the court starts calling for substantive compliance with an emergent best-practice consensus, in the name of the constitutional right. The screws tighten on what can count as a reasonable, sincere governmental response. The court serves as arbiter but it never has or claims a door-closing last word.*"

27 Gerstenberg Oliver; *Negative/positive constitutionalism, "fair balance," and the problem of justiciability;* International Journal of Constitutional Law, Volume 10, Issue 4, Pages 904–925, (October 2012); page 904.

28 Michelman Frank; *Legitimacy, The Social Turn and Constitutional Review: What Political Liberalism Suggests.*

Judicial interpretation and recognition of rights, however, are not without danger. Every time a court interprets or revises the meaning of the Constitution, it may spark public disagreement and erode trust in the political system.[29] It is easier to ascribe to a vaguer meaning of coercive norms than a detailed, precise one.

This is where the "*experimentalist*" model of judicial review could come into play to alleviate the concerns. It is important to note that climate and environmental rights are, in a sense, also connected to the socioeconomic rights debate. Although climate protection primarily concerns collective rights, such as the right to a healthy environment, it may impact all three generations of rights. As a matter of fact, the destruction of our life-supporting ecosystems even threatens our incontestable first-generation rights, such as the right to life or family life.[30] Many of the world's contemporary constitutions were adopted at a time when climate protection and climate-relevant rights were not yet significant concerns, or at the very least not recognised as such.

Especially in the case of entrenched constitutions, climate-related judicial review may play a significant role in interpreting the constitution and its essentials, thereby affecting the respectworthiness of the politico-legal system and the three branches of government.

Even though it is not a climate protection case, it is worth noting the judicial developments in the U.S. federal abortion case, *Dobbs v. Jackson Women's Health Organisation.*[31] That case highlights that a judicial review decision might lead to deep disagreement because it favours some interests and disadvantages others (possibly those of the actual political majority). The U.S. Supreme Court's opinion in *Roe v. Wade*[32] could not solve the abortion rights controversy. The people questioned the respectworthiness and reasonableness of *Roe v. Wade* to the extent that in 2018, the State of Mississippi's legislature enacted an "*unconstitutional*" law prohibiting abortion beyond the 15th week of pregnancy. The Jackson Women's Health Organisation, running the sole abortion Clinic in Mississippi, challenged this law.

According to the Supreme Court's opinion in *Dobbs v. Jackson Women's Health Organisation*, the precedent of *Roe v. Wade* would stand on weak reasoning, as the Constitution does not mention abortion, and neither American law nor common law recognised such a right. In favour of the State of Missis-

29 Michelman Frank; *Constitutional Legitimation for Political Acts;* The Modern Law Review 66 (2003); page 11.

30 See notably the ECtHR's *KlimaSeniorinnen* ruling.

31 *Dobbs v. Jackson Women's Health Organisation,* Supreme Court, 597 U.S. (2022); 24.06.2022.

32 *Roe v. Wade*, 410 U.S. 113 (1973); Supreme Court; 22.01.1973.

sippi, the U.S. Supreme Court opinion concluded that it should overrule *Roe v. Wade* and *Casey*[33] *to give back* the authority to the states to regulate abortion according to their moral code. According to the Supreme Court's opinion in *Roe v. Wade*, it was wrong because it would have halted an ongoing process of political liberalisation.

The leak of the first draft of the U.S. Supreme Court opinion written by Justice Alito[34] caused an uproar in American society. Pro-choice and pro-life demonstrators protested outside the U.S. Supreme Court. The leak highlighted the debate and made apparent the deep social division about abortion rights. It is crucial that courts base their decisions on sound, reasonable, and respectable reasons. If not, the court decision could generate ongoing dissent, affecting the constitutional and judicial branches' legitimacy and credibility. It might endanger what Michelman referred to as "*the convergence of citizens on an institutional service whose judgments regarding such questions are trusted by all to fall within the bounds of reasonable acceptability.*"[35]

∵

33 *Planned Parenthood of Southeastern Pa. v. Casey*, 505 U.S. 833 (1992), 112 S. Ct. 2791; Supreme Court; 29.06.1992.

34 *Dobbs v. Jackson Women's Health Organisation*, first draft circulated among the Supreme Court Justices; Supreme Court, 10.02.2022.

35 Michelman Frank; *Constitutional Essentials: On the Constitutional Theory of Political Liberalism*; pages 54 & 55.

## Section 3: Intermediary Conclusion and Outlook

Climate change threatens the democratic project. In the past, political branches were generally rather reluctant to take consistent climate protection measures. This reluctance is related to the rival interests inherent in a (liberal) democracy. General, economic, and individual interests compete. The clash of interests between current and future generations has led to an increasing number of judicial review petitions.

In climate-based judicial review, courts must navigate between the democratic ideals of self-government by the people and government bound by law. If a workable compromise is possible, it should consider both democratic ideals outlined above. Courts themselves alleviated the counter-majoritarian nature of judicial review, typically by applying rules and tests developed by the judicial branch to avoid judicial overreach, thereby favouring self-government by the people but neglecting the rule of law. Courts, as a coequal branch of government, must safeguard the Constitution. Exercising judicial self-restraint at the pre-trial stage hinders scrutiny of the case's merits and, over time, might undermine the system's respectworthiness. It renders access to justice ineffective.

Once a case enters the trial phase, discussions about procedural and substantive climate-related judicial review gain momentum. In the U.S., petitioners have struggled to meet the standing requirements, despite a trend towards loosening them. In Europe, in addition to the significant national court decisions discussed in Part 1, the ECtHR's ruling in *KlimaSeniorinnen* has increased the pressure on its member states. The latter must render the climate dimensions of articles 2, 6 and 8 effective. Moreover, the ECtHR expanded access to court in climate matters by introducing two tests: one to determine victim status and another to assess the standing of non-governmental organisations in climate protection, thereby allowing greater recourse to legal action by associations in climate litigation.[36]

---

36 *Verein KlimaSeniorinnen Schweiz and Others v. Switzerland*, application no. 53600/20, 09.04.2024; ECtHR; point 502: To have standing, the association must be "(*a*) *lawfully established in the jurisdiction concerned or have standing to act there;* (*b*) *able to demonstrate that it pursues a dedicated purpose in accordance with its statutory objectives in the defence of the human rights of its members or other affected individuals within the jurisdiction concerned, whether limited to or including collective action for the protection of those rights against the threats arising from climate change; and* (*c*) *able to demonstrate that it can be regarded as genuinely qualified and representative to act on behalf of members or other affected individuals within the jurisdiction who are subject to specific threats or adverse effects of climate change on their lives, health or well-being as protected under the Convention.*"

The fear that courts become overly involved in climate protection, as we discussed above, is particularly evident when courts take a firm stance. This could blur the lines of demarcation between the state branches and endanger democracy.[37]

Part 3, referencing Frank Michelman and Mark Tushnet, argues that the form of judicial review matters and that dynamic forms of judicial review could enable courts to handle climate-related judicial review in a reasonable and respectful manner. Utilising the full range of weak-form judicial review stances could foster a respectful dialogue among the three branches of government.

∴

37 Colby Heather et al.; *Judging Climate Change: The Role of the Judiciary in the Fight Against Climate Change*; page 174.

# PART 3

# The Possibilities of Democracy

"The belief that judicially affirmed rights are a force of social change removed from the constraints of political power has attained near-sacred status in public discussion. National high courts and supranational tribunals have become increasingly important, even crucial, political decision-making bodies."[1]

1 Hirschl Ran; *Towards Juristocracy: The Origins and Consequences of the New Constitutionalism;* page 1.

 | HTTPS://DOI.ORG/10.1163/9789004771710-012

# Introduction

Following our discussions about judicial review of socioeconomic rights in a liberal democratic system, the current part commits itself to continuing the quest for a benchmark for climate-based judicial review that should help sustain democracy through the climate crisis without overly impairing either of the two rival democratic ideals of government by the laws of the people and of government bound by law, that we pointed out before.

We have already begun elaborating on a workable compromise, holding that courts should only exceptionally interfere in the political realm to preserve the respectability of the political system. We have also discussed relevant court techniques to avoid undue judicial interference, such as standing and justiciability. As we pointed out, those techniques hinder the case from reaching the trial stage, thereby preventing a court assessment of its merits. This, however, may be insufficient to protect the democratic project throughout the climate crisis. To alleviate the counter-majoritarian concerns that arise when courts interfere with political decisions, we have also begun distinguishing between declaratory and injunctive relief, holding that the latter can be more problematic.

Chapter 6 distinguishes between judicial activism and judicial self-restraint and examines the various forms of judicial review available to the court. The question of judicial activism and self-restraint is crucial at both the preliminary and trial stages. In contrast, the court's decision-making form (weak form versus strong form) becomes significant once a climate case enters the trial stage. Weak-form judicial review promotes the democratic ideal of self-government of the people, while strong-form judicial review adheres more to the rival ideal of government constrained by law. Depending on its posture, the court can alleviate or aggravate concerns about the separation of powers.

Chapter 7 considers all concerns developed thus far to propose a framework for climate-based judicial review. Recalling that the form of judicial review matters, we shall argue that courts should grant the most extensive political discretion to political government that preserving constitutional essentials allows.

Chapter 8 argues that climate-based judicial review need not endanger democracy and could even promote and protect the democratic project. Court intervention based on legal questions, distinguished from political ones and grounded in well-explained considerations, could enhance the respectworthi-

 | HTTPS://DOI.ORG/10.1163/9789004771710-013

ness of judicial review and the political setting. This matters because the climate crisis poses a grave threat to the democratic project, particularly to the peaceful coexistence of people with rival interests grounded in equality, tolerance, and civility.

CHAPTER 6

# Judicial Stances and Decision-Making Forms

## Introduction

Judicial review has become an essential feature in modern constitutional democracies.[1] According to Alexander Bickel, there are three possible outcomes of judicial review: the court strikes down the legislative policy, legitimises it, or stays its hand without legitimising it. The first option is problematic because there is an actual difference between political and legal reasoning. A court must base its decision on legal principles rather than policy considerations. A court decision should differ significantly from a political one; it rests on legal arguments and does not involve balancing or prioritising interests.[2]

Differences may exist in the judicial branch's competencies. Some states have a robust legislative system rooted in parliamentary sovereignty, while others have a more vital Executive or a more assertive Judiciary. They all share the commonality that the three branches of government are distinct, and the judicial branch reviews the legality of the acts and decisions of the political branches. A state's constitutional framework might affect the court's powers, posture, and the forms of judicial review available to it. This chapter deals with these concerns in three sections.

Section 1 engages with the debate over judicial activism and judicial self-restraint. We will argue that an activist court stance does not necessarily pose counter-majoritarian dangers. It could enable people to participate more actively in the political decision-making process, and this participation extends beyond casting a ballot on Election Day. However, this is only possible if the court chooses to hear the case and does not exercise self-restraint from the outset. A court could permit the case to proceed to trial and yet refrain from ultimately issuing a counter-majoritarian decision. A court taking an activist posture can still avoid excessive interference with the political branches.

Section 2 distinguishes between strong-form and weak-form judicial review, and between declaratory and injunctive relief. Weak-form judicial review can help overcome democratic deficits that may arise during the trial stage. The court would do more than stay its hand and less than substitute majority decisions. It could promote the democratising process and contribute to the

1 Grimm Dieter; *Verfassungsgerichtsbarkeit.*

2 See Bickel Alexander; *The Least Dangerous Branch.*

 | HTTPS://DOI.ORG/10.1163/9789004771710-014

respectworthiness of the liberal democratic system; the moment of restraint matters. Even if a court is powerful, it can nonetheless take a weak stance. The moment at which judicial restraint is exercised need not be at the pre-trial stage.

Section 3 concludes the chapter by exploring whether the idea of *experimentalist* or *dynamic* forms of judicial review could serve as a workable compromise for substantive judicial review in liberal democratic systems.

∴

## Section 1: Judicial Activism versus Judicial Self-Restraint

### Introduction

The debate between judicial activism and self-restraint echoes the debate between self-government by the laws of the people and government bound by law. Frank Michelman schematically distinguishes between two kinds of judges. The first type is more likely to exercise judicial self-restraint because judges adhere to the literal interpretation of constitutional texts, thereby fostering self-restraint. The second type is more likely to adopt an activist stance, prioritising moral values over the written text.[3] Judges who are open to moral interpretations of the Constitution are more likely to close constitutional gaps by providing new or broader interpretations of the text. Such gaps arise whenever the constitution fails to address a specific question. This is especially apparent when interpreting entrenched constitutions, such as the U.S. Constitution, in light of changing social needs. The interpretation of international treaties and conventions evinces the same problem. The ECtHR, for instance, evidently closes conventional gaps by interpreting the ECHR as a living instrument, binding the 46 member states of the Council of Europe.

We shall argue that courts cannot always sidestep the counter-majoritarian difficulty. Some issues may require urgent relief, especially when deferring the petitioners to the polls for a necessary political course correction appears unreasonable.

### 1 Court Activism

Court activism serves as a corrective to abuses of political discretion. The strongest argument for judicial activism and substantive judicial review would probably be the Second World War Holocaust crimes. Such situations are exceptional, and most people likely accept that courts can and should intervene in such circumstances.[4]

Judges sometimes adopt a more activist stance to allow for new constitutional interpretations. An evolving approach could enable courts to read environmental or climate rights and obligations into the founding text. Activist judges give the constitution a moral reading. The moral approach goes

3 Michelman Frank; *Constitutional Essentials: On the Constitutional Theory of Political Liberalism;* page 128.

4 In the following section, we will return to this point when discussing strong and weak forms of judicial review.

beyond procedural due process control by disallowing a "*witless, vicious, unjust or all the above*" norm from remaining validly in force.[5] Constitutional morality is based on the idea that certain fundamental rights, such as the protection of life, dignity, freedom, equality, and protection against arbitrary actions, cannot be denied by the government.

The court's extension of existing rights and obligations, and the recognition or declaration of new rights through judicial review, are of particular concern in climate-based judicial review. A specific constitutional right may arise through an activist court decision that recognises it and declares its violation.[6]

Especially when dealing with old texts, such as the entrenched U.S. federal constitution or the ECHR, a living-instrument approach might sometimes be necessary, even though it is controversial.[7] Constitutions and international conventions can be abstract, so courts must address interpretive divergences and discussions regarding scope, justiciability, and enforceability. Court interpretations of the Constitution as a living instrument pivot on the idea that current people should not, at all costs, submit to the words of those who are dead or no longer in power. Preceding generations should enable succeeding generations to govern themselves in accordance with the realities of their time.

In practice, some courts have rendered activist decisions. The Court of Justice of the European Union (*CJEU*) was a notable example of an activist court, especially in its early rulings on the direct effect and primacy of EU law.[8] With these decisions, the CJEU created general principles of EU law that promoted European integration beyond the treaty provisions. These decisions clearly exceeded the court's institutional powers and had a profound impact on the sovereignty of Member States. Nevertheless, the EU Member States accepted those decisions, and the Union became a more integrated system.

In the climate protection cases we discussed, the petitioners urged the courts to take an activist stance. Claimants pointed to climate rights, even though the constitutional drafters did not write them into the text. The claimants, nevertheless, expected the courts to recognise "*new*" constitutional rights,

---

5 Michelman Frank; *IDA's Way: Constructing the Respect-Worthy Governmental System;* page 346.

6 See, for instance, Luhmann Niklas; *Gibt es in unserer Gesellschaft noch unverzichtbare Normen?;* Heidelberger Universitätsreden (Heidelberg, Müller Jurist. Verlag, 1993).

7 Pulliam Mark; *Unleashing The "Least Dangerous" Branch: Quis Custodiet Ipsos Custodes?;* Texas Review of Law & Politics, vol. 22, no. 3, 2018; pages 423–468. Pulliam is one of the more recent authors who discuss the risks of the living instruments approach and the court recognition of unenumerated rights.

8 See, for instance, CJEU *Van Gend & Loos* (26/62), *Costa/Enel*, (6/64), *Winner Wetten* (C-409/06) & *Von Colson* (14/83).

such as the *right to a climate system capable of sustaining human life* in *Juliana*. They also requested that courts extend public trust obligations to encompass the atmosphere. The plaintiffs even sought injunctive relief, asking the court to order the adoption and implementation of an adequate climate mitigation plan.

## 2 Judicial Self-Restraint

If a court has control over its agenda, it can select only those cases that fit its limited agenda and refuse to take on others. In some systems, apex courts have discretion over their docket. They may ignore controversial cases, failing to address issues such as justiciability, redressability, or standing that petitioners must overcome at the pre-trial stage. Therefore, there is no guarantee that such a High Court will even pick up the case.[9]

Judicial self-restraint refers to a more conservative or restrictive approach to the courts' role. It concerns the idea that courts should stick to the Constitution's traditional meanings and refrain from innovation. According to textualists, if a qualified majority does not amend the Constitution to establish a new right, that right does not exist. The literal meaning of the constitutional content binds the courts. For this reason, they should exercise self-restraint and defer political questions to the political branches, as judges lack both the capacity and legitimacy to make political decisions. Elected representatives are the appropriate decision-makers. If the People are unhappy with political choices, they should elect other politicians to govern them.[10] The Alaska Supreme Court's decision in *Sagoonick v. State of Alaska* illustrates the capacity argument. The court used this argument to dismiss the lawsuit.[11]

---

9 Michelman Frank; *Constitutional Essentials: On the Constitutional Theory of Political Liberalism*; page 15.

10 See, for instance, Waldron Jeremy; *The Core of the Case against Judicial Review* & Landau David; *A Dynamic Theory of Judicial Role*; 55 B.C. L. REV. 1501 (2014); 63; page 4.

11 *Sagoonick v. State of Alaska*; No. S-17297, Opinion No. 7583; Supreme Court of the State of Alaska; 28.01.2022; page 45: "*In truth, a dynamic acceleration of climate change would reinforce the reality that the judiciary is the least competent branch to address climate challenges because we 'lack scientific, economic, and technological resources' and 'may not commission scientific studies or convene groups of experts' essential to understanding evolving complexities.*"

In the next section, we will reflect on the strong and weak forms of judicial review, which my research views as an extension of the debate on court activism and judicial self-restraint.

## Section 2: Strong-Form versus Weak-Form Judicial Review

### Introduction

The level of acceptance of strong-form judicial review and the powers allotted to the court might be connected to the state's history. In the United States, liberal democracy has a long history, and judicial review was introduced into an already established democratic system. The U.S. Supreme Court is a strong institution, and since its inception, scholars have controversially debated judicial review and court activism. In Germany, the Federal Constitutional Court also has extensive competencies. It began functioning two years after the entry into force of the Grundgesetz on May 24, 1949. The political branches conferred more extensive powers on the Bundesverfassungsgericht than on its predecessor, the *Staatsgerichtshof* of the Weimar Republic. The experiences of Nazi Germany during the Second World War and the writings of scholars such as Gustav Radbruch on judicial passivism have led to greater acceptance of judicial activism. Court activism was considered a way of avoiding grave human rights violations, such as those committed by the Nazi authorities.[12] Hence, the idea that the Bundesverfassungsgericht should firmly safeguard the constitution, fundamental rights, and human dignity against political abuse. If, in the aftermath of the Second World War, the debate centred on judicial inertia, discussions of judicial overreach later became important in Germany as well.[13]

In circumstances such as the aftermath of the Second World War, firm court intervention creates little tension because people reasonably understand and respect it. Keith E. Whittington argues that the same individuals, namely politicians, can both accept and reject court intervention. Sometimes, the court is applauded for striking down legislation; sometimes, the same actors criticise it. Every court decision could generate criticism. Therefore, courts must carefully determine when and how to intervene.[14] The "*how to intervene*" concerns the court's posture when deciding on the merits. The question of the

---

12 Radbruch Gustav; *Statutory Lawlessness and Supra-Statutory Law* (1946); Oxford Journal of Legal Studies 26, No. 1 (Spring 2006); 1–11; translated by Bonnie Litsachewski Paulson and Stanley L. Paulson; page 6: "*Positivism, with its principle that 'a law is a law', has in fact rendered the German legal profession defenceless against statutes that are arbitrary and criminal. Positivism is, moreover, in and of itself wholly incapable of establishing the validity of statutes.*"

13 See, for instance, Grimm Dieter; *Verfassungsgerichtsbarkeit*; pages 8-9 & 127.

14 Whittington Keith; *Repugnant Laws: Judicial Review of Acts of Congress from the Founding to the Present*; pages 1–2.

appropriate judicial review decision form (strong form or weak form) becomes vital once the court decides to admit a case to the trial stage. Suppose a court takes an activist stance and allows a case to proceed to trial by loosening the standing requirements. This does not mean that the court's decision will eventually disrupt the ideal of self-government by the people. The counter-majoritarian effect of judicial review primarily depends on the form the court adopts for its decision. Depending on the legal system, the court could intervene by substituting democratic decisions through injunctive court orders, which I consider a strong-form decision. It could, however, also refrain from disproportionately interfering with the political branches and merely declare the law and what it requires of the branches. I consider *declaratory relief* to be a weak form of judicial review because it does not give the final word on the subject, but it opens a political debate.

∴

## 1 Weak-Form Judicial Review

Mark Tushnet refers to weak-form judicial review as the "*managerial model.*" This model is open to short-term legislative amendments and fosters a discourse between the judiciary and the legislature, a form of cooperation between powers that allows for reasonable disagreement.[15] Weak-form judicial review raises awareness of the dangers of politics, but ultimately, the political branches remain in charge.

Weak-form judicial review consists of courts determining the applicable law and stating whether government actions comply with constitutional and international law requirements. Such a declaration could also be oriented towards the future by stating that there is a risk or threat to human rights if the political branches do not take legal or political corrective measures. Thereon, the court defers the question to the political branches to take appropriate measures. It is then up to the political government to decide whether and how to address the issues outlined in the judicial ruling. Political representatives (majorities and minorities) can henceforth advance their arguments, balance, and prioritise the relevant interests in the political debate. This solution typically amounts to a political compromise.

---

15 Tushnet Mark; *Weak Courts, Strong Rights: Judicial Review and Social Welfare Rights in Comparative Constitutional Law* (Princeton, N.J. Woodstock: Princeton University Press, 2009), pages 36, 37 & 228.

In other words, the weak-form judicial review posture allows for political dialogue and does not shut down the discourse. It appears to be more compatible with (liberal) democracy. The political branches remain responsible for crafting and deciding remedies following the court's opinion.[16] A weak form of judicial review amounts nonetheless to judicial review of a political decision and allegedly still protects against potential political abuses of discretion. A declaratory judgment could entail sufficient authority to create a disturbance in society. It can raise public awareness, pressure competent authorities to act adequately and inspire legal and political change.

The primary difference between a strong-form stance and a weak-form stance is that the former compels the political branches to execute the order in both spirit and letter. In contrast, a court declaration interferes less and preserves considerable political discretion. Declaratory relief may also give rise to state liability if the political branches remain inert and damage results from this inaction. The fact that a court has already found political shortcomings in a prior case could help prove the government's fault in subsequent litigation.[17]

In U.S. climate-based judicial review, declaratory relief appears more acceptable than injunctive relief because the former does not necessarily raise political questions.[18] In the U.S., there may still be ongoing barriers to declaratory judgments. In youth cases, several courts refused to grant declaratory relief because it would not provide adequate redress. This was, for instance, a concern of the Supreme Court of the State of Alaska in *Sagoonick v. State of Alaska.*[19] In their partly dissenting opinion, Justices Maassen and

16 Patricia Popelier in Napel Hans-Martien and Voermans Wim; *The powers that be: rethinking the separation of powers: a Leiden response to Möllers* (Leiden, Leiden University Press, 2015); page 70.

17 Moules Richard; *Environmental Judicial Review* (Oxford , Hart Publishing, 2011); page 150.

18 In *Navahine F. v. Hawai'i Department of Transportation* (1CCV-22-0000631; 06.04.2023), the First District Court of the State of Hawai'i held that declaratory relief, unlike injunctive relief, would not likely lead to counter-majoritarian difficulties: "*The State argues that three of the Baker factors are met.* [...] *To the court, the issue of a political question is not yet and likely will not be formed unless and until a specific motion for injunctive relief is filed. Then, we will see if the requested relief improperly trespasses into political questions. In the meantime, the court concludes that the Baker factors are not automatically triggered by the declaratory relief requested. Depending on where the constitutional arguments and claimed relief end up, Defendants are free to bring up the political question argument again.*"

19 *Sagoonick v. State of Alaska*, No. S-17297 Opinion No. 7583; Supreme Court of the State of Alaska; 28.01.2022; page 46: "*Declaratory relief alone still would 'have no immediate impact on* [*carbon*] *emissions,' 'would not compel the State to take any particular action,' and would not 'protect the plaintiffs from the injuries they allege.' It also would not tell the State*

Carney emphasised that declaratory relief would matter and suffice.[20] Notwithstanding, the court in *Natalie R. v. State of Utah* held that declaratory relief could not effectively redress the plaintiffs' harms. In *Held v. State of Montana,* the court provided declaratory and even injunctive relief.

Judicial promotion of participatory rights also constitutes a weak form of judicial review, because it does not conclude the discursive process. Instead, it ensures that political rights are effectively protected. John Ely Hart's reference to the *"representation-reinforcing theory of judicial review"* concerns a check on political representatives to ensure they genuinely represent the people, thereby promoting effective political representation and supporting representative democracy.[21] In matters of global warming, this representation-reinforcing theory of judicial review could mean that courts primarily review whether there was a proper democratic discourse. Was the public well-informed, and could it participate in the decision-making process? Political discourse and policy choices ought to be transparent and foreseeable. Climate change measures span over time, and the public needs to know how the state intends to address this challenge and how it will impact their rights and freedoms over time. Only when these conditions are met can voters assess whether their political representatives are doing a reasonably good job. The transparency of state climate protection policies was a concern for the courts in *Neubauer* and *Friends of the Irish Environment.*

In summary, a climate protection case that proceeds to trial does not necessarily result in invalidation and replacement of a political decision. The court could examine the merits of the case and conclude that the political decision at issue is not yet manifestly unreasonable but that, without political amendments, there remains a risk of impairing rights. Especially in climate protection, the fact that the political branches adopted a climate protection law or a climate recovery plan is already a positive political step that deserves recognition.

---

*how to fulfil its constitutional obligations or help plaintiffs determine when their constitutional rights have been violated."*

20 Ibid, partially dissenting opinion of Justices Maassen and Carney, 28.01.2022; page 61: *"This same important question is before us for the second time in six years. It has been thoroughly briefed by committed parties and three groups of amici. Our failure to answer the question now will not eliminate it but will only postpone our answer, in the meantime putting the burden of redundantly litigating it on plaintiffs, the State, and the trial courts, potentially to return to us on appeal again and again until we conclude that prudence finally requires an answer. Given the urgency of the issue, I would conclude that "practicality and wise judicial administration" militate strongly in favour of limited declaratory relief identifying the constitutional source of the right plaintiffs claim."*

21 Ely John Hart; *Democracy and Distrust: A Theory of Judicial Review*; pages 102 & 181.

With a rights-endangerment finding, the court does not invalidate the majoritarian act; instead, it creates a disturbance that promotes political amendments and accountability. Justice Walters argued in his dissenting opinion in *Chernaik v. Brown that* even invalidating a political decision must not necessarily amount to counter-majoritarian difficulties if the court does not itself make a policy decision.[22] This reasoning aligns with the weak-form review as contemplated by this research, as the invalidation of an act does not provide a definitive answer to the subject; it is a dialogical form and remains so, even if the court orders the political decision-maker to amend the act within a specific timeframe.

I argue that declaratory relief, as a weak form of judicial relief, is neither incompatible with judicial activism nor with judicial self-restraint but could serve as a compromise by providing an adequate dose of court intervention. In *Neubauer,* the German Federal Constitutional Court took recourse to precisely this kind of compromise. It did not invalidate the German climate protection law but held that there could be a fundamental rights risk if the state postpones GHG reduction measures into the future. Ultimately, the legislator amended the Klimaschutzgesetz. The court thereby alleviated the counter-majoritarian difficulty and promoted the democratic dialogue.

Additionally, when a court demands compliance with national or international obligations but does not specify how to achieve the objective, it evidently acknowledges political discretion. In a French pollution case, for instance, the Council of State (*Conseil d'État*) urged the Prime Minister and the Minister for the Environment to take all necessary measures to develop and implement an air quality plan to bring concentrations of nitrogen dioxide and Fine PM10 particles below the limits set by the state.[23]

## 2 Strong-Form Judicial Review

Strong-form judicial review supports the view that an act approved by the democratic majority can be considered constitutionally unacceptable. However, a finding of constitutional unacceptability remains problematic. It leads to judicial substitution for democratic decisions and fuels the ongoing debate

22 *Chernaik v. Brown,* docket number: S066564, 367 Or 143 (2020); Supreme Court of the State of Oregon; 22.10.2022; dissenting opinion by Judge C.J. Walters, page 184:"[*J*]*udicial review for compliance with the law may have the effect of invalidating a policy decision of another branch, but in exercising that function, a court does not itself make a policy decision.*"

23 *Association Les Amis de la Terre France c/ Etat français,* Decision N°394254; France; Council of State; 12.07.2017.

over judicial supremacy.[24] It concerns the legitimacy of unaccountable judges overruling public choices.

Strong-form court decisions can potentially bind the state over time. If the court authoritatively and extensively interprets the constitution, that interpretation might remain in force unless the legislature amends it or the competent High Court or the Constitutional Court shifts its stance. This could also happen in the case of an apex court reading climate rights into an entrenched constitution. We will return to this issue when discussing the possibility of a compromise through an *experimentalist* model of judicial review.

If a sizable contingent of people disagrees with a strong-form court interpretation, it increases the tension between democratic self-governance and judicial review. Moreover, strong-form judicial decisions could influence the executive branch's bargaining power in international negotiations.[25] In other words, it affects state sovereignty and interests.

Jeremy Waldron argues that if four assumptions hold, there would be no reason to believe that courts are better positioned to protect rights than the People's legitimate representatives:

> We are to imagine a society with (1) democratic institutions in reasonably good working order, including a representative legislature elected on the basis of universal adult suffrage; (2) a set of judicial institutions, again in reasonably good order, set up on a nonrepresentative basis to hear individual lawsuits, settle disputes, and uphold the rule of law; (3) a commitment on the part of most members of the society and most of its officials to the idea of individual and minority rights; and (4) persisting, substantial, and good faith disagreement about rights (i.e., about what the commitment to rights actually amounts to and what its implications are) among the members of the society who are committed to the idea of rights.[26]

So if society, including its democratic institutions, functions reasonably well and most people take their rights seriously,[27] they should not seek judicial review of legislation, but rather pursue resolution through ordinary legislative processes. Courts, a panel composed of unelected and unaccountable judges, should defer political questions to political institutions and not replace the

---

24 Friedman Barry; *The History of the Counter-majoritarian Difficulty, Part One; The Road to Judicial Supremacy*; page 341.

25 Stone Christopher; *Should trees have standing?;* page 34.

26 Waldron Jeremy; *The Core of the Case against Judicial Review*; page 1360.

27 Ibid, page 1346.

will of the democratic majority.[28] Waldron mainly criticises strong-form judicial review (*the mode of final decision-making*).

We shall see below that a strong-form judicial decision could sometimes still be necessary to stop ongoing unconstitutional behaviour. In cases of manifest political abuse, most people will either agree with or even demand a strong-form court decision.

28 Landau David; *A Dynamic Theory of Judicial Role.*

## Section 3: The Prospects of a Compromise

The difference between strong-form and weak-form judicial review relates to how quickly the courts' interpretation of the Constitution can be changed.[29] In the short term, the political branches can overturn judgments based on weak-form review, whereas they cannot simply override decisions under strong-form judicial review.

Depending on the issue before the court, judges may sometimes make maximalist decisions and, at other times, minimalist ones.[30] Combining different review forms for different purposes and shifting between weak- and strong-form judicial review could better protect people's rights and strengthen the democratic process. Courts could utilise the advantages of all forms of judicial review and select the most suitable for each case. An *experimentalist* model of judicial review is even possible in a state offering strong-form judicial review. Strong courts could restrain themselves and adopt a weak stance while still retaining the power to revert to stronger forms of review. Weak-form judicial review grants the political branches discretion in responding to the ruling. The Court does not make policy decisions; it refers the matter to the political branches for consideration and holds them accountable. If a court declares a new right, it could do so in relatively vague terms, allowing the political branches to define its content.

This prudent judicial approach could prevent the state from becoming either an unchecked system of political sovereignty or a *juristocracy*. Democratic representatives would have the opportunity to decide how to comply with the constitutional requirements set by the court before the court resorts to a more potent form of enforcement, if necessary.

Mark Tushnet differentiates between different constitutional rights and argues that strong-form review may be less contentious when addressing non-controversial issues involving liberal democratic essentials such as the right to life or the protection against torture and ill-treatment. Strong-form judicial review could be more appropriate for protecting core constitutional safeguards, as it is grounded in a comprehensive agreement and an overlapping consensus. This decreases the likelihood that such court decisions will be perceived as unreasonable or disrespectful. Weaker forms of judicial review would be more appropriate for more controversial rights, such as socioeconomic rights. Ultimately, Tushnet argues that weak-form review may be the

---

29 Tushnet Mark; *Weak-Form Judicial Review and Core Civil Liberties Essay;* page 20.

30 See Tushnet Mark, with reference to Sunstein Cass, in Mourtada-Sabbah Nada; *The Political Question Doctrine and the Supreme Court of the United States*; page 72.

most suitable solution for all three generations of human rights, as it accommodates reasonable disagreement and serves as a check on both the political branches and the judiciary.[31]

Let us recall Frank Michelman's argument that weak-form judicial review might be appropriate for socioeconomic rights (second-generation rights) because these rights can have a greater impact on the budget than first-generation rights. Following this cue, weak-form judicial review could be more effective in contentious matters where there is less consensus among states or the public. The state is entitled to more leeway until consensus is reached.

Let us take the ECtHR as an example to illustrate the matter. It evidently adopts a differentiated approach in its jurisprudence, developing the *margin-of-appreciation* doctrine. For instance, it grants the states leeway when there is no consensus among the member states, such as on property rights. Conversely, it provides the fiercest protection against torture and inhuman or degrading treatment or punishment. The court accepts no justification for ill-treatment that breaches Article 3 of the ECHR, even if the justification involves the right to life.[32]

This differential approach is particularly relevant to climate protection, as global warming can affect all three generations of rights. Weak-form judicial review appears suitable for addressing controversial third-generation rights. In some states, these rights may qualify as constitutional objectives rather than justiciable ones. The amended constitution of Luxembourg that entered into force on July 1, 2023, has, for instance, a provision on climate protection: „*L'État garantit la protection de l'environnement humain et naturel, en œuvrant à l'établissement d'un équilibre durable entre la conservation de la nature, en particulier sa capacité de renouvellement, ainsi que la sauvegarde de la biodiversité, et la satisfaction des besoins des générations présentes et futures. L'État s'engage à lutter contre le dérèglement climatique et à œuvrer en faveur de la neutralité climatique*". That provision, however, is a constitutional objective rather than an enforceable right.

Why then introduce such a constitutional provision? Even if people cannot derive a right from the provision, the Constitutional Court could use it to assess the reasonableness of governmental measures. Weak-form judicial review fosters a discursive process in which political decision-makers consider

31 Tushnet Marc, *Weak Courts, Strong Rights*, pages 36, 37, 228.

32 See, for instance, *Gäfgen v. Germany* (Application no. 22978/05; ECtHR; 03.06.2010); or *Jalloh v. Germany* (Application no. 54810/00; ECtHR; 11.07.2006).

the court's reasoning and can thereby take into account elements and issues they might not have anticipated in the making process.

One should also consider the possibility of a dynamic relationship between judicial postures and political discretion. The demand for self-restraint and weak-form judicial review could be higher when political discretion is high, such as in foreign, economic, and social policies. Acceptance and reasonableness of court activism could increase if personal rights or liberties are at stake.[33] The more the public agrees with the court's interpretation of the Constitution, the less controversial the decision will be, and the less debate there will be about the counter-majoritarian difficulty.[34] Such a connection was evident in *Friends of the Irish Environment*. The court differentiated between judicial review of secondary and primary legislation. In the latter case, judicial review would be more problematic, as it results from a deliberative will-forming process involving many actors. Court interference with executive decisions would be less problematic than with legislative decisions.[35]

The dynamic relationship between judicial stance and political discretion also relates to the distinction between higher and lower courts. Lower courts should issue weak-form decisions and reserve strong-form judicial review for the Apex or Constitutional Courts.

In other words, dynamic forms of judicial review could employ both approaches, thereby alleviating the democratic caveats. Courts could, especially when confronted with a controversial issue, first issue a weak-form decision and resort to strong-form judicial review only after proper discourse within the political branches, allowing the people to appreciate the reasonableness and respectworthiness of state policies. The dynamic approach could alleviate concerns expressed by U.S. courts that declaratory relief does not guarantee sufficient redress. Declaratory relief is often the first step towards obtaining redress. When the government and the legislator respond adequately to this first step, it evidently provides redress. Declaratory relief requires supplementation by subsequent injunctive relief only in cases of inadequate response from the political branches.

We shall argue that even if a court issues such injunctive relief, for instance, by striking down a governmental act or decision, it can still ultimately support political discourse. Oliver Gerstenberg, for instance, argues that strong- and

---

33 Grimm Dieter; *Verfassungsgerichtsbarkeit*; page 55.

34 Friedman Barry; *The History of the Counter-majoritarian Difficulty, Part One; The Road to Judicial Supremacy*; pages 349 & 351.

35 See, for instance, Habermas Jürgen referring to Sunstein Cass in *Between Facts and Norms: Contributions to a Discourse Theory of Law and Democracy;* page 276.

weak-form judicial review go hand in hand. Strong-form review (such as the court establishment of a fundamental principle) can open up a deliberative process, but does not need to close the door to *"ongoing experimentation."*[36]

For example, the Irish Supreme Court struck down the climate recovery plan in *Friends of the Irish Environment* and refrained from further interfering with political decisions. It returned the ball to the government to adopt a new plan in light of the court's considerations. The Dutch Supreme Court adopted a similar approach in *Urgenda*, ruling that the Dutch state must meet its 2020 intermediate GHG reduction target. However, it remained silent on the question of how to achieve that goal.[37]

∴

36 Gerstenberg Oliver; *Negative/positive constitutionalism, "fair balance," and the problem of justiciability;* International Journal of Constitutional Law, Volume 10, Issue 4, Pages 904–925 (October 2012); pages 914–915.

37 *Urgenda* (2020).

CHAPTER 7

# A Cooperation Rather than a Separation of Powers Approach

## Introduction

Considering the socioeconomic rights debate in the U.S. and our discussions of experimentalist judicial review, we shall now critically assess whether *prima facie* weak forms of judicial review could promote climate protection without overly impairing either of the two ideals of democracy. Since judicial review cases regarding participatory rights are less likely to raise counter-majoritarian issues, our primary focus will be on climate lawsuits related to the state's climate protection plans and those involving climate rights or public trust obligations.

We shall argue that even in substantive climate-related judicial review cases, courts can help preserve democracy if the three branches of government engage in respectful dialogue and reasonable cooperation. Courts cannot turn the tide on their own; it requires the support of political actors to enforce their rulings. They rely on the executive and legislative branches to enforce these rulings and allocate sufficient resources. This could boost climate protection if the political branches align with the court's rulings.

With appropriate levels of court intervention, we could transition from a separation of powers to a cooperation of powers approach, leading to more effective climate protection measures. An *experimentalist* model of judicial review could foster exchanges and consultations among the different branches, thereby alleviating the tension between the separation of powers and the rule of law. This chapter will elaborate on this point in three sections.

Section 1 discusses the challenges courts face when intervening in climate-related lawsuits, identifying the most contentious cases, the courts' stances, and the forms of judicial decision-making.

Section 2 argues that dynamic forms of climate-related judicial review can effectively address climate protection cases in a democratically respectful manner. Prima facie weak-form judicial review might promote the progressive realisation of climate-relevant rights.

Section 3 explores whether the climate crisis could lead to a shift from a traditional separation of powers approach towards a conception of powers pivoting on a respectful discourse among the three branches that respects democracy, on the one hand, but also allows courts to play a significant role in guiding the political branches by highlighting legal risks and obligations and by shielding our rights against unchecked climate threats.

## Section 1: Climate Litigation and Judicial Postures

The question of whether a court should take an activist stance or adhere to judicial self-restraint becomes crucial when discussing GHG regulation, climate recovery plans, climate-relevant rights, or public trust obligations.

In the U.S. court system, presenting a climate case at an open trial was challenging because, apart from *Held v. State of Montana*, these cases were typically dismissed before they could proceed to trial. If the courts must engage with climate protection cases with great care, this does not mean they should not engage with them at all. Quite the opposite, the careful choice of the moment of self-restraint matters, meaning it must not be made already during the preliminary proceedings. At the trial stage, the court could still consider the best form of judicial review for the case at bar. Its posture could be weaker or stronger depending on the constitutional setting and the questions at bar. The higher the controversy, the weaker the court's posture could be.

Courts in Europe issued rather weak-form decisions, yet they still improved the states' stance on climate protection. In *Neubauer*, the court issued a declaratory judgment highlighting the risk to constitutional and human rights, promoting participatory rights, but did not invalidate the climate protection law. The court's approach was also relatively tolerant in *Friends of the Irish Environment*. It granted discretion to the political branches without disregarding the climate recovery plan. The Irish Supreme Court held that it could review the plan because it had evolved from policy to law. The court quashed the plan and guided the executive branch without interfering in the interest-balancing process. Even in *Urgenda*, the most controversial climate protection case, one could perhaps argue that the court still issued a type of weak-form judicial review decision by assessing and declaring what the law requires the government to do. It evaluated the state's legal obligations and told the political representatives that, considering its international commitments, the state should at least meet the lower level of the defined GHG reduction target. The court did not interfere with the policies beyond ordering compliance with the state's legal obligations. It left the political branches with the discretion over how to reach the legal target. The ECHR adopted the same stance in *Klimaseniorinnen*.

Let us differentiate between three current climate-based judicial review types: public participation cases (1), public trust cases (2), and climate rights cases (3). Drawing these distinctions enables us to understand the counter-majoritarian risks associated with each type of climate-based judicial review. This is particularly significant when considering the reasonableness of court intervention and dynamic forms of judicial review. We shall see that public acceptance is greater for some types and less for others.

## 1 Participatory Rights

The participatory cases relate to the level of public involvement. There appears to be a shared consensus on participatory rights, including the rights to information, participation, and access to justice. Participatory rights are also protected by international law, as outlined in the Aarhus Convention on Access to Information, Public Participation in Decision-Making, and Access to Justice in Environmental Matters. See also Article 6 of the ECtHR (the right to a fair trial) and the ruling in *KlimaSeniorinnen.*

People deserve to know, in sufficient detail, how projected policy decisions will affect them over time, thereby promoting political participation beyond Election Day. The right to access information enables people to address informed petitions to their political representatives or, as a last resort, to a court of law. Hence, participatory rights can foster good politics and promote climate protection. According to U.S. environmental lawyer Robert Kennedy, the effectiveness of democracy depends on the public's right to information and participation, access to justice, and the equitable distribution of public goods.[1]

We saw courts promoting participatory rights in *Neubauer* and *Friends of the Irish Environment*. Both court decisions eventually led to more precise and bolder climate protection plans. The political branches needed to set out in sufficient detail how they intended to meet their climate protection objectives over time, thereby providing economic sectors and the public with the planning security and transparency they needed. When courts strengthen participatory rights, they promote climate protection, as the state needs to plan and communicate effectively.

## 2 The Public Trust Cases

A common law framework already exists for cases involving public trust. In Europe, courts impose positive obligations on the state to preserve the envir-

1 Kennedy Robert Jr., *Crimes Against Nature: How George W. Bush and His Corporate Pals Are Plundering the Country and Hijacking Our Democracy; page* 43:

"There are several ways to measure the effectiveness of a democracy. One is to look at how much public is included in community decision making. Another is to evaluate access to justice. The most telling aspect of a government, however, is how it distributes the goods of the land. Does it safeguard the commonwealth- the public trust assets- on behalf of the public? Or does it allow the shared wealth of our communities to be stolen by corporate power?"

onment.[2] Public trust requires the State to preserve its public resources, which could create tension with the State's de facto management of natural wealth and its delay in deciding and implementing adequate climate protection measures. Public trust is connected to sovereignty. Theodore Roosevelt famously argued that "[*t*]*he nation behaves well if it treats the natural resources as assets which it must turn over to the next generation increased, and not impaired, in value.*"[3] For instance, in *Massachusetts v. EPA*, the Supreme Court held that a state is entitled to special *parens patriae* standing to protect its environment.

Public trust cases involve assessing whether the political branches have adequately considered environmental interests when making policy decisions. This form of judicial review is procedural and often referred to as the "*hard look*" standard. It involves reviewing administrative acts. The court determines whether the political branches properly considered ecological factors and incorporated them into their decision-making. This type of judicial review is widely accepted and differs from judicial review of individual constitutional rights.[4]

If the public trust case involves extending the public trust doctrine to new natural resources, it becomes more controversial. Still, in the U.S., the public trust doctrine is rooted in common law, and court intervention and equitable relief have a long tradition within this framework.[5] Therefore, court interven-

---

2 See the positive obligations that the ECtHR derived from Articles 2 and 8 of the ECHR or the public trust doctrine developed in the U.S. under a common law approach.

3 Theodore Roosevelt; 1858–1919, 26th President of the United States (Republican, NY), Speech, Colorado Live Stock Association, Denver, Colorado, August 29, 1910.

4 See, for example, *Sagoonick v. State of Alaska*, No. S-17297, Opinion No. 7583; Supreme Court of the State of Alaska; 28.01.2022, page 17:

"The "hard look" doctrine for reviewing DNR's decisions first appeared in Hammond v. North Slope Borough, when we referenced a United States Supreme Court statement that the "court cannot substitute its judgment as to environmental consequences, but should only ensure that the agency has taken a 'hard look.'" A year later, in Southeast Alaska Conservation Council, Inc. v. State, we stated that our role is to ensure that the agency "has given reasoned discretion to all the material facts and issues." The court exercises this aspect of its supervisory role with particular vigilance if it "becomes aware, especially from a combination of danger signals, that the agency has not really taken a 'hard look' at the salient problems and has not genuinely engaged in reasoned decision making." Since then, we have used the "hard look" standard when reviewing agency decisions on resource uses. This is in stark contrast to how we review claims about individual constitutional rights violations."

5 See, for instance, Wood Mary Christina; *On the Eve of Destruction: Courts Confronting the Climate Emergency*; Indiana Law Journal: Vol. 97: Iss. 1, Article 5 (Winter 2022); pages 239–295.

tion and equitable relief are generally considered more acceptable in these cases. Public trust cases are on the rise. Similar to extending standing, a court could extend nature's trust obligations to the atmosphere. The court could do so by issuing a declaratory judgment (a weak-form judicial decision) and leaving the political branches to determine the consequences. The political branches would then have the opportunity to consider the judicial decision and make a political choice after public discourse.[6] In *Sagoonick v. State of Alaska* and *Navahine F. v. Hawai'i Department of Transportation*, the claimants argued that extending the public trust to the atmosphere would not be necessary because global warming impairs the already protected public trust resources.[7]

## 3 The Climate Rights Cases

The most controversial cases involve petitions for judicial review that seek activist court intervention to declare and enforce specific climate rights, such as the right to a sustainable environment or the right to a stable climate. These cases may raise questions about their existence if the constitutional text is silent and about their scope and justiciability if they are labelled as constitutional objectives. Constitutional protection of environmental rights, specifically climate rights, is a recent development, and entrenched constitutions probably do not entail such dispositions. Judicial review petitions seeking declaratory relief place the courts in a difficult position. Any decision to take them to trial is bound to raise counter-majoritarian concerns. The petitioners, after all, are asking the court to interpret the founding text in light of changing conditions, thereby deriving climate rights that are not explicitly stated in the text but implied from other rights. Some seek recognition of distinctive standalone ecological rights. This technique seems paradoxical, as human rights

6 See, for instance, Justice Walters's dissenting opinion in *Chernaik v. Brown* (docket number: S066564, 367 Or 143 (2020); Supreme Court of the State of Oregon; 22.10.2022; page 183): "Similarly, here, the state does not cite any cases limiting the authority of the judicial branch to declare the common-law obligations of the other two branches or to review their acts or omissions for compliance with the applicable legal standard. Here, the declaration of an affirmative fiduciary obligation to protect and manage public trust property would allow a court to review the actions or omissions of those in the legislative and executive branches for objective reasonableness, but the exercise of that review function would not necessarily usurp or interfere with the policymaking functions of the other two branches."

7 See, for instance, *Sagoonick v. State of Alaska,* No. S-17297, Opinion No. 7583; Supreme Court of the State of Alaska, 28.01.2022, page 46; and *Navahine F. v. Hawai'i Department of Transportation,* 1CCV-22-0000631, 06.04.2023; First Circuit Court of the State of Hawai'i; page 3.

require an environment that sustains life, not the other way around. Therefore, one could argue that those highly controversial ecological rights must be presupposed to make our world's societies possible; they are a *sine qua non* condition, for example, to the right to life. This is the position adopted by the Supreme Court of the Philippines in the *Minors Oposa* case.[8]

In *Juliana*, the youth petitioners aimed, on the one hand, at judicial recognition of a stand-alone right to a climate, and, on the other hand, at the respect of public trust obligations. In the U.S., District Court Judge Ann Akin was the first to recognise a federal right to a life-sustaining climate. Until now, that court decision stands alone at the federal-state level. At the state level, the Hawai'i Supreme Court in 2023 also declared the existence and protection of such a right to a life-sustaining climate system.[9]

Courts could, and perhaps should, adopt a more lenient stance in this matter. If they declare a right as a constitutional essential that must be protected, they could do so without providing a too specific definition. In other words, they could limit themselves to developing broad standards. By referring the matter back to the political branches, they solicit a pivotal discourse on the implications of the rights at stake. This, in turn, allows the political branches to develop a more explicit definition of the right and make follow-up decisions to enforce it.

This proceeding could help achieve the gradual realisation of climate rights and protection. It is to this idea that we now turn.

∴

8 *Minors Oposa v. Factoran, G.R. No. 101083, 33 I.L.M. 173;* the Philippines, Supreme Court; 30.07.1993.

9 *Navahine F. v. Hawai'i Electric Light Company, Inc.*, SCOT-22-0000418; Supreme Court of the State of Hawai'i; 13.03.2023.

## Section 2: Progressive Realisation of Climate Rights and Climate Protection

Courts play a crucial role in declaring and protecting individual rights. However, they cannot initiate cases on their own. They have to wait for a case to come to them. Therefore, the development of rights needs a supportive structure. Lawyers and organisations' rising assertion of rights is crucial to making judicial developments possible. Even if judicial declarations of new constitutional rights in cases brought by civil society might seem undemocratic,[10] the declared rights can eventually strengthen democracy.[11]

Following Frank Michelman's and Mark Tushnet's cues, we argue that if courts adopt a weak-form judicial review stance, they can declare what the law is or what constitutional law requires without making policy decisions. I agree with Frank Michelman that even weak-form judicial review decisions entail sufficient authority. Our judicial review analysis in Part 1 evidently supports Michelman's view in this regard.

Tushnet's "*managerial model*" of judicial review[12] could foster deliberation without usurping the powers of government. Courts could issue a declaratory judgment on the merits and then refer the matter back to the political branches for further consideration. This proceeding could leave the political branches with sufficient discretion to implement the judicial decision while remaining politically accountable to the people. The court decision would still create a disturbance that political leaders would need to address, which might stimulate the political discourse. Hence, this approach could lead to a situation in which the court decision opens the door to ongoing political discourse, which is necessary to address climate change in the short and long term. Courts could resort to more robust versions of judicial review if weaker options have failed to affect political outcomes.

A court declaring, in a bottom-up approach, the existence of a constitutional right could serve as a corrective to a state's inadequate or insufficient climate protection actions and encourage the progressive adoption and realisation of science-based climate protection measures. The court is not required to define the content of climate rights in detail, nor is it obligated to invalidate the state's climate protection policies. It could refer those questions back to

---

10 Epp Charles; *The Rights Revolution: Lawyers, Activists, and Supreme Courts in Comparative Perspective*; Illustrated Edition (Chicago, University of Chicago Press, 1998); page 197.

11 bid pages 2–4. Epp called this "*the democratization of access to courts.*"

12 Tushnet Mark; *Weak-Form Judicial Review and Core Civil Liberties Essay;* Harvard Civil Rights-Civil Liberties Law Review 41, No. 1 (2006); 1–22.

the political branches for further consideration. The branches of government should then take responsibility and decide on appropriate policies, duly considering the court's decision.[13]

A weak form of judicial review could affect the state's stance on climate protection in two ways. First, it may lead to the (re-)formation of public opinion on climate issues, and second, it may affect the (dis)approval of governmental climate protection efforts. Political pressure could increase if climate rights find support in civil society.[14]

Would that be sufficient? I would answer that question affirmatively. Declaring that a state has infringed, or might infringe, on a specific environmental right might suffice to trigger policy changes by the political branches themselves.[15] Even after judicial review, the state could promote settlement negotiations, which could lead to a reasonable compromise.[16] Not only is the discursive process re-engaged in court, but the process also becomes more transparent. A widely discussed judicial process will likely leave public debates more informed about relevant facts than before. Therefore, an independent authority that reviews political decisions and issues an opinion might reopen political discourse and reinforce political participation.

I disagree with the view that a weak-form court order is merely symbolic if it lacks support from political leaders, the public, or market forces. According to Ran Hirschl, even if courts intervene actively, court decisions can only have an impact if extrajudicial factors, such as support from the political branches or market forces, contribute to this change. The judicial branch has limited resources and no independent enforcement powers. Referring to *Brown v. Board of Education*,[17] Hirschl emphasised that the court's ruling alone could not induce significant reform, as opposition forces had hampered social progress for a decade.[18]

In matters of climate protection, there are undoubtedly also opposition forces within the political branches, market forces, and the public that attempt

13 Hirschl Ran; *The New Constitution and the Judicialization of Pure Politics;* pages 744–746.

14 Epp Charles; *The Rights Revolution: Lawyers, Activists, and Supreme Courts in Comparative Perspective*; page 13.

15 See, for instance, Posner Eric; *Climate Change and International Human Rights Litigation: A Critical Appraisal* (January 2007). University of Chicago Law & Economics, Olin Working Paper No. 329; University of Chicago, Public Law Working Paper No. 148; page 7.

16 See, for instance, *Navahine F.* v *Hawai'i Electric Light Company, Inc.*, CIVIL NO. 1CCV-22-0000631; Circuit Court of the First Circuit, State of Hawai'i; 20.06.2024.

17 *Brown v. Board of Education of Topeka*, 347 U.S. 483 (1954); United States Supreme Court; 17.05.1954 ("*Brown v. Board of Education*").

18 Hirschl Ran; *Towards Juristocracy: The Origins and Consequences of the New Constitutionalism* (Cambridge London, Harvard University Press, 2007); page 208.

to delay the energy system transformation or the impacts on their way of life. However, I believe that court rulings and judicial review still matter, as the political branches cannot simply discard judicial outcomes. If the political branches do not adequately heed the court's decision, their institutional credibility will be at risk. In other words, ignoring judicial decisions could jeopardise their legitimacy and respectability in the eyes of the public. Raising public support and the mediatisation of the court decision could promote subsequent endorsement, as political branches would generally avoid perceptions that they are falling foul of the rule of law. Even if there is no guarantee that court decisions will make headlines, they are still likely to attract some press and social media coverage.

Although I emphasise the benefits of weak-form judicial review, courts may need to shift to a more assertive approach in future cases. If courts recognised a constitutional right to a stable climate, they could, in subsequent cases, order government action that complies with the science if the political branches fail to act. The court has already laid a solid foundation for subsequent cases in the first, weak-form judgment. The political branches could intervene, adopt policies, or further define broadly declared rights. However, they could also remain inert, as the court did not issue injunctive orders. This political posture would likely lead to further judicial review petitions. The court could then navigate along the spectrum of available judicial review postures between the boundaries of strong-form and weak-form judicial review. Case by case, the court could, if necessary, shift from weaker to stronger postures and progressively promote climate rights and climate protection. In other words, if political decision-makers deliberately neglect to address shortcomings in climate protection, the time might be ripe for a shift in judicial posture.

## The Multi-step Approach and *res judicata* or *stare decisis*

Whether a court would revisit an issue is a significant consideration for the multistep approach I propose. A first weak-form judicial review decision should, in principle, not stop the debate but promote its continuation. Doing so would alleviate the counter-majoritarian difficulties and, quite the contrary, promote and safeguard the democratisation process throughout the climate crisis. A judicial declaration of public trust obligations or environmental rights, in broad terms, is likely to ignite political debate. All of this should contribute to the normative understanding of the key matters involved in the dispute.

If the court, on the other hand, refuses to declare such rights and obligations, it is also not the end of the road. The case could easily be queued again when the time ripens to do so, given that the *res judicata* principle would not have been triggered. A multi-step approach could, however, be more difficult if the Supreme Court or the Plenary of a Human Rights Court were to have their say. If, for instance, the U.S. Supreme Court ruled that the federal constitution does not entail a right to a viable climate, it might not be willing to take up a similar case, which would bar the multistep approach, at least in the short run.

Considering the living-instrument approach to a constitution or convention, an initial decision on the subject matter does not definitively prevent a change in jurisprudence. The discussion could continue at the level of individual states and their constitutions. We observed this in the youth climate protection cases, where the federal court exercised judicial self-restraint in *Juliana*. That decision did not end the debate. State courts eventually revisited the core grievances and ultimately provided relief under their state constitutions. Moreover, these subsequent developments are likely to return to the federal courts, and possibly even to the Supreme Court. In *Juliana,* the U.S. Supreme Court dismissed the petition for a *writ of certiorari*.[19]

19 Kelsey Cascadia Rose Juliana et al. v. United States et al.; docket 24–645; order list 604 U.S.; United States Supreme Court; 24.03.2025; ["*Juliana* (2025)"].

## Section 3: From Separation of Powers to Cooperation among Powers

The "*cooperation of powers*" conceptualised in this work avoids the pitfalls commonly associated with judicial supremacy. The court is not a leader but a partner that collaborates with the political branches to promote climate protection:

> In constitutional government, the ultimate power cannot be left to the legislature or even a supreme court, which is only the highest judicial interpreter of the constitution. Ultimate power is held by the three branches in a duly specified relation with one another with each responsible to the people.[20]

This idea of cooperation among powers is not new and is already part of the "*dialogue theory*" of constitutional review, which posits that courts can broadly interpret constitutional rights and defer political questions to the political branches. According to this theory, courts are fully entitled to intervene if political branches stay inert. It is a form of dialogue between the branches of the state. In the words of Rosalind Dixon:

> As with the other theories of cooperative constitutionalism considered here, dialogue theory does not assume that courts should intervene in the political process only in the event of clear error or patent unreasonableness or irrationality on the part of the legislature or the executive. Rather, it assumes that courts are entitled to intervene either coercively or communicatively (or, potentially, in both ways), where there are arguable failures of foresight, perspective, accommodation, or responsiveness. From a dialogic perspective, in particular, such intervention will be aimed at introducing new ideas, perspectives, or even equilibriums into the political process, all with a view to encouraging the legislature and the broader constitutional culture to 'reconsider its allegiance to the previous status quo. It will thus be inevitable that, at least in some cases, courts will uphold rights-based claims that do not find broad support within the culture.[21]

---

20 Michelman Frank; *Constitutional Essentials: On the Constitutional Theory of Political Liberalism; page* 168 referring to John Rawls, *Political Liberalism* (Columbia University Press, 1993, 232).

21 Dixon Rosalind; *Creating Dialogue about Socioeconomic Rights: Strong-Form versus Weak-Form Judicial Review Revisited; page* 393.

The court decision enlarges the political discourse by adding new considerations.[22] Generally, the branches of government take rights seriously and implement appropriate corrective measures following a ruling that provides a constitutional rights perspective on a state's stance on climate change and outlines the risks to constitutional rights.

Fostering exchanges or consultations between state branches could be highly beneficial and help alleviate the tension between the separation of powers and the rule of law. Courts can ensure that the elected branches of government incorporate the climate dimension into their decision-making processes and fulfil their statutory duties.

Progressive realisation of climate protection through prima facie weak-form climate-based judicial review could promote such cooperation of the state branches. Recalling first that courts lack both the financial means and the enforcement powers (the sword and the purse).[23] And second, that efficient climate change protection requires the state to restructure society, the concept of cooperation of powers could become essential during the climate crisis.

In *Massachusetts v. EPA*, the Supreme Court issued its opinion on the administrative decision and remanded the matter to the EPA for reconsideration. Following the court's opinion, the EPA issued an endangerment finding, regulated GHG from new motor vehicles, and even addressed GHG emissions from stationary sources, such as power plants and factories.[24]

In *Neubauer*, the Federal Constitutional Court of Germany neither struck down the *Klimaschutzgesetz* nor imposed a zero-emission target; instead, it gave the legislature leeway to take supplementary measures. The German Federal Constitutional Court balanced climate protection requirements with economic concerns about planning security by holding that the legislator should establish the reduction targets from 2031 onwards, and it set a deadline (by 31 December 2022 at the latest). The legislator pledged to amend its *KSG* in line with the Constitutional Court's opinion, to reinforce its GHG reduction targets, and to provide greater planning security to the various economic sectors.

Also, a court can offer guidance without directly imposing measures. For example, the Bangladesh Supreme Court offered such guidance concerning

---

22 Ibid, page 407.

23 Rosenberg Gerald; *The Hollow Hope: Can Courts Bring About Social Change?*; page 3.

24 Meltz Robert; Federal Agency Actions Following the Supreme Court's Climate Change Decision in *Massachusetts v. EPA: A Chronology*; Congressional Research Service Report; 09.01.2014; pages 6–10.

industrial pollution in *Farooque v. Government of Bangladesh*. It proposed to advise the government on how to effectively and satisfactorily achieve the objectives of the 1995 Environmental Protection Act. It was up to the government to decide whether it wished to approach the Supreme Court "*for directions as and when necessary, so that the objectives of the Act can be achieved effectively and satisfactorily.*"[25]

25 *Farooque v. Government of Bangladesh*; WP 891 of 1994; Bangladesh, Supreme Court; 15.07.2001 ("*Industrial Pollution Case*").

CHAPTER 8

# Climate Protection, Court Legitimacy, and Democracy

## Introduction

This chapter addresses the question of whether climate-related judicial review invariably endangers the liberal democratic project. We contend that climate change can be so significant that courts need to intervene to strengthen and protect democracy. We shall consider a climate-related judicial review decision as a democratic moment between elections, where citizens do not have to wait until the next election to evaluate whether political representatives govern the state reasonably and responsibly. Judicial review, especially in an experimentalist mode, can strengthen (liberal) democracy. Oliver Gerstenberg expounds on Frank Michelman and the idea that courts can play a significant "*legitimacy-sustaining*" and "*democracy-enhancing*" role. Courts provide a mutually shared forum for the ongoing interpretation of the constitution, including the so-called constitutional essentials. The constitution is interpreted through an interplay between the courts, the legislatures, the plaintiffs, the citizens and the wider public. An *experimentalist* mode of judicial review encourages this open-ended, reasoned, and deliberative process in which the court does not impose a final say. The court provides "*an argumentative setting where all participants appear, procedurally, as equals and are required to defend their interpretations of law with reference to reasons that are capable of being acknowledged by all others involved.*"[1]

Judicial promotion of participatory rights in ecological matters could reconnect citizens with democracy. Since participatory rights also encompass access to justice, courts could serve as a platform for people, including those who are politically underrepresented, to voice their concerns, access information, and challenge governmental decisions. Petitioners might receive documentation that was previously unavailable to them. Open trials raise public awareness and hold the branches of government accountable beyond Election Day. The risk of a public trial and a court order unfavourable to the government fosters

1 Gerstenberg Oliver; *Negative/positive constitutionalism, "fair balance," and the problem of justiciability;* International Journal of Constitutional Law, Volume 10, Issue 4, Pages 904–925 (October 2012); page 925.

 | HTTPS://DOI.ORG/10.1163/9789004771710-016

good politics. The government, for example, must assess and consider the projected climatic impacts of its political decisions.

Even court interventions in the more controversial climate protection cases can strengthen the democratic project if they are legitimate, reasonable, and respectful. Declaring the law or outlining risks to human or constitutional rights is not making political decisions. Such court rulings offer guidance to the government, which then must make difficult political decisions.

This chapter again unfolds in three sections. Given the dichotomy between legal and political questions, Section 1 examines the legitimacy of climate-related court decisions. In addition to the judicial branch's role as a protector of the rule of law, judges can derive legitimacy from their appointment process and oath to uphold the Constitution.

Section 2 argues that courts support democracy by ensuring the effectiveness of participatory rights, which are essential in ecological matters. In climate-related judicial review, access to justice can be problematic if courts systematically dismiss climate protection cases at the pre-trial stage.

Section 3 returns to the topic of substantive climate-based judicial review. We will argue that the democratic project could be at risk if states and, in the last line of defence, also the courts disregard the protection of constitutional principles, rights, and duties. In a trial, vulnerable minorities, including those who do not yet have a political say, could have a voice. This is where our proposal for dynamic forms of climate-based judicial review gains significance, as the climate threat might challenge the traditional court approach to climate-relevant matters.

## Section 1: Court Legitimacy

Climate-related judicial review indeed entails counter-majoritarian risks, but court intervention may still be legitimate and necessary. Perhaps the concerns about the separation of powers can be eased. Henceforth, we will assess the counter-majoritarian risks and then examine arguments that might justify court intervention within a democratic system grounded in the rule of law.

### Counter-Majoritarian Risks of Judicial Review

In the U.S., if five Supreme Court Justices support one's claim, the constitutional content can be changed. According to Justice Brennan, the most crucial rule in U.S. constitutional law would not be due process, equal protection, free speech, the right to vote, the privilege against self-incrimination, or the prohibition on cruel and unusual punishment, but the "*Rule of Five.*" All it would take to change the Constitution is the votes of five of the nine Supreme Court justices, the majority needed for a Supreme Court opinion. In other words, five judges get to decide on what the law is.[2] "*If you have five votes here, you can do anything,*" Brennan famously said.[3]

When crafting their policies, the political branches must strive for a compromise that the people can accept. Of concern here is the notion of the "*at least reasonable*" that can be derived from Rawls's understanding of political liberalism. It is not the role of a court to effect or articulate such a compromise: "[…] *when judges rule this or that policy unconstitutional, there's little room for compromise: One side must win, the other must lose.*"[4] The judicial decision invariably favours one of the parties' positions and is issued on the basis of a limited view of the facts of the case at bar. The court cannot take into account other considerations than those flowing from the case before it.[5]

Despite the dangers of getting involved in controversial policy issues,[6] a court can still contribute to reaching a compromise when it outlines a gross

---

2 Lazarus Richard; *The Rule of Five: Making Climate History at the Supreme Court*; pages 181 & 182. See also Kuh Katrina Fischer; *The Legitimacy of Judicial Climate Engagement*; page 18.

3 Brennan William, quoted in Kaplan David; *The Most Dangerous Branch: Inside the Supreme Court's Assault on the Constitution* (New York, Crown, 2018); page VII.

4 Kaplan David; *The Most Dangerous Branch: Inside the Supreme Court's Assault on the Constitution*; page 47.

5 Bickel Alexander; *The Least Dangerous Branch: The Supreme Court at the Bar of Politics;* pages 69–70.

6 See, for example, Kaplan David; *The Most Dangerous Branch: Inside the Supreme Court's Assault on the Constitution*; page 47.

and manifest failure to do so, namely a manifestly disproportionate disregard for minority rights in the political process.

### Legitimacy of Court Intervention

Failing to make a decision could be perceived as flagrantly unjust and may compromise the system's credibility. An activist court interpretation might be controversial, but it still avoids denying *justice.*[7] Also, access to justice is allegedly ineffective if courts systematically dismiss cases already at the standing stage. When this happens, the court fails to address the legal questions of the lawsuit, forcing petitioners to continue litigating. This could render the administration of justice excessively costly and impede effective access to justice.

Some arguments justify the counter-majoritarian nature of judicial review. One concern is long-term legitimacy. Courts would rely more on the original constitutional drafters than on the current legislators, rendering political representatives accountable beyond Election Day. Even if Alexander Bickel exposed the counter-majoritarian nature of judicial review as the central concern, he still believed that the judiciary, notably the Supreme Court, was the best placed to protect society's values over time.[8]

In the literature, some supporters of judicial review invert the counter-majoritarian argument, emphasising that court intervention would not endanger democracy but would instead promote it. Since the judge does not control the purse or the sword of the state, the judicial branch would be the least dangerous, and court abuses would be less likely and less far-reaching. These arguments are not new. They were already a concern of the drafters of the Constitutional Convention in the U.S. after the American Revolution, as documented in the Federalist and Anti-Federalist Papers:

> Whoever attentively considers the different departments of power must perceive, that, in a government in which they are separated from each other, the judiciary, from the nature of its functions, will always be the least dangerous to the political rights of the Constitution; because it will be the least in a capacity to annoy or injure them. The Executive not only dispenses the honours but holds the sword of the community. The legislature not only commands the

---

7 Jacqueline Lucienne Lafon, France in Tate Neal and Vallinder Torbjorn; *The Global Expansion of Judicial Power;* page 291.

8 Harry H. Wellington in Bickel Alexander; *The Least Dangerous Branch: The Supreme Court at the Bar of Politics*; page xi.

> purse; no direction either the strength or the wealth of the society; and can take no active resolution whatever. It may truly be said to have neither FORCE nor WILL, but merely judgment; and must ultimately depend upon the aid of the executive arm even for the efficacy of its judgments.[9]

Another legitimising aspect could relate to the links between the judiciary and the political branches. The process of appointing judges might involve the political branches. For example, the executive and legislative branches are involved in the selection process for federal Supreme Court justices in the United States: The acting President nominates and appoints the federal judges, and the Senate confirms or rejects the nominees. The electors can foresee what type of judges a presidential candidate might select as President. By carefully selecting the Justices for the Supreme Court, political decision-makers can perhaps serve their party's (Republican or Democratic) interests for quite some time.[10] For instance, U.S. President Trump was "*very committed to nominating and appointing committed originalists and textualists*" to the Supreme Court during his first term.[11]

Jeremy Waldron rejects this legitimacy argument. According to him, the appointment process of legislatures, i.e. elections, is more democratic and obviously more accountable to the public. A majoritarian legislative decision requires more than five votes out of nine, and this wider majority would provide greater legitimacy than any judiciary can claim.[12]

Judges could also draw legitimacy from their oath to uphold the Constitution and the rule of law. The Bangladesh Supreme Court, in *Farooque v. Government of Bangladesh*, observed that this oath is more than merely a formality; it is a duty and a constitutional obligation:

> The oath of office of the Judges of the Supreme Court requires that they will preserve, protect and defend the Constitution and the laws of Bangladesh. These are not mere ornamental empty words. These glorifying words of oath eulogizes the supremacy of judiciary. It is by now well settled that if the Government or its functionaries fails to act and perform its duties cast upon them by the laws of this Republic, the High Court Division of the Supreme Court,

---

9 Hamilton Alexander, James Madison, John Jay, and Patrick Henry; *The Complete Federalist and Anti-Federalist Papers* (Independently published, 2020); page 235.

10 See, for instance, Whittington Keith; *Repugnant Laws: Judicial Review of Acts of Congress from the Founding to the Present*; page 10.

11 Tushnet Mark; *Taking Back the Constitution: Activist Judges and the Next Age of American Law* (London, Yale University Press, 2020); page 19.

12 Waldron Jeremy; *The Core of the Case against Judicial Review*; page 1391.

> shall not remain a silent spectator to the inertness of the part of the Government or its officials, rather, in order to vindicate its oath of office can issue, in its discretion, necessary orders and directions, under Article 102 of the Constitution to carry out the intents and purpose of any law to its letter, in the interest of the people of Bangladesh because all powers in the Republic belong to the people, and their exercise on behalf of the people shall be effected only under, and by the authority of the Constitution.[13]

Protecting the rule of law and ensuring that court decisions are grounded in sound reasoning are essential to legitimate court intervention.

My research does not ignore the counter-majoritarian risks of court interventions in climate protection matters, but argues that, even if such risks exist, they do not justify courts sidestepping or abstaining from intervening. Court engagement with climate cases could help preserve democracy.[14] Changing social exigencies matter. Sometimes, the written text of constitutions no longer aligns with practice or social reality. Courts would not create counter-majoritarian tensions when the interpretation is already socially accepted, provided they proceed in the carefully analogical fashion described above.

A clear example is the Supreme Court's rulings on U.S. racial segregation. In *Brown v. Board of Education*, the court overruled *Plessy v. Ferguson*, holding that racial segregation in public schools was no longer consistent with the U.S. Constitution. Social realities underwent significant changes between 1896 and 1956, and the court responded to these changes.[15] Given the effects of dangerous climate change and related social realities, judicial review petitioners could argue that a significant portion of society believes the state should do more to protect climate-relevant rights and fulfil its obligations.[16]

Access to courts can strengthen democracy by ensuring that relatively autonomous environmental agencies are accountable. Some systems empower unelected, politically unaccountable administrative bodies to oversee environmental government action. The latter might act under the broad discretion granted by legislative texts. They may lack political legitimacy as their decision-makers are not elected political representatives. Political links could be weak and indirect.[17] Therefore, a court ruling sanctioning the abuse of

---

13 *Farooque v. Government of Bangladesh*, WP 891 of 1994; Bangladesh, Supreme Court; 15.07.2001; point 33.

14 See, for instance, Kuh Katrina Fischer; *The Legitimacy of Judicial Climate Engagement;* page 43.

15 Burgers Laura; *Should Judges Make Climate Change Law?*; page 63.

16 Ibid, page 69.

17 Moules Richard; *Environmental Judicial Review*; page 17.

discretion provides a check on the agencies; the people cannot hold them accountable by voting at the polls.[18] According to the *non-delegation* principle, the legislative branch cannot delegate its power to other institutions. After a proper deliberative process, only the legislative branch can issue a legally binding act, and certain decisions require one. This process provides further legitimacy to the act and, therefore, deserves more discretion than an executive act based on less or no prior democratic debate.

As defenders of the rule of law, courts uphold respect for "*minimum standards of fairness, both procedural and substantive.*"[19] The rule of law also connects to the constitutional and international human rights framework, which limits the discretion of political authorities. The judicial branch thereby prioritises the rule of law over the rule of the people and protects vulnerable, often underrepresented people from abuse by the majority.[20] This could also legitimise more substantial forms of judicial review. The separation of powers safeguards not only against judicial supremacy but also against political abuse. Courts must intervene in cases of manifest abuse of discretion in the exercise of political power. This kind of *safety valve* might enable courts to set aside abusive legislation.[21] It is the idea that unjust law is not law and does not deserve normative effects: "*Lex iniusta non est lex.*"[22] These essential features of constitutional democracies are, of course, well-known. Nevertheless, it is crucial to emphasise the critical role they can and will likely play in the face of global and potentially catastrophic climate change.

The rule of law has gained importance in (liberal) democracies, with some states explicitly enshrining it in their constitutions. Even international organisations, such as the European Union, adhere to it. Unpacking the distinction between legal and political questions is crucial, as courts have more extensive powers and obligations in a democratic system operating under the rule of law. In his dissent in *Chernaik v. Brown*, Judge C.J. Walters argued that the court must assess what the rule of law requires, establishing the framework within which political branches must operate.[23]

---

18 See, for example *Massachusetts v. EPA* and the EPA's decision to revoke the endangerment finding of carbon dioxide under the Clean Air Act leading to *Venner v. EPA*.

19 Ibid, page 6.

20 Boyd David; *The environmental rights revolution: a global study of constitutions, human rights, and the environment;* page 5.

21 See *Greenpeace Nordic Ass'n and Natur og Ungdom v. Ministry of Petroleum and Energy*, 20-051052SIV-HRET; Norway, Supreme Court; 22.12.2020 ("*People v. Arctic Oil*").

22 Bulloch Penelope, Raz Joseph, and Hart. H. L. A.; *The Concept of Law;* Second Edition (Oxford, Oxford University Press, 1997); page 156.

23 *Chernaik v. Brown*, docket number: S066564, 367 Or 143 (2020); Supreme Court of the State of Oregon; 22.10.2022; dissenting opinion by Judge C.J. Walters:

The demarcation between political and legal questions is sometimes unclear and subject to debate. Courts need to draw a line. We saw, for instance, in *Friends of the Irish Environment* that the court distinguished between law and policy. The Irish Supreme Court held that it could review the climate protection plan because political representatives had made it a legal instrument. Once a final decision is made, the political question becomes a legal matter.

Courts must explain[24] which legal arguments they rely on to justify their decisions. Especially if a court issues an activist ruling, it must provide sufficient reasons for stakeholders to endorse it. If judicial review is to promote democracy and contribute to climate protection, it must base its rulings on established legal norms and principles. Scientific evidence may support these legal arguments.

---

All parties to this case, including the state, agree that climate change "is causing, and will continue to cause, harm to our planet and the State of Oregon." All parties to this case, including plaintiffs, agree that the legislative and executive branches of our state government have taken steps to address and prevent that harm. I conclude that the judicial branch also has a role to play: This court can and should determine the law that governs the other two branches as they undertake their essential work. This court can and should issue a declaration that the state has an affirmative fiduciary duty to act reasonably to prevent substantial impairment of public trust resources. Because the majority declines to issue that declaration in this case, I dissent.

24 Benvindo Juliano Zaiden; *On the Limits of Constitutional Adjudication: Deconstructing Balancing and Judicial Activism* (Heidelberg, Springer, 2010); page 110.

## Section 2: Promoting Participatory Rights

Climate-based judicial review promotes democracy by upholding participatory rights and increasing transparency and foreseeability of state actions. More than other policies, environmental matters empower citizens beyond Election Day. This largely depends on effective access to justice. Loosened standing criteria permit broader access to the courts and increase the likelihood of a day in court, allowing a court to assess the case's merits. Furthermore, broader access to courts reduces the costs of lengthy pre-trial proceedings, whereas a judicial posture of self-restraint increases them. Petitioners must carry the costs of those lengthy pre-trial proceedings, and few individuals can afford to do so. Therefore, economic access to justice in climate cases may be problematic; crowdfunding and donations play a significant role in climate protection cases, particularly for those representing younger and future generations.

Especially in climate matters, courts could become essential actors in protecting deliberative democracy. They could support the political participation of young people who lack a voice.[25] Courts can legitimately do so, as multiple national and international legal texts and principles could allow the recognition and declaration of intergenerational responsibilities.[26]

Courts could promote public transparency by requiring the government to provide sufficient detail on its plans to address climate change.[27] In court proceedings, plaintiffs get access to reliable information. Moreover, climate-relevant court decisions are public and receive coverage in the literature and the media. Altogether, this might contribute to democracy and the discursive political process. Climate-relevant court decisions thus increase public awareness, which might foster dialogue between the branches of government.

---

25 Colby Heather et al.; *Judging Climate Change: The Role of the Judiciary in the Fight Against Climate Change*; page 175.

26 Kuh Katrina Fischer; *The Legitimacy of Judicial Climate Engagement*; pages 21–23.

27 According to the Supreme Court in *Friends of the Irish Environment* (2020); point 9.2, this needs to be done so that "*a reasonable and interested person could make a judgment both as to whether the plan in question is realistic and as to whether they agree with the policy options for achieving the NTO which such a plan specifies. The 2015 Act as a whole involves both public participation in the process leading to the adoption of a plan but also transparency as to the formal government policy, adopted in accordance with a statutory regime, for achieving what is now the statutory policy of meeting the NTO by 2050. A compliant plan is not a five-year plan but rather a plan covering the full period remaining to 2050. While the detail of what is intended to happen in later years may understandably be less complete, a compliant plan must be sufficiently specific as to policy over the whole period to 2050.*"

In a French criminal case, the Lyon Appeal Court (*Cour d'appel de Lyon*)[28] gave participatory rights a new dimension, thereby strengthening public participation amid the climate emergency. Members of an *NGO* stole a picture of the French President from the town hall. They used it to raise public awareness about climate change and the failure to meet commitments under the Paris Agreement. The court stated that in a democratic state, when the government fails to respect its obligations, political participation must not be limited to voting in elections; alternative forms of participation must also be permitted. Since the picture was stolen to raise public awareness, the accused were not punished for this theft. Hence, according to this French judgment, elements of civil disobedience could qualify as participatory rights. Perhaps one could understand this manifestation of participatory rights in terms of the criminal defence of necessity (*état de nécessité*).

28 Jugement correctionnel N° 19168000015; France, Cour d'Appel de Lyon; 26.09.2019 (*"Macron Portrait criminal case"*).

## Section 3: Promoting Substantive Rights

Substantive due process judicial review involves perhaps the greatest risk to the separation of powers. Nonetheless, we argue that substantive review can be necessary, consistent with the basic principles of liberal democracy, and even promote the democratic project.

The counter-majoritarian difficulty arises when courts design climate-relevant remedies, as this would involve intervening *ex-ante* in the political process and legislative outcomes. Our proposed *prima facie* weak-form mode for judicial review could alleviate some of the counter-majoritarian concerns. Although courts must issue a decision, that does not necessarily mean judges must end the ongoing democratic debate.[29] Weak-form judicial review could protect and even encourage deliberative democracy. Even a subsequent strong-form decision, such as an injunctive court order, could address democratic shortcomings by putting representative democracy back on track. An injunctive court order must not terminate the political process, as we saw in *Urgenda*. The Dutch courts, in addition to scientific insight, based their ruling on existing legal principles and drew a line between declaring the law and intervening on the political level. The court did not specify how to implement the legal GHG reduction target of 25%, which is a political question, whereas interpreting and declaring the law are legal questions.

It appears that climate-relevant rights have become increasingly relevant in climate-based judicial review. The claim is that such rights could be constitutional essentials and prerequisites for democracy.[30] In protecting climate rights, courts could enhance the rule of law and the respectworthiness of the democratic system. In return, failing to address climate-relevant rights could be perceived as unworthy and unreasonable.

*Prima facie* weak forms of judicial review permit courts to intervene in climate matters because their flexible stance allows for reasonable disagreement and safeguards substantive rights, as seen in *Neubauer*. Suppose the constitution is silent about climate-based rights and climate protection obligations. In that case, a court laying down a broad standard does not disproportionately interfere with the government, as the political branches remain responsible for defining the specific content and its subsequent implications.

The dynamic approach to climate-based judicial review permits a departure from the systematic dismissal of climate protection cases at the pre-trial stage. It is a compromise between a rigid separation of powers approach and

29 Michelman Frank; *Brennan and Democracy;* page 75.

30 Burgers Laura; *Should Judges Make Climate Change Law?;* page 56.

judicial supremacy, enabling the judicial branch to fulfil its controlling function while preserving a significant degree of political autonomy. More vigorous forms of court intervention may be required in cases of manifest wrongdoing or unreasonable political inertia.

# General Conclusion

Our analysis of climate protection judicial review shows that people are increasingly concerned about their governments' climate policies and have challenged them in court. These complaints place the judicial branch in a difficult position for two main reasons: (1) Constitutional texts may be silent on climate rights and obligations, and (2) Court rules and procedures are often unsuitable for climate protection cases.

Under these circumstances, courts that deem it necessary to act may well need to innovate and depart from current court practices or precedents. The diffuse and delayed effects of anthropogenic GHG emissions test our traditional understanding of state sovereignty, political responsibility, the separation of powers, and the role of courts. For instance, it is difficult to determine whose fault or neglect directly caused the alleged harm to the climate. Climate effects are delayed, meaning that today's harms are linked to past GHG emissions. Some harms are common to humanity and not specific to any particular group or individual. Future populations in distant regions may suffer the harms of our current climate policies, as GHG emissions persist in the atmosphere for prolonged periods. Who can eventually be held responsible for global warming when there is a lack of direct causality because the causal links are so diffuse? The harms of the current ineffective stance on climate protection may not yet be apparent or ascertainable, and today's decision-makers might no longer be available when they occur.

In other words, climate protection hinges on states' precautionary measures to prevent future harm. We are, therefore, principally dealing with the state's positive obligations to safeguard rights and liberties. Climate rights and public trust obligations are thus future-oriented as well. The potential benefits of our current protection efforts lie ahead as well.

In our assessment of climate protection lawsuits and court decisions, we identified two main tendencies in judicial review.

In the U.S., federal courts have generally avoided counter-majoritarian difficulties by steering clear of substantive climate protection questions and dismissing cases on standing grounds, as the redressability prong often entails political questions. In *Juliana,* the leading federal court climate protection case, the government has successfully prevented the case from reaching the trial stage. However, we have also noticed that an increasing number of judges are issuing dissenting opinions in favour of climate petitions. At the state level, the trend shifted from dismissing cases for lack of standing at the preliminary

 | HTTPS://DOI.ORG/10.1163/9789004771710-017

stage to admitting them to trial, culminating in the first ruling on the merits in *Held v. Montana*.

In Europe, the courts have so far been more proactive. They have shown a greater willingness to admit climate protection cases to the trial stage and issue decisions on the merits. An explanation for this more active stance could be their more limited internal discretion. EU Member States have endorsed the UN's climate protection instruments, and the EU, as an international organisation, has emerged as a leader in climate protection. They are also signatories to the European Convention on Human Rights, another significant source of climate rights that they would need to consider binding. The *ICJ*'s advisory opinion further confirmed states' obligations in the context of climate matters.

The climate protection lawsuits that we previously discussed have already triggered new judicial developments in several fields:

First, regarding state sovereignty, the U.S. Supreme Court softened its standing criteria by granting *parens patriae* standing to the federated states in *Massachusetts v. EPA*. As quasi-sovereign entities, they would deserve privileged access to federal courts. In Germany, courts even granted standing to people from Bangladesh and Nepal in *Neubauer*. In *Luciano Lliuya v. RWE*, the Oberlandesgericht in Hamm, Germany, accepted the lawsuit of the Peruvian plaintiff, Saúl Luciano Lliuya, against the German energy company RWE for its share in global GHG emissions. Although the plaintiff ultimately did not prevail because the probability of damage occurring within the next thirty years was considered to be too low, this case nevertheless established that large GHG emitters can be held liable under German law for the damage they cause, even when such harm arises in the long term, over a great distance, and result from GHG emissions that are themselves lawful. The *ICJ* advisory opinion on the obligations of States in respect of Climate Change outlined the states' climate related obligations, thereby further limiting the discretion of individual states.

Second, regarding the political transparency of projected state measures, judicial promotion of participatory rights has led to more detailed climate recovery plans and stronger climate protection measures. *Neubauer* and *Friends of the Irish Environment* were exemplary in this regard.

Third, we have also noticed a greater willingness to engage in substantive judicial review in European jurisdictions. EU member state courts were not averse to considering people's substantive rights and positive state duties in their rulings. Even before the ECtHR ruled on the climate dimension of Articles 2 and 8, some EU states had already held, domestically, that both apply to climate protection and had even declared their violation. A similar tendency is evident in the United States as well. A case in point is *Juliana v. United States*.

Although the case did not proceed to trial, District Judge Ann Akin declared at the pre-trial stage that there is a federal *right to a climate system capable of sustaining human life*.

Fourth, regarding extraordinary measures, we observed that the Irish Supreme Court granted a *leapfrog appeal* in the Friends of the Irish Environment case. During the pre-trial proceedings *in Duarte Agostinho and Others v. Portugal and Others*, the Fourth Section of the ECtHR directly admitted the case, granting a fast-track procedure that bypassed national court proceedings. It also allowed the petitioners to litigate against 32 other states. Later, the Plenary of the ECtHR nevertheless dismissed the case, ruling that it did not intend to extend extraterritorial jurisdiction as requested by the applicants. It also held that the complaint against Portugal was inadmissible for non-exhaustion of domestic remedies, citing the available remedies within the domestic system.[1]

Even though some of the court decisions we analysed appear to be activist, the courts arguably avoided judicial supremacy by limiting themselves to outlining constitutional and human rights risks, promoting good politics, and upholding the rule of law. They have guided the political branches without overly interfering with their prerogatives to balance interests as they deem fit.

Despite their substantive historical GHG emissions, developed states have generally not served as prime examples of effective climate protection. Their inadequate climate protection records have brought judicial review to the centre of people's attention. The increasing number of lawsuits entering court dockets worldwide prompted a search for a benchmark for reasonable court intervention in climate matters that squares with fundamental principles of democracy.

We distinguished between two rival ideals of democracy: the ideal of self-government, or government by laws of the people, and the ideal of government bound by law.

The ideal of self-government by laws enacted by the people limits judicial review primarily to procedural due process. Due to the inherent political questions involved in climate change cases, a court adhering to this ideal would grant extensive political discretion and exercise judicial self-restraint. Judicial self-restraint can hinder climate protection measures, typically by preventing cases from reaching the trial stage.

The democratic ideal of government bound by law, on the other hand, grants courts greater leeway. It encourages judges to protect substantive con-

1 ECtHR, *Duarte Agostinho and Others v. Portugal and Others*, Application no. 39371/20; 09.04.2024.

stitutional essentials beyond just the procedural constitutional validity of political decisions. However, this encouragement raises counter-majoritarian difficulties. An authoritative court interpretation of the constitution can potentially bind the political branches of government over time, which could be perceived as a form of judicial supremacy. Similarly, a court order that overrides political decisions also raises counter-majoritarian concerns.

Once a climate case reaches the trial stage, the debate over whether to pursue procedural or substantive climate-based judicial review intensifies. Procedural judicial review, which aims to render participatory rights effective, is less controversial than substantive judicial review. Courts conducting climate-based procedural judicial review in this manner essentially verify whether the political decision-maker adequately assessed and considered climate impacts before making a climate-relevant decision. They may also require the political branches to specify how they plan to address the climate crisis over time. The effect of this kind of requirement on the political process is significant, but it is not easily accusable of interfering with the process.

Therefore, procedural due process aimed at enforcing participatory rights is essential and may lead to satisfactory results in some cases. It may nevertheless not suffice in others where substantive review is the only remedy against manifest abuse of political discretion. In climate protection, this substantive due process approach may, despite the counter-majoritarian risks, necessitate a living-instrument approach, thereby widening the scope of constitutional rights and obligations. Acknowledging the risks to the separation of powers, we turned to the doctrinal debate about the judicial enforcement of socioeconomic rights to illuminate the dangers of substantive review and to show how these risks can be mitigated.

We referred to Frank Michelman's "*experimentalist*" model of judicial review, which allows courts to intervene in socioeconomic matters while limiting themselves to declaring a broad standard and leaving the detailed definition to political discourse. In this way, courts can promote socioeconomic rights on a case-by-case basis. Some cases might eventually require a more assertive judicial stance. Therefore, Michelman's "*experimentalist*" model of judicial review can be considered a dynamic approach that allows for shifting between weaker and firmer court postures.

We then turned to Mark Tushnet's views on strong and weak judicial stances. Stronger court stances could be taken on less contested first-class rights, while weaker postures could be adopted for more controversial rights. Tushnet eventually concluded that weak-form judicial review might be the most appropriate approach for all generations of rights. In a liberal democratic system with an entrenched constitution, weak-form judicial review fosters political discourse and alleviates counter-majoritarian concerns, whereas a strong stance does the opposite. A strong form of judicial review substitutes political decisions and binds the political actors for a long time.

Acknowledging that an unhealthy climate potentially affects all three generations of rights, a dynamic judicial review approach could enable courts to address climate rights and public trust obligations in a reasonable and respectful manner. Through *prima facie* weak forms of judicial review, the court could intervene while still respecting the political branches' authority to define climate rights and determine their implications.

In response to the debate over court activism and judicial self-restraint, we argued that admitting a climate protection case to the trial stage need not, *per se*, violate the separation of powers. It could even promote the democratic project. The systematic dismissal of climate protection lawsuits at the pre-trial stage could render the system unreasonable and subject claimants to lengthy and costly proceedings, potentially impeding access to justice.

We stressed the importance of an appropriate "*dose*" of court activism and the right form of judgment. We showed that even more contentious climate cases, which recognise substantive climate rights and atmospheric public trust obligations, can be reconciled with the fundamental principle of democracy if courts intervene with a relatively weak stance, as Frank Michelman and Mark Tushnet describe in the context of socioeconomic rights.

We also argued that through *prima facie* weak form decisions, courts could effectively address the state's positive climate protection obligations and the questions about climate-based rights. Declaratory judgments outlining the risks and highlighting the state obligations could suffice as an impetus for more ambitious policies. This approach is not counter-majoritarian, as the court does not dictate policy but exercises its controlling function, throwing the ball back to the political branches to decide on an adequate response to the court's decision, thereby rendering them accountable to the public.

We showed that even a first injunctive court order grounded in law need not be unreasonable or end the discursive political process if the court continues to respect political discretion, as the Dutch Supreme Court did in *Urgenda and the ECtHR did in KlimaSeniorinnen.*

Time will show whether and when courts would need to shift to more assertive forms of judicial review, or whether the cooperation between powers that should result from our proposed benchmark in climate-based judicial review will be able to establish a respectable discourse among state branches for the sake of sustaining democracy and the democratic essentials throughout the climate crisis. Be it as it may, we nevertheless conclude that the cooperation of powers of the kind proposed in this work could accelerate climate protection. The collaboration of powers established through *prima facie* weak forms of judicial review could be a workable compromise in which courts navigate between the democratic ideal of self-government by the people and the ideal of government bound by law without completely neglecting either.

Climate litigation has given young people a voice and has prompted some states to implement stronger climate protection measures. These follow-up decisions are significant for the future of our rights and freedoms, underscoring the importance of climate litigation. They further encourage the conclusion that the framework for court intervention in climate matters proposed in this research can strengthen rather than undermine democracy.

In Europe, important court rulings on GHG regulation have already been issued in several cases. Also, the ECtHR's *KlimaSeniorinnen* ruling again shows that climate litigation can achieve significant outcomes.

In the United States, the federal courts' stance remains a significant obstacle for climate-related judicial review, as illustrated by cases such as *Juliana* or *Lighthiser v. Trump*. To date, there is still no federally mandated climate protection plan, nor has any federal court definitely recognised a constitutional right to a climate system capable of sustaining human life. At the same time, the Trump administration has continued to promote fossil-fuel development and restrict energy transition and climate measures. EPA's withdrawal of the endangerment finding for carbon dioxide under the Clean Air Act prompted a new youth-led climate petition seeking judicial review (*Venner v. EPA*). Defendants in youth-led climate cases have thus far succeeded these actions from proceeding to the trial stage. By contrast, some state courts have issued rulings on the merits. Although based on state constitutions, these rulings may nonetheless influence future developments at the federal level.

Everything considered, we can reasonably conclude that the cumulative effect of significant U.S. state court rulings, rulings of the EU State Courts, the recent ruling of the ECtHR and the ICJ advisory opinion on the obligations of States in respect of Climate Change may well be pointing to a future in which courts will more regularly allow climate cases to go to trial on the merits. The cooperation of powers approach to judicial review, proposed in this work, shows that this development need not raise counter-majoritarian concerns. Sticking to what we call the cooperation of powers can preserve political discretion while still promoting our rights and liberties.

# Acknowledgements

## Support of Extraordinary People

Without the ongoing support of several significant and cherished people, this book would not have been possible. This work originates from a part-time PhD project that I pursued on a self-funded basis. It has been a long journey, from returning to school to finish the *bachalauréat* to doing the bachelor's degree in law and the master's degree in European economic and financial criminal law at the University of Luxembourg, to completing the Cours Complémentaires en Droit Luxembourgeois and eventually starting a PhD in law while working full-time. Conducting the PhD research as a part-time doctoral candidate consumed much of my free time and time with my family. Days were long, and nights were short. Pursuing my scholarly work presupposed their comprehension and acceptance over the last six years.

I would like to thank all the lecturers, thinkers, jurists, judges, philosophers, and colleagues with whom I have had the opportunity to discuss and exchange my thoughts.

I am profoundly grateful to Professor Van der Walt for welcoming me as a part-time PhD candidate and for accompanying me throughout this scholarly journey. Please allow me to refer to the *Goldilocks problem* once again. Prof. Van der Walt could strike a fair balance between granting me too much and insufficient leeway. I could work on my research in a climate of mutual trust and civility, which required confidence in my skills and myself. In the final phase of my PhD, Prof. Van der Walt offered valuable advice on refining the text and fixing language and style issues. Thank you for your advice and guidance.

The guidance of my CET committee, consisting of Prof. Séverine Ménétrey, Prof. David Hiez, and Prof. Van der Walt, was crucial in shaping the main focus of my research. Each CET meeting kept me on course and provided helpful guidance, which was vital for a self-funded PhD candidate writing a thesis outside the university's premises.

I also thank my defence jury, comprising Prof. Johan VAN DER WALT, Prof. David HIEZ, Prof. Séverine MENETREY, Prof. Hans LINDAHL, and Prof. Oliver GERSTENBERG, who challenged my ideas with inspiring questions.

I wish to express my sincere gratitude to Mr Francis Delaporte, President of the Luxembourg Administrative Court (Cour administrative) and Deputy President of the Luxembourg Constitutional Court. Mr Delaporte kindly inv-

 | HTTPS://DOI.ORG/10.1163/9789004771710-018

ited me to discuss and present my findings, and our conversations were truly inspiring.

Lastly, but equally important, I wish to express my sincere gratitude to Koninklijke Brill BV for accepting my work for publication. I am also thankful to Selma Hoedt, whose exchanges I greatly valued.

From the early stages of writing, I aimed to make it accessible to a broader audience. I did not write for the jury but for the general public. When I began the PhD project, my goal was to contribute meaningfully to a highly important subject. Thank you to Koninklijke Brill BV for making this possible.

## Valuable Tools and Databases

For this work, I used *Zotero* for my references and Grammarly for proofreading. Together, these tools significantly improved the efficiency of my writing and review process.

Regarding databases for case selection, I used the following five: *ClimateCaseChart* was the most frequently used. It results from a joint project between the Sabin Centre for Climate Change Law at Columbia Law School and the law firm Arnold & Porter[1]. The second database I have been using is the website of the NGO *Our Children's Trust*, which supports legal youth actions worldwide. This website provides information on youth-driven climate cases.[2] The Environmental Law Association Worldwide (*ELAW*) runs the third database. It updates petitions and court rulings on the full range of environmental litigation.[3] *Ecolex*, the fourth database, offers information services on environmental law. It is operated jointly by the Food and Agriculture Organisation (*FAO*), the International Union for Conservation of Nature (*IUCN*), and the United Nations Environment Programme (*UNEP*).[4] Finally, cases from the Indiankanoon database have also been accessed.[5] This database is essential for our inquiry, given the widespread perception of the Indian Supreme Court as activist and progressive.

I started by selecting climate change–related cases from the *ELAW* website, focusing on the most recent ones and then moving backwards in reverse-chronological order. I looked for a more comprehensive database for two

1 Climatecasechart: https://www.climatecasechart.com <11.10.2021>.

2 Ourchildrenstrust: https://www.ourchildrenstrust.org/global-legal-actions >.

3 Environmental Law Association: https://www.elaw.org/notablecases <11.10.2021>.

4 Ecolex: https://www.ecolex.org <11.10.2021>.

5 Indiankanoon: https://indiankanoon.org <11.10.2021>.

reasons: first, to reduce selection bias caused by ELAW's preselection of cases; and second, to gain a fuller understanding of the many climate-related cases. I found the *ClimateCaseChart* website, which provides a detailed, up-to-date database of climate litigation. Research in these databases showed that youth petitioners were involved in a large number of cases, leading to the discovery of the NGO Our Children's Trust (*Youth v. Gov*) database and the notable youth climate cases it has brought to court. Another observation was that cases could be categorised as either reducing GHG emissions or protecting and enhancing carbon sinks. Finally, and crucially, since human rights and specific climate rights underpin most climate cases, I began exploring human rights cases in both national and international contexts.

# References

## Bibliography


Ackerman Bruce; *Good-bye, Montesquieu in* Rose-Ackerman Susan and Lindseth Peter; *Comparative Administrative Law;* Research Handbooks in Comparative Law series (Edward Elgar Publishing, 25.08.2017).

Ackerman Bruce; *The Storrs Lectures: Discovering the Constitution;* The Yale Law Journal 93, No. 6 (May 1984); 1013; https://doi.org/10.2307/796204.

Adams Sam; Earth Journalism Network; *A Way Forward: Agreements Reached in Cancun*; 10.12.2010; https://earthjournalism.net/stories/a-way-forward-agreements-reached-in-cancun. <07.01.2024>.

Anton Don; *Is the Environment a Human Rights Issue?;* SSRN Scholarly Paper, Rochester, Social Science Research Network, 29.04.2008; https://papers.ssrn.com/abstract=1126470.

Anton Don and Shelton Dinah; *Problems in Environmental Protection and Human Rights: A Human Right to the Environment*; SSRN Scholarly Paper. Rochester, NY, Social Science Research Network, 26.06.2011; https://papers.ssrn.com/abstract=1872937.

AP News; *Germany pledges to adjust climate law after the court verdict;* 30.04.2021; https://apnews.com/article/germany-europe-climate-climate-change-environment-and-nature-191b8ffca5ba6994ebd402b04432e6c8.

Ballotpedia; Arbitrary-or-Capricious Test; https://ballotpedia.org/Arbitrary-or-capricious_test, <29092021>.

Bellinger Nate and Howell Isak; Oral Arguments Held in Virginia Youth Climate Case; Youth to Appeal Decision; Our Children's Trust <16.09.2022>.

Benvindo Juliano Zaiden; *On the Limits of Constitutional Adjudication: Deconstructing Balancing and Judicial Activism* (Heidelberg, Springer, 2010). https://doi.org/10.1007/978-3-642-11434-2.

Bickel Alexander; *The Least Dangerous Branch: The Supreme Court at the Bar of Politics*; 2nd Edition (New Haven, Yale Univ. Press, 1986).

Bingham Tom; *The Rule of Law*, Reprint Edition (London, Penguin, 2011).

Blumm Michael and Wood Mary Christina; *The Public Trust Doctrine in Environmental and Natural Resources Law;* 3rd edition (Durham, Carolina Academic Press, 2021).

Boyd David; *The environmental rights revolution: a global study of constitutions, human rights, and the environment*; Law and Society series. (Vancouver, UBC Press, 2012).

Brennan Jason; *Against Democracy*; (Princeton Oxford, Princeton University Press, 2017).


 | HTTPS://DOI.ORG/10.1163/9789004771710-019

Brown Wendy; *Walled states, waning sovereignty;* (New York, Zone Books, 2017).

Broswimmer Franz; *Ecocide: a short history of mass extinction of species.* (London, Pluto Press, 2002).

Bulloch Penelope, Raz Joseph and Hart. H. L. A.; *The Concept of Law;* Second Edition (Oxford, Oxford University Press, 1997).

Burgers Laura and Staal Tim; *Climate Action as Positive Human Rights Obligation: The Appeals Judgment in Urgenda v The Netherlands;* SSRN Scholarly Paper; Rochester, NY; Social Science Research Network; 11.01.2019; https://papers.ssrn.com/abstract=3314008.

Burgers Laura; *Should Judges Make Climate Change Law?;* Transnational Environmental Law 9, No. 1 (March 2020); 55–75; https://doi.org/10.1017/S2047102519000360.

Cabanes Valérie; *Un nouveau droit pour la Terre: pour en finir avec l'écocide;* Anthropocène Seuil; (Paris, Éditions du Seuil, 2016).

Carson, Rachel, Shackleton, Julian Huxley, and Lear Linda; *Silent Spring*; Reprinted; (London: Penguin, 2000).

Castagno Davide; *Challenging Legal Standing in Climate Change Litigation: A Comparative Approach to the Italian Case 'Giudizio Universale*; International Journal of Procedural Law 14, No 1; (5 September 2024); 47–72.

Center for International Environmental Law; *2008 International Environmental Law Award Recipient – Antonio A. Oposa Jr.*; https://www.ciel.org <08.01.2022>.

Colby Heather, Ebbersmeyer Ana Stella, Heim Lisa Marie, and Røssaak Kielland Marthe; *Judging Climate Change: The Role of the Judiciary in the Fight against Climate Change;* Oslo Law Review 7, No. 3 (17 December 2020); 168–185.

Collier Ute, Löfstedt Ragnar; *Cases in Climate Change Policy: Political Reality in the European Union*; (London, Routledge, 1997).

Council of Europe; *Manual on Human Rights and the Environment;* 2nd edition; (Strasbourg, Council of Europe Publishing, 2012).

Derrida Jacques; *Gesetzeskraft: Der mystische Grund der Autorität*; Translated by Düttmann Alexander García; (Frankfurt am Main, Suhrkamp Verlag, 1991).

Deutscher Bundestag; Gesetzentwurf der Bundesregierung, Entwurf eines Ersten Gesetzes zur Änderung des Bundes-Klimaschutzgesetzes, Drucksache 19/30230; 02.06.2021; https://dserver.bundestag.de/btd/19/302/1930230.pdf.

Deutscher Bundestag; Amendment KSG; Drucksache 30949, 22.06.2021; https://dserver.bundestag.de/btd/19/309/1930949.pdf.

Diamond Jared; *Collapse: How Societies Choose to Fail or Survive* (New York, Penguin Books, 2011).

Dixon Rosalind; *Creating Dialogue about Socioeconomic Rights: Strong-Form versus Weak-Form Judicial Review Revisited*; International Journal of Constitutional Law 5, No. 3 (2007); 391–418.

Ely John Hart; *Democracy and Distrust: A Theory of Judicial Review*; (Cambridge, Harvard Univ. Press, 1980).

Environmental Protection Agency; *The Clean Air Act – Highlights of the 1990 Amendments*; o. J.; https://www.epa.gov.

Epp Charles; *The Rights Revolution: Lawyers, Activists, and Supreme Courts in Comparative Perspective*; Illustrated Edition, (Chicago, University of Chicago Press, 1998).

Federal Ministry of Justice and the Federal Office of Justice; Basic Law for the Federal Republic of Germany, https://www.gesetze-im-internet.de/englisch_gg/englisch_gg.pdf

Felli Romain; *La grande adaptation: climat, capitalisme et catastrophe;* Anthropocène Seuil; (Paris, Éditions du Seuil, 2016).

Freeman Jody and Vermeule Adrian; *Massachusetts v EPA: From Politics to Expertise,* Supreme Court Review (2007); 51–110.

Friedman Barry; *The History of the Counter-majoritarian Difficulty, Part One*; The Road to Judicial Supremacy; NYU Law Review 73, Number 2 (May 1998); 333–433.

Fritsch Matthias; *Taking Turns: Democracy to Come and Intergenerational Justice*; Derrida Today 4, no. 2; (November 2011); 148–72; https://doi.org/10.3366/drt.2011.0015.

Fritsch Matthias; *Taking Turns with the Earth: Phenomenology, Deconstruction, and Intergenerational Justice*; (Stanford California, Stanford University Press, 2018).

Fuller Lon and Winston Kenneth; *The Forms and Limits of Adjudication*; Harvard Law Review, Dec. 1978, Vol. 92, No. 2 (Dec. 1978); pp. 353–409.

Geel Oliver; *Urgenda and Beyond: The past, present and future of climate change public interest litigation,* Maastricht University Journal of Sustainability Studies, Vol. 3; (01.07.2017).

Gelbspan Ross; *The Heat Is On: The Climate Crisis, The Cover-up, The Prescription*; updated Edition; (Basic Books, 1998).

Gerstenberg Oliver; *Negative/positive constitutionalism, "fair balance," and the problem of justiciability;* International Journal of Constitutional Law, Volume 10, Issue 4, (October 2012); Pages 904–925.

Gerstenberg Oliver; *The constitution as a law of lawmaking: Comments on Frank Michelman's Constitutional Essentials*; Philosophy & Social Criticism, 50(7); (September 2024);1014–1022.

Glicksman Robert, Daniel Kim and Keziah Groth-Tuft; *Judicial Review of Scientific Uncertainty in Climate Change Lawsuits: Deferential and Nondeferential Evaluation of Agency Factual and Policy Determinations*; 2022.

Gore Albert; *Earth in the Balance: Forging a New Common Purpose*; (London, Earthscan, 2008).

Gore Albert; *An Inconvenient Truth: The Planetary Emergency of Global Warming and What We Can Do About It*; Book Club Ed Edition; (Bloomsbury Publishing PLC, 2006).

Graver Hans Petter; *Judges against Justice: On Judges When the Rule of Law Is Under Attack* (Heidelberg, Springer Berlin Heidelberg, 2015); https://doi.org/10.1007/978-3-662-44293-7.

Grimm Dieter; *Verfassungsgerichtsbarkeit;* (Berlin, Suhrkamp Verlag, 2021).

Grimm Dieter and Cooper Belinda; *Sovereignty: The Origin and Future of a Political and Legal Concept;* Columbia Studies in Political Thought / Political History; (New York, Columbia Univ. Press, 2015).

Habermas Jürgen; *Between Facts and Norms: Contributions to a Discourse Theory of Law and Democracy*; New Edition; (Cambridge, Blackwell Publishers, 1997).

Hamilton Alexander, Madison James, Jay John and Henry Patrick; *The Complete Federalist and Anti-Federalist Papers;* (Independently published, 2020).

Hassan Parvez; *Role of the South in the Development of International Environmental Law*; Chinese Journal of Environmental Law 1, No. 2 (7 February 2017); 133–157; https://doi.org/10.1163/24686042-12340011.

Heuschling Luc; *État de droit, Rechtsstaat, Rule of law* ; (Paris: Dalloz, 2002).

Higgins Polly; *Earth Is Our Business: Changing the Rules of the Game*; (Shepheard-Walwyn, 2012).

Higgins Polly; *Eradicating ecocide: laws and governance to prevent the destruction of our planet;* 2nd edition; (London, Shepheard-Walwyn, 2015).

Hirschl Ran; *Towards Juristocracy: The Origins and Consequences of the New Constitutionalism*; (Cambridge London, Harvard University Press, 2007).

Hirschl Ran; *The New Constitution and the Judicialization of Pure Politics Worldwide*; Fordham Law Review Vol. 75, Issue 2, Article 14 (2006).

Hussain Faquir; *Public Interest Litigation in Pakistan;* Sustainable Development Policy Institute, Work Paper Series, 5; (1993).

Intergovernmental Panel on Climate Change; *6th Assessment report*; 2023: https://www.ipcc.ch/report/ar6/syr/ <01.08.2023>.

International Court of Justice; Advisory Opinion on the obligations of States in respect of Climate Change; General List No. 187; 23.07.2025.

Ireland; Department of the Environment, Climate and Communications; (Department of the Taoiseach); *Climate action plan 2021*; https://www.gov.ie/en/publication/6223e-climate-action-plan-2021.

Kagan Robert, Cartwright Bliss, Friedman Lawrence and Wheeler Stanton; *The Evolution of State Supreme Courts;* Michigan Law Review 76, No. 6; (May 1978); https://doi.org/10.2307/1287860.

Kaplan David; *The Most Dangerous Branch: Inside the Supreme Court's Assault on the Constitution*; (New York, Crown, 2018).

Kelsen Hans and Zeleny Klaus; *Vom Wesen und Wert der Demokratie*; (Ditzingen, Reclam, 2018).

Kennedy Jr. Robert; *Crimes against Nature: How George W. Bush and His Corporate Pals Are Plundering the Country and Hijacking Our Democracy*; New title Edition; (New York, Harper, 2004).

Kmiec Keenan; *The Origin and Current Meanings of Judicial Activism;* California Law Review 92, No. 5; (2004); 1441–1477. https://doi.org/10.2307/3481421.

Kuh Katrina Fischer*; The Legitimacy of Judicial Climate Engagement*; Ecology Law Quarterly 63; (2019).

Le Moult Craig; "*Mass. Officials, Environmentalists Criticise EPA's Revocation of Scientific Finding*"; GBH News; 12.02.2026; https://www.wgbh.org/news/local/2026-02-12/mass-officials-environmentalists-criticize-epas-revocation-of-scientific-finding; <16.02.2026>.

Landau David; *A Dynamic Theory of Judicial Role*; 55 B.C. L. REV. 1501; (2014).

Laramée de Tannenberg Valéry; *Le changement climatique: menace pour la démocratie?;* Collection Dans le vif; (Paris, Buchet-Chastel, 2017).

Laski, Gregory; *Untimely Democracy: The Politics of Progress After Slavery*; (Oxford University Press Inc, 2021).

Lazarus Richard; *The Rule of Five: Making Climate History at the Supreme Court;* (Cambridge, Massachusetts, Belknap Press, 2020).

Legal Information Institute; „*Nondelegation Doctrine*"; https://www.law.cornell.edu/wex/nondelegation_doctrine.

Levitsky Steven and Ziblatt Daniel; *How Democracies Die*; First edition; (New York, Broadway Books, 2019).

Lomborg Bjorn; *False Alarm: How Climate Change Panic Costs Us Trillions, Hurts the Poor, and Fails to Fix the Planet*; Reprint Edition; (New York, Basic Books, 2021).

Luhmann Niklas; *Gibt es in unserer Gesellschaft noch unverzichtbare Normen?;* Heidelberger Universitätsreden; (Heidelberg, Müller Jurist. Verlag, 1993).

MacLean Nancy; *Democracy in Chains: The Deep History of the Radical Right's Stealth Plan for America*; (Melbourne London, Scribe, 2017).

Maslin Mark; *Climate change: a very short introduction;* Third edition; (Oxford, Oxford University Press, 2014).

Meltz Robert; *Climate Change Litigation: A Growing Phenomenon*; (Bibliogov, 2013).

Meltz Robert; Federal Agency Actions Following the Supreme Court's Climate Change Decision in *Massachusetts v. EPA: A Chronology*; Congressional Research Service Report; 09.01.2014.

Michelman Frank; *Constitutional Authorship by the People*; Notre Dame Law Review 74; (1999), 1605.

Michelman Frank; *Dilemmas of Belonging: Moral Truth, Human Rights, and Why We Might Not Want a Representative Judiciary*; UCLA Law Review 47, No. 5; (2000 1999); 1221–1252.

Michelman Frank; *IDA's Way: Constructing the Respect-Worthy Governmental System*; 72 Fordham Law Review; (2003).

Michelman Frank; *Constitutional Legitimation for Political Acts;* The Modern Law Review 66; (2003).

Michelman Frank; *Brennan and Democracy;* Revised Edition (Princeton University Press, 2005).

Michelman Frank; *Legitimacy, The Social Turn and Constitutional Review: What Political Liberalism Suggests;* Kritische Vierteljahresschrift Für Gesetzgebung Und Rechtswissenschaft 98, No. 3 (2015); 183–205; https://doi.org/10.5771/2193-7869-2015-3-183.

Michelman Frank; *Human Rights and Constitutional Rights: A Proceduralizing Function for Substantive Constitutional Law?*; Human Rights, Democracy, and Legitimacy in a World of Disorder; Gerald L. Neuman and Silja Voeneky; 73–96. (Cambridge; Cambridge University Press; 2018).

Michelman Frank; *Constitutional Essentials: On the Constitutional Theory of Political Liberalism*; (New York, Oxford University Press, 2022).

Möllers Christoph; *Die drei Gewalten: Legitimation der Gewaltengliederung in Verfassungsstaat, Europäischer Integration und Internationalisierung;* (Weilerswist, Velbrück Wissenschaft, 2008).

Moules Richard; *Environmental Judicial Review*; (Oxford , Hart Publishing, 2011).

Mourtada-Sabbah Nada; *The Political Question Doctrine and the Supreme Court of the United States*; (Lanham, Lexington Books, 2007).

Napel Hans-Martien and Voermans Wim; *The powers that be: rethinking the separation of powers: a Leiden response to Möllers*; (Leiden, Leiden University Press, 2015).

Neyret Laurent and Delmas-Marty Mireille; *Des écocrimes à l'écocide: le droit pénal au secours de l'environnement;* Droit(s) et développement durable; (Bruxelles, Bruylant, 2015).

Our children's Trust; *Action Alert: Save America's Climate Case!*; 27.02.2024.

Our children's Trust; *Venner v. EPA*; https://www.ourchildrenstrust.org/venner-v-epa <26.02.2026>.

Paid to Pollute campaign (UK); *This year, Paid To Pollute will leave the courtroom and take to the streets*; 23.02.2022; https://paidtopollute.org.uk/news/next-steps/; <03.07.2022>.

Peel Jacqueline and Osofsky Hari; *A Rights Turn in Climate Change Litigation?;* Symposium: Rights-Based Approaches to Climate Change; Transnational Environmental Law 7, No. 1 (March 2018); 37–67; published online by Cambridge University Press; 29.12.2017; https://doi.org/10.1017/S2047102517000292.

Posner Eric; *Climate Change and International Human Rights Litigation: A Critical Appraisal*; University of Chicago Law & Economics; Olin Working Paper No. 329; University of Chicago, Public Law Working Paper No. 148; (January 2007).

Pottier Antonin and Gaël Giraud; *Comment les économistes réchauffent la planète*; Anthropocène; (Paris, Éditions du Seuil, 2016).

Pulliam Mark; *Unleashing The "Least Dangerous" Branch: Quis Custodiet Ipsos Custodes?;* Texas Review of Law & Politics, vol. 22, no. 3; 2018; pages 423–468.

Radbruch Gustav; *Statutory Lawlessness and Supra-Statutory Law (1946)*; *Oxford Journal of Legal Studies* 26, No. 1; (Spring 2006); 1–11; https://doi.org/10.1093/ojls/gqi041.

Rawls John; *A Theory of Justice*;. (Cambridge, Belknap Press, 2005).

Rawls John; *Political Liberalism*; (New York; Columbia University Press, 2005).

Rawls John; *The Law of Peoples*; (Cambridge, Harvard University Press, 1999).

Rifkin Jeremy; *The Zero Marginal Cost Society: The Internet of Things, the Collaborative Commons, and the Eclipse of Capitalism*; (New York, Palgrave Macmillan, 2015).

Rochfeld Judith; *Justice pour le climat: Les nouvelles formes de mobilisation citoyenne;* (Paris, Jacob, 2019).

Ropivia Marc-Louis; *Manuel d'épistémologie de la géographie: écocide et déterminisme anthropique*; (Paris, L'Harmattan, 2007).

Rosenberg Gerald; *The Hollow Hope: Can Courts Bring About Social Change?*; (Chicago, University of Chicago Press, 1991).

Rousseau Jean-Jacques, Tozer Henry John, and Matavers Derek; *The Social Contract or Principles of Political Right*; (Hertfordshire, Wordsworth, 1998).

Runciman David; *How Democracy Ends*; (London, Profile Books, 2019).

Schrijver Nico and Weiss Friedl; *International law and sustainable development: principles and practice;* Developments in international law; (Boston, Martinus Nijhoff Publishers, 2004).

Shaw Carlita; *The Silent Ecocide: The Environmental Crisis Is a Crisis of Human Consciousness*; (CreateSpace Independent Publishing Platform, 2015).

Shellenberger Michael and Nordhaus Ted; *Break Through: From the Death of Environmentalism to the Politics of Possibility;* First Printing Edition; (Houghton Mifflin Harcourt, 2007).

Smith Don; *Held v Montana: the beginning of a climate change lawsuit trend in US state level courts or a one-shot wonder?;* Journal of Energy & Natural Resources Law, 41:4; (2023); 369–378.

Smith Joel; *Massachusetts v. EPA: A Change of Climate at EPA Clouds the D.C. Circuit's Review of Risk-Based Policy Decisions*; Ecology Law Quarterly 33, No. 3; (2006); 653–74.

Smith Thurman Leonard; *Supreme Damage: Rescuing Representative Government from Judicial Overreach*; (Smithurmann Publishing, 2020).

Spentzou Danai; *Climate Change Litigation as a means to address Intergenerational Equity and Climate Change*; Queen Mary Law Journal 2; (2021); DOI: 10.26494/QMLJ3944.

Speth James Gustave; *The Bridge at the End of the World*; (New Haven, Yale University Press, 2008).

Speth James Gustave; *They Knew: The Federal Government's Fifty-Year Role in Causing the Climate Crisis* (Massachusetts, MIT Press, 2021).

Spier Jaap; *The "Strongest" Climate Ruling Yet: The Dutch Supreme Court's Urgenda Judgment;* Netherlands International Law Review 67, No. 2; (September 2020); 319–91; https://doi.org/10.1007/s40802-020-00172-5.

Stefanelli Justine; *Convention on Access to Information, Public Participation in Decision-Making and Access to Justice in Environmental Matters*; International Legal Materials 38; No. 3; (May 1999); 517–533; https://doi.org/10.1017/S0020782900019203.

Stone Christopher; *Should trees have standing? Law, morality, and the environment;* 3rd edition; (New York, Oxford University Press, 2010).

Sumudu Atapattu and Schapper Andrea; *Human rights and the environment: key issues*, key issues in environment and sustainability; (New York, Routledge, 2019).

Sunstein Cass; *Designing Democracy: What Constitutions Do*; (Oxford, Oxford Univ. Press, 2002).

Tate Neal and Vallinder Torbjorn; *The Global Expansion of Judicial Power;* New Edition (New York, New York University Press, 1997).

The New York Times; T*he White House and the Greenhouse;* 09.05.1989; https://www.nytimes.com/1989/05/09/opinion/the-white-house-and-the-greenhouse.html.

The Seattle Times; Hill Hollis; *Let Youth Have Day in Court over Climate Change*; https://www.seattletimes.com/opinion/let-youth-have-day-in-court-over-climate-change; <01.10.2021>.

The United Nations; *Secretary-General Calls on States to Tackle Climate Change 'Time Bomb' through New Solidarity Pact*, Acceleration Agenda, at Launch of Intergovernmental Panel Report; https://press.un.org/en/2023/sgsm21730.doc.htm <25.03.2023>.

The United Nations; Secretary-General's remarks to High-Level opening of COP27 United Nations Secretary-General; https://www.un.org/sg/en/content/sg/speeches/2022-11-07/secretary-generals-remarks-high-level-opening-of-cop27 <31.03.2023>.

The United Nations; *IPCC Adaptation Report 'a Damning Indictment of Failed Global Leadership on Climate*; https://news.un.org/en/story/2022/02/1112852; <28.02.2022>.

The United Nations; UN Climate Report: *It's 'Now or Never' to Limit Global Warming to 1.5 Degrees*; https://news.un.org/en/story/2022/04/1115452; <04.04.2022>.

The United Nations, OHCR; *Bachelet welcomes top court's landmark decision to protect human rights from climate change;* https://www.ohchr.org/EN/NewsEvents/Pages/DisplayNews.aspx?NewsID=25450&LangID=E; <12.10.2021>.

The United Nations, OHCR, Committee on the Rights of the Child; https://www.ohchr.org/EN/NewsEvents/Pages/DisplayNews.aspx?NewsID=27139&LangID=E; <23.06.2021>.

The United Nations, OHCR, Committee on the Rights of the Child; CRC/C/GC/26; General comment No. 26 (2023) on children's rights and the environment with a special focus on climate change; 22.08.2023; https://www.ohchr.org/en/documents/general-comments-and-recommendations/crccgc26-general-comment-no-26-2023-childrens-rights.

Tushnet Mark; *Weak-Form Judicial Review and Core Civil Liberties Essay;* Harvard Civil Rights-Civil Liberties Law Review 41, No. 1; (2006); 1–22.

Tushnet Mark; *Taking Back the Constitution: Activist Judges and the Next Age of American Law*; (London, Yale University Press, 2020).

Tushnet Mark; *Weak Courts, Strong Rights; Judicial Review and Social Welfare Rights in Comparative Constitutional Law*; (Woodstock, Princeton University Press, 2009).

Urgenda Homepage; https://www.urgenda.nl/en/themas/climate-case/global-climate-litigation; <14.04.2023>.

Van der Vyver Johan; *The Environment: State Sovereignty, Human Rights, and Armed Conflict;* SSRN Scholarly Paper. Rochester, NY: Social Science Research Network; 14.05.2009; https://papers.ssrn.com/abstract=1944200.

Van der Walt Johan; *The horizontal effect revolution and the question of sovereignty;* (Berlin, De Gruyter, 2014).

Van der Walt Johan; *The Concept of Liberal Democratic Law*; (New York, Routledge, 2019).

Verschuuren Jonathan; *Contribution of the Case Law of the European Court of Human Rights to Sustainable Development in Europe*; SSRN Scholarly Paper; Rochester NY; Social Science Research Network; 06.09.2013; https://papers.ssrn.com/abstract=2321663.

Waldron Jeremy; *The Core of the Case against Judicial Review;* The Yale Law Journal 115, No. 6; (2006); 1346–1406; https://doi.org/10.2307/20455656.

Waldron Jeremy; *The Dignity of Legislation*; (New York, Cambridge University Press, 2008).

Whittington Keith; *Repugnant Laws: Judicial Review of Acts of Congress from the Founding to the Present*; Illustrated Edition. (Kansas, Univ. Press of Kansas, 2019).

Wood Mary Christina; *Nature's Trust: Environmental Law For A New Ecological Age* (New York, Cambridge University Press, 2013).

Wood Mary Christina; *On the Eve of Destruction: Courts Confronting the Climate Emergency*; Indiana Law Journal, Volume 97, Issue 1, Article 5; (Winter 2022).

Žatková Sandra and Paľuchová Petra; *ECtHR: Verein KlimaSeniorinnen Schweiz and Others v. Switzerland (Application No. 53600/20, 9 April 2024): Insufficient Measures to Combat Climate Change Resulting in Violation of Human Rights*; Bratislava Law Review 8, Nr. 1; (07 July 2024); 227–244.

Zierler David; *The invention of ecocide: Agent Orange, Vietnam, and the scientists who changed the way we think about the environment*; (Athens, University of Georgia Press, 2011).

## Case Law

### Australia

*Gloucester Resources Limited v. Minister for Planning*, NSWLEC 7; Land and Environment Court; 08.02.2019.

### Bangladesh

*Farooque v. Government of Bangladesh*, WP 891 of 1994; Supreme Court; 15.07.2001; (*"Industrial Pollution Case"*).

### Belgium

*VZW Klimaatzaak v. Kingdom of Belgium and Others*, No. 167, 83, 2015/4585/A; Court of First Instance of Brussels;17.06.2021.

*VZW Klimaatzaak v. Kingdom of Belgium and Others*, 2021/AR/1589, 2022/AR/737 and 2022/AR/891; Court of Appeal of Brussels; 30.11.2023.

### Czech Republic

*Klimatická žaloba ČR v. Czech Republic*, 14A 101/2021 – 248; Municipal Court in Prague; 15.06.2022.

*Klimatická žaloba ČR v. Czech Republic*, 9 As 116/2022; Supreme Administrative Court of the Czech Republic; 20.02.2023.

### Court of Justice of the European Union

*Carvalho and Others v Parliament and Council*; C-565/19; 25.03.2021; (*"The People's Climate Case"*).

*Costa v. Enel*; 6/64; 15.07.1964.

*Sabine von Colson AND Elisabeth Kamann v. North-Rhine Westphalia*, 14/83; 10,.04.1984 (*"Von Colson"*)
*Van Gend & Loos v Netherlands Inland Revenue Administration*, 26/62; 05.02.1963; (*"Van Gend & Loos"*).
*Winner Wetten GmbH v. Bürgermeisterin der Stadt Bergheim*; C-409/06; 08.09.2010; (*"Winner Wetten"*).

## European Court of Human Rights

*Carême v. France*, Application no. 7189/21; 09.04.2024.
*Duarte Agostinho and Others v. Portugal and Others*, Application no. 39371/20; Fourth Section; 13.11.2020.
*Duarte Agostinho and Others v. Portugal and Others*, Application no. 39371/20; 09.04.2024.
*Gäfgen v. Germany*, Application no. 22978/05; 03.06.2010.
*Greenpeace Nordic and others v. Norway*, Application no. 34068/21*; the* case is still pending.
*Jalloh v. Germany*, Application no. 54810/00; 11.07.2006.
*Öneryıldız v. Turkey*, Application no. 48939/99; 30.11.2004.
*Verein KlimaSeniorinnen and others v. Switzerland*, Application no. 53600/20; 09.04.2024.

## France

*Association Les Amis de la Terre France c/ Etat français;* décision N°394254; Council of State; 12.07.2017.
*Association Les Amis de la Terre France et autres c/ Etat français;* décision N° 428409; Council of State; 10.07.2020.
*Commune de Grande Synthe et autre;* décision N° 427301; Council of State; 19.11.2020.
Jugement correctionnel N° 19168000015; Cour d'Appel de Lyon; 26.09.2019. (*"Macron Portrait criminal case"*).

## Germany

*Luciano Lliuya v. RWE*, No. 2 O 285/15; Oberlandesgericht Hamm; 28.05.2025; (*"Huaraz case"*).
*Neubauer, et al. v. Germany*, ECLI:DE:BVerfG:2021:rs20210324. 1bvr265618; Bundesverfassungsgericht; 24.03.2021 (*"Neubauer"*).

## India

*Ridhima Pandey v. Union of India*, Application No. 187 of 2017; National Green Tribunal; 15.01.2019.

*Sudiep Shrivastava v. Union of India, No. 73/2012;* National Green Tribunal; 24.03.2014.

## International Criminal Court

*The Planet against Bolsenaro;* court reference unknown, *filed by AllRise on October 12, 2021; the* case is still pending.

## International Court of Justice

*Advisory Opinion on the obligations of States in respect of Climate Change; General List No. 187; 23.07.2025.*

## Ireland

*Friends of the Irish Environment CLG v. the Government of Ireland, Ireland and the Attorney General*, [2017 No. 793 JR]; High Court, 19.09.2019; ["*Friends of the Irish Environment (2019)*"].

*Friends of the Irish Environment CLG v. the Government of Ireland, Ireland and the Attorney General*, [Appeal No: 205/19]; Supreme Court; 31.07.2020; ["*Friends of the Irish Environment* (2020)"].

*Friends of the Irish Environment v. the Minister for the Environment, Climate and Communications, the Government of Ireland, Ireland and the Attorney General*, [2025] IEHC 61, [H.JR.2023.0000627]; High Court, 07.02.2025; ["*Friends II*"].

## Norway

*Greenpeace Norway v. Government of Norway*, 16-166674TVI-OTIR/06; Oslo District Court, 04.01.2018; ("*People v. Arctic Oil*").

*Natur og Ungdom v. Norway*, 18-060499ASD-BORG/03; Borgarting Court of Appeal; 23.01.2020; ("*People v. Arctic Oil*").

*Greenpeace Nordic Ass'n and Natur og Ungdom v. Ministry of Petroleum and Energy*, 20-051052SIV-HRET; Supreme Court; 22.12.2020 ("*People v. Arctic Oil*").

## Pakistan

*Ashgar Leghari v Federation of Pakistan*, W.P. No. 25501/2015; Lahore High Court; 25/01/2018.

*Maple Leaf Cement Factory Ltd v. Environmental Protection Agency*, Case No: W. P. No.115949/2017; Lahore High Court; 21.12.2017.

*MS. Shehla Zia and others v. Wapda*, PLD 1994 SC 693; Supreme Court; 12.02.1994.

*Sheikh Asim Farooq v. Federation of Pakistan*, W.P. No. 192069 of 2018; Lahore High Court; 03.08.2019.

## South Africa

*Earthlife Africa Johannesburg v. Minister of Environmental Affairs and others*, Case no. 65662/16 (2017); High Court in Pretoria; 06.02.2017 &19.11.2020; (*"Thabametsi Power Project case"*)

## The Netherlands

*Greenpeace Netherlands v. State of the Netherlands*, C/09/600364 / KG ZA 20-933, ECLI:NL:RBDHA:2020:12440; The Hague District Court; 12.09.2020.

*Greenpeace Netherlands and eight citizens of Bonaire v.State of the Netherlands;* C/09/659832 / HA ZA 24-53 (ENG); the Hague District Court (Rechtbank Den Haag); 28.01.2026.

*Milieudefensie et al. v. Royal Dutch Shell plc;* C/09/571932 / HA ZA 19-379, ECLI:NL:RBDHA:2021:5339; The Hague District Court (Rechtbank Den Haag); 26.05.2021.

*Milieudefensie et al. v. Royal Dutch Shell plc; 200.302.332/01, ECLI:NL:GHDHA:2024:2100; The Hague Court of Appeal (Gerechtshof Den Haag); 12.11.2024.*

*The Urgenda Foundation v. the State of the Netherlands*, C/09/456689 / HA ZA 13-1396, ECLI:NL:RBDHA:2015:7196; the Hague District Court (Rechtbank Den Haag); 24.06.2015; ("Urgenda 2015").

*The State of the Netherlands v. the Urgenda Foundation*, C/09/456689 / HA ZA 13-1396, ECLI:NL:GHDHA:2018:2610; the Hague Court of Appeal (Gerechtshof Den Haag); 09.10.2018; ("Urgenda 2018").

*The State of the Netherlands v. the Urgenda Foundation*, 19/00135, ECLI:NL:HR:2019:2007; Supreme Court (Hoge Raad); 13.01.2020; ("Urgenda 2020").

## The Philippines

*Minors Oposa v. Sec'y of the Dep't of Envt'l & Natural Res*, G.R. No. 101083, 33 I.L.M. 173; Supreme Court; 30.07.1993; ("Minors Oposa v. Factoran").

## United Kingdom

*Roao Cox & Others v Oil and Gas Authority & Others*, Case No: CO/1624/2021 [2022] EWHC 75 (Admin); England and Wales High Court (Administrative Court); 18. 01.2021 ("*Paid to Pollute case*").

## United States

*Aji P. v. State of Washington*, No. 80007-8-I; Supreme Court of the State of Washington;10.06.2021.

*American Electric Power Co. v. Connecticut*; 04 Civ. 5669, 04 Civ. 5670; District Court of New York (Southern District); 19.09.2005.

*Baker v. Carr.*, 369 U.S. 186 (1962); Supreme Court; 26.03.1962; ("*Baker*").

*Brown v. Board of Education of Topeka*, 347 U.S. 483 (1954); Supreme Court; 17.05.1954; ("*Brown v. Board of Education*").

*Chernaik v. Brown*, Docket number: S066564, 367 Or 143 (2020); Supreme Court of the State of Oregon; 22.10.2022.

*Commonwealth of Massachusetts, et al. v. EPA and alliance of automobile manufacturers et al.*, 415 F.3d 50 (2005); Court of Appeals for the District of Columbia Circuit; 15.07.2005; ["*Massachusetts v EPA (2005)*"].

*Connecticut v. American Electric Power Co*, 05-5104-cv, 05-5119-cv; Court of Appeals 2nd Circuit; 21.09.2009.

*Dobbs v. Jackson Women's Health Organisation*, first draft circulated among the Supreme Court Justices; Supreme Court, 10.02.2022.

*Dobbs v. Jackson Women's Health Organisation*, 597 U. S. (2022); Supreme Court; 24.06.2022.

*Eva Lighthiser et al v. Donald J. Trump*; United States District Court for the District of Montana; CV 25-54-BU-DLC; 15.10.2025; (*Lighthiser v. Trump*).

*G. B., et al. v. United States Environmental Protection Agency, et al.*, Case No. CV 23-10345-MWF (AGRx); District Court of the Central District of California; 08.05.2024.

*G. B., et al. v. United States Environmental Protection Agency, et al.*, Case No. CV 23-10345-MWF (AGRx); District Court of the Central District of California; 11.02.2025.

*Georgia v. Tennessee Copper Co.*, 206 U.S. 230 (1907); Supreme Court 13.05.1907.

*High Country Conservation Advocates v. USFS*, 52 F.Supp.3d 1174; Colorado District Court; 27.06.2014.

*Ilioulaokalani Coalition v. Rumsfeld*, 464 F.3d 1083 (9th Cir. 2006); United States Court of Appeals, 9th Circuit; 06.10.2006.

*Kelsey Cascadia Rose Juliana, et al. v. United States et al.*, Case 6:15-cv-01517-TC; District Court of Oregon; 10.11.2016. ["*Juliana (2016)*"].

*Kelsey Cascadia Rose Juliana, et al. v. United States et al.*, Case No. 6:15-cv-01517-AA, (D. Or. Apr. 19, 2024), Case 6:15-cv-01517-AA; District Court of Oregon; 15.10.2018; ["*Juliana (2018)*"].

*Kelsey Cascadia Rose Juliana, et al. v. United States et al.*, Case: 18-36082, D.C. No. 6:15-cv-01517-AA; United States Court of Appeals for the Ninth Circuit; 17.01.2020; ["*Juliana (2020)*"].

*United States v. U.S. District Court for the District of Oregon*, Case: 24-684, DktEntry: 46.1; United States Court of Appeals for the Ninth Circuit; 12.07.2024; ["*Juliana (2024)*"].

*Kelsey Cascadia Rose Juliana et al. v. United States et al.*; docket 24-645; order list:604 U.S.; United States Supreme Court; 24.03.2025; ["*Juliana (2025)*"].

*Layla H. v. Commonwealth of Virginia*, CL22000632-00; Richmond Circuit Court (Commonwealth of Virginia); 16.09.2022.

Massachusetts v. EPA, 49 U.S. 497; Supreme Court; 02.04.2007; ["*Massachusetts v EPA (2007)*"].

*Navahine F. v. Hawai'i Department of Transportation*, 1CCV-22-0000631; First Circuit Court of the State of Hawai'i; 06.04.2023.

*Navahine F. v. Hawai'i Electric Light Company*, Inc., CIVIL NO. 1CCV-22-0000631; Circuit Court of the First Circuit, State of Hawai'i; 20.06.2024.

*Natalie R. v. State of Utah*, Case no. 220901658; Utah District Court of the Third Judicial District; 09.11.2022.

*Natalie R. v. State of Utah*; 2025 UT 5; Utah, Supreme Court of the State of Utah; 20.03.2025.

*Marbury v. Madison*, 5 U.S. (1 Branch) 137 (1803); Supreme Court; 24.02.1803.

*Native Village of Kivalina v. ExxonMobil Corporation*, 663 F. Supp. 2d 863 (N.D. Cal. 2009); California District Court; 30.09.2009.

*Native Village of Kivalina v. ExxonMobil Corporation*, No. 09-17490, United States Court of Appeals for the Ninth Circuit; 21.09.2012.

*New York v. EPA*, USCA case number 06-1322; Court of Appeals for the District of Columbia Circuit; 24.09.2007.

*New York State Rifle & Pistol Assoc. v. Bruen*, 597 U. S. __ (2022); Supreme Court; 23.06.2022.

*Obergefell v. Hodges*, 576 U. S. (2015); Supreme Court; 26.06.2015.

*Planned Parenthood of Southeastern Pa. v. Casey*, 505 U.S. 833 (1992), 112 S. Ct. 2791; Supreme Court; 29.06.1992.

*Plessy v. Ferguson*, 163 U.S. 537 (1896); Supreme Court; 18.05.1896.

*Rikki Held, et al. v. State of Montana, et al*, CDV-2020-307; Montana 1st Judicial District Court, Lewis & Clark County, 04.08.2021; ["*Held v. State of Montana (2021)*"].

*Rikki Held, et al. v. State of Montana, et al.*, CDV-2020-307; Montana 1st Judicial District Court, Lewis & Clark County, 14.08.2023; ["*Held v. State of Montana (2023)*"].

*Rikki Held, et al. v. State of Montana, et al.*, DA 23-0575; Supreme Court of the State of Montana, 16.01.2024; ["*Held v. State of Montana (2024-1)*"].

*Rikki Held, et al. v. State of Montana, et al.*, DA 23-0575; Supreme Court of the State of Montana, 18.12.2024; ["*Held v. State of Montana (2024-2)*"].

*Rikki Held, et al. v. State of Montana, et al.*; Montana 1st Judicial District Court, Lewis & Clark County; (*Held v. State of Montana II*).

*Roe v. Wade*, 410 U.S. 113 (1973); Supreme Court; 22.01.1973.

*Sagoonick v. State of Alaska*, No. S-17297, Opinion No. 7583; Supreme Court of the State of Alaska; 28.01.2022.

*Stop H-3 Ass'n v. Dole*, 870 F.2d 1419; District Court of Hawai'i; 30.03.1989.

*West Virginia v. EPA*, USCA Case 15-1363; Court of Appeals for the District of Columbia Circuit; 21.01.2016; ["*West Virginia v. EPA (2016)*"].

*West Virginia v. EPA*, USCA Case 15-1363; Court of Appeals for the District of Columbia Circuit; 17.09.2019, ["*West Virginia v. EPA (2019)*"].

*West Virginia v. EPA*, 597 U. S. _(2022); Supreme Court; 30.06.2022; ["*West Virginia v. EPA (2022)*"].

*Wildearth Guardians v. U.S. BLM et al.*, D.C. No. 2:13-CV-00042-ABJ; the United States Court of Appeals 10th Circuit; 15.09.2017.

## Databases

Climatecasechart; https://www.climatecasechart.com; <11.10.2021>.

Ourchildrenstrust; https://www.ourchildrenstrust.org/global-legal-actions; <11.10.2021>.

Environmental Law Association; https://www.elaw.org/notablecases <11.10.2021>.

Ecolex; https://www.ecolex.org; <11.10.2021>.

Indiankanoon; https://indiankanoon.org; <11.10.2021>.

# Person Index



 | HTTPS://DOI.ORG/10.1163/9789004771710-020

# Subject Index



 | HTTPS://DOI.ORG/10.1163/9789004771710-021

www.ingramcontent.com/pod-product-compliance
Lightning Source LLC
LaVergne TN
LVHW082058151026
850117LV00003B/17
* 9 7 8 9 0 0 4 7 6 5 3 2 0 *